ACCEPTING TRUTH, FINDING HOPE!

ACCEPTING TRUTH, FINDING HOPE!

RICKY D. SLUDER

XULON PRESS

Xulon Press
2301 Lucien Way #415
Maitland, FL 32751
407.339.4217
www.xulonpress.com

Paperback ISBN-13: 978-1-66283-927-6
Hard Cover ISBN-13: 978-1-6628-4210-8
Ebook ISBN-13: 978-1-66283-928-3

TABLE OF CONTENTS

Introduction

Joy in Heaven

15 *Many tax collectors and sinners came to listen to Jesus.* *²Then the Pharisees and the teachers of the law began to complain, "Look, this man welcomes sinners and even eats with them."*

³ Then Jesus told them this story:

⁴ "Suppose one of you has 100 sheep, but one of them gets lost. What will you do? You will leave the other 99 sheep there in the field and go out and look for the lost sheep. You will continue to search for it until you find it. ⁵ And when you find it, you will be very happy. You will carry it ⁶ home, go to your friends and neighbors and say to them, 'Be happy with me because I found my lost sheep.'

⁷ In the same way, I tell you, heaven is a happy place when one sinner decides to change. There is more joy for that one sinner than for 99 good people who don't need to change.

Luke 15: 1-7

ACKNOWLEDGMENTS

To Scott Pricket:
Thank you for being obedient to the Holy Spirit's calling and for being willing to help a lost and broken man like me. Thank you for standing in the place of my father so I could begin to heal from the wounds of my childhood. Thank you for telling me what I didn't want to hear but needed to hear. I owe you an apology for being angry with you the day I left your office. I took offense to your words and began to boil with anger. But the more I processed them, the more I realized you were right. Scott, I am sorry for being offended and for being angry with you. I knew your heart and I should have given you the benefit of the doubt in the moment instead of letting anger consume me. Ultimately, God used you to move me out of the Valley of Hopelessness and to get me back on my Path of Purpose.

Forever grateful,
Ricky

To Rachel Ginger:
After reading all your edits and comments in my rough draft, I knew precisely why God chose you to be my editor. Thank you for enduring the extra rawness of my rough draft and helping me to soften it. I believe this book is a polished stone that God will use to help many slay the giants of fear and failure in their lives. I am grateful for the many hours you sacrificed to help me make this book a reality!

Your friend,
Ricky

To Amber Sluder:

You met me and married me during one of the hardest chapters of my life. Actually, you married Robert… that will never stop being funny. I want to say again Amber that I have a lot of regret for how I handled myself when I was your husband. I am sorry for all the times I hurt you, spoke ugly to you, and for all those seasons of life where you got rained on because of the storms that surrounded me. Thank you for Kylie! Thank you for standing next to me as we endured countless hardships as it related to our daughter. Thank you for your forgiveness for my transgressions and for your willingness to be my friend! I will forever be grateful for the bond we formed after our divorce that is still growing stronger with each new year. Thank you for allowing me to share the stories I did in this book. Your support means a lot to me!

Your friend, co-parent, and favorite ex-husband,
Rick-Rick

To Ashley and Michael Davis:

Michael, I cannot begin to express how much your friendship means to me. I am so grateful to God for placing you in my life when He did. Whether you knew it or not when you said it, those words you spoke to me in that Minnesota steakhouse were prophetic. I cannot wait to see what all God is going to do through TRM.

Ashley, thank you for being my friend and moreover, for being Amy's friend. I know your prayers were for us to succeed in marriage when it looked like we wouldn't. You will always hold a special place in my heart. Last, thank you for loving Michael the way you do. TRM never could have happened without you. Here is to many years in service together!

I love you both,
Ricky Dale

To Tess Davis:

I am so glad you weren't the student or niece I had hoped you would be when I first saw the picture of you and Amy. While our relationship is still blooming, I want you to know that I am truly grateful that God chose you to be my bonus daughter. While I am still learning my way as a Bonus Dad,

I want to make you a promise that I will never give up on loving you. Thank you for all the amazing hugs and for loving me so sweetly. Finally, don't ever forget that I see you! To me, you're never invisible!

I love you with my whole heart,
Ricky ("Dad")

To Kylie Sluder:
God used you to change my selfish heart, and I am so grateful that I was chosen by Him to be your Daddy. Thanks to our relationship, I understand what unconditional love means. I understand why Jesus chose to die for us. Until you, I simply couldn't grasp it. You have changed me for the better in so many ways Kylie, and I am so glad God left you here with me instead of taking you home when doctors said you couldn't recover. No matter how old you get, you'll always by my KylieBear Taylor!

I love you to the furthest star and back,
DaddyBear

To Bennett Asher:
As I write this for you son, you are eight months old. It's still hard to believe you are here. When I heard God say He would give me a son several years ago, I honestly didn't believe it was a real message from Him. Over the course of a five-year period, random people approached me prophetically, telling me that God would give me a son. When I met your mother in January of 2020, I suspended all my disbelief because I knew I had just met the woman God had been telling me about. Sure enough, no sooner than we were married God began to weave you in your mother's womb. You are a blessed and happy boy, just as your name implies. I am so glad God trusted me to be your Daddy. As much as I enjoy watching you grow, I cannot wait to see the man you become. I promise to be there each step of the way!

I love you son,
Daddy

To Amy Kate:
We met, married, got pregnant, and blended a family in less than six months. At the same time, we were sued, disowned, navigated the COVID-19

pandemic, we both encountered serious health issues, we were dealt financial woes, and we lived in what seemed like persistent conflict almost every day that first year. It was hard, but we made it! If I had to do it all over again, I would still pick you to do life with. I am so grateful for your patience and love. You've experienced me at my best and my worst, and regardless of which version of me you wake up to, you choose to love me well. The pain and the storms we endured together only served to make us better as individuals and as a couple. You are and will always be my forever love! Thank you for the support and encouragement you gave me along the way as I spent countless hours studying and writing. Thank you for our son, Bennett Asher, and for all you have sacrificed to be the mommy he needs. Thank you for being an outstanding mother to Tess and a fantastic Bonus Mom to Kylie. Your influence is stamped on every aspect of my life and our family, and I am beyond grateful. I will love you forever Amy!

Your husband, lover, and best friend,
Ricky Dale

THE OUTLAW DISCIPLE

Outlaw Disciple Defined

> "An unlikely sheepdog of the Shepherd, Jesus Christ,
> born into darkness and raised with wolves, but drawn to
> the Light with a heart to leave the 99 in search for the one
> who is lost. A broken vessel with rough edges that lives
> in the refining fires of adversity; fed up with legalism and
> masks of religiosity, walking boldly through the valley of
> the shadow of death proclaiming hope through a mes-
> sage of grace to the walking wounded among us."

— Ricky D. Sluder

On a cold and wet December morning in 2008, at approximately 1:30 AM, I pulled into the parking lot of an abandoned supermarket in Arlington, TX. With sleet pelleting my windshield, I saw three additional sets of headlights enter the parking lot from different directions. All three cars converged on mine, lights blacked out, trunk lids popped open, and I knew it was 'go time.'

In each of our trunks were a collection of shotguns, assault rifles, evidence bags, zip ties, and tactical vests. Last, but not least, I had my .40 caliber Smith & Wesson Military and Police Semi-Automatic handgun with Trijicon night sights and hollow point ammunition on my right hip.

As we say in Texas, we were loaded for bear.

We had everything a team of highly trained law enforcement professionals could possibly need to execute the search and arrest warrant for the...um... gentleman we had probable cause to believe had committed a felony.

We huddled up and began to discuss our tactical plan. The FBI agent leading the case began to go over the intelligence he had on the apartment and whom he believed would be inside. The schematic of the apartment didn't give us much information, but we had one very important detail that made this entry very dangerous - a single stairway that led up to the second-floor apartment with a 4'x 4' landing at the entrance to the apartment. This meant we had to squeeze together tightly along the brick facade and officer safety went out the window once we reached the door. The first guy in had to mount up squarely in front of that door and if you have ever executed a high-risk search and arrest warrant you know exactly how badly this situation sucked. The officer responsible for the knock-and-announce is always the one who gets shot either through the door or as soon as the team enters. And that, my friend, is precisely why I always volunteered to be the first one in the door. I wasn't consciously trying to die, but I didn't really care if I did either. After all, I had two realities I faced everyday as a police officer in Dallas County, Texas: die a hero or go home a racist.

After a decade of serving my state as a Texas Peace Officer, I found my worth in the badge I wore and, in the sacrifice, I was willing to make for others each day.

After a decade of serving my state as a Texas Peace Officer, I found my worth in the badge I wore and, in the sacrifice, I was willing to make for others each day. My title had become my identity. My gun and each less-than-lethal weapon on my belt were my security. Protecting and serving the people of the state of Texas was my purported purpose for living.

In law enforcement and military circles alike, those of us who volunteer to stand in the gap for everyone else are the sheepdogs of society. What the sheep run away from in fear of their lives, we run toward. Wolves don't frighten us, they excite us. We live to pursue the wolf, to protect the sheep, and while we say we don't care about the "thank you" we rarely receive, we secretly strive for it. We long for the acceptance of the sheep, hoping they will notice our acts of bravery and service on their behalf.

My name is Ricky D. Sluder, and I am an Outlaw Disciple of Jesus Christ. I grew up in bondage, a member of the walking-wounded, caught-up in the cycle of brokering lies and stealing thrones. Because refining fires of adversity raged like wildfires through the forests of my pretended contentment, I falsely believed I was cursed by God and doomed to roam the earth alone striving to meet my own needs. I lived in constant fear due to terrible theology and an overwhelming desire to find the happiness that seemed to evade me. Satan has worked long and hard to silence my voice and destroy my ministry before it could ever begin; to separate me from the Shepherd and to isolate me in hopes I would give up and die. But as I walked through the valley of the shadow of death, I found hope buried under the rubble of my own inse-

> *Because refining fires of adversity raged like wildfires through the forests of my pretended contentment, I falsely believed I was cursed by God and doomed to roam the earth alone striving to meet my own needs.*

curities. When the light of God pierced the darkness of my idolatrous veil and I found the *Truth*, it was then that God called me His son and I drew near to Him, and now I have *Hope*.

For most of my Christian walk, I have hoped that He would supernaturally move me out of the darkest places and allow me to enjoy the manna of Heaven from a mountaintop of joy, but that is not where Outlaw Disciples work.

Instead, He raised me up out of the ashes of my pretended contentment from the refining fires of adversity; out of the rubble of the mess I made from thousands of wrong decisions over the course of my life. He resurrected me from the casualty of my own sin. He asked me to stand firm in the face of the enemy as I walked through the darkest of valleys, and He fitted my feet with the readiness that comes from the gospel of peace. He stripped me of my false identity that was held up by a duty belt bearing all the weapons I relied on to defend others and myself in the course of my duty, and He buckled about my waist the belt of truth. He asked me to trade in my shield from the force and replaced it with a shield of faith to extinguish the fiery arrows of the enemy. He unstrapped my Kevlar vest and replaced it with a breastplate of righteousness. In humble surrender, I took off my cowboy hat, a symbol of my own independence and pride, and He adorned my head with the helmet of salvation. Lastly, He taught me to rely on a new weapon, the sword of the Spirit, which is the Word of God. He called me to a life of discipleship carrying the light of God into the darkest of places, sharing all of my scars openly, offering *Hope* to the hopeless, a *Father* to the fatherless, and *Grace* to everyone who would receive it.

He sent me to reclaim the lost sheep, that *YOU* might be reconciled to Him.

Before I came to terms with my true identity, fear, pride, and idolatrous living blinded me from finding the *Truth*. "I knew Jesus", but I couldn't have picked Him out of a line-up. I called Him God, Lord, Savior, and a whole host of other names, but I had never taken the time away from pursuing my will to spend a single day with Him.

> *I said all the right religious things in all the right religious circles, but I didn't want His will to be done in my life. I wanted my will to be done and I demanded that He bless it.*

I said all the right religious things in all the right religious circles, but I didn't want His will to be done in my life. I wanted my will to be done and I demanded that He bless it. I said repeatedly to Him, "I will do anything you want me to do Lord, as long as I can continue being a Detective". Furthermore, I indulged in secret sins, vehemently refusing to give them up in my heart.

I had about as much control of my life as a drunken man in the backseat of a car careening over a cliff. But just like that drunken man, I had diluted my thinking to the point of believing my own *bullsh***. I truly thought I was behind the wheel and in full control of my life. Instead of trusting God, I wore my salvation like a lifejacket, treating prayer like a 911 call. Although I had my transfer ticket from this world to eternity validated by the blood of Christ, I didn't have a real relationship with Him. Instead, I was striving to be the god of my own life, constantly fighting for control over all the things no man or woman can.

Then on March 17, 2008, He finally got my attention. Wrapped in extreme adversity, He gave me the greatest gift I have ever received in the flesh - a daughter that doctors said would die from congestive heart failure at three weeks old and there was nothing anyone could do to change that reality.

You see, He wasn't punishing me for all I had done wrong, which I would have more than deserved. He was leading me to a place of surrender, a place where grace and mercy abound, and His love always triumphs. All I needed to do in that moment was give up control and let Him have His way, something I had never done before.

While you haven't heard my story yet, I'll confess up front that I am very stubborn. So, why would a stubborn control freak like me give up during this battle when I had refused to give up so many times before?

Have you ever heard the adage, "you can lead a horse to water, but you can't make him drink"?

For now, let's just say, Daddy put some salt in the oats, and I was thirsty for surrender.

Accepting Truth, Finding Hope!

Will You Accept the Challenge?

It's Time to Get Real with Yourself

Insanity

> "Insanity is doing the same thing, over and over again, but expecting different results."

— Narcotics Anonymous

Before I tell you my story, I need to explain some things to you. Whether you chose to read this book on your own or this book chose you, I'm glad you're here. You are about to embark on a life-changing journey with me.

I hope you are skeptical of my claim. Being skeptical will cause you to pay closer attention to the words on each page of this book. As you examine the content, I hope you will dig deep within yourself and examine your own heart.

This book isn't intended for the passive reader. It will require deep thought and reflection on your part. So, if you want a fun and easy read, this isn't it. It will, however, shed light on four areas of your life that are critically important to you.

1. Acceptance
2. Identity
3. Security
4. Purpose

This book is written for the purpose of helping you *accept Truth,* that you may *find Hope.* To do this for real in your own life, you need to understand

Acceptance, Identity, Security and Purpose. I capitalized the *Truth* because I am referring to a proper noun. Many in our culture today would argue that truth is relative, but I argue that it is an absolute. Relative truth is intellectual dishonesty at best, and moral corruption at worst.

I am a Christ follower writing this book from a Christ-centered worldview. If that bothers you, you can set the book down and it won't hurt my feelings. But I sincerely hope you won't do that. This isn't about me though. This message is designed specifically for you. It's not a coincidence or an accident that you are reading this book. Whether you're a Christian of 10 decades or a self-proclaiming agnostic, it really doesn't matter. Where you are right now relative to the questions you will ask yourself in a minute is where you are right now. All I ask of you is to examine the information presented to you in this book. It's that simple.

> *"Insanity is doing the same thing, over and over again, but expecting different results."* — *Narcotics Anonymous*

To evaluate these four areas, you need to answer four questions.

1. Why are you striving for acceptance?
2. Who are you?
3. Why are you so insecure?
4. What is your purpose for living?

The answers you give will explain the foundation upon which you have built your entire life. These questions and the following information you read about them will also give you ample opportunity to change the foundation on which your life is built. That is, should you choose to.

Did you notice the definition I placed at the top of the page at the beginning of this chapter? Or did you skip over it?

Let's examine it together really quick:

"Insanity is doing the same thing, over and over again, but expecting different results." — Narcotics Anonymous

If you are anything like me, you have lived this definition in at least one of these four key areas of your life. Maybe you've lived it in all of them. As for me, I got tired of running on the hamster wheel of insanity. It took me a long time to truly accept the *Truth* and discover that I had it all wrong when it came to these four areas of my life.

Are you tired of doing the same thing and expecting a different result when it comes to acceptance? What about when it comes to your identity or security? How does all of this impact your purpose for being alive?

Does your life really have meaning, or do you just exist?

Before I get too deep, I need you to decide. Are you ready to accept The Challenge?

Accepting *The Challenge* means you will write down your answers to the four questions on Acceptance, Identity, Security, and Purpose. You will then read the book, re-evaluating the answers you gave here when you get to the end.

Many people believe the Bible is fable or allegorical, and maybe that's you. But I will present evidence to you that leads you to the *Truth*, showing you what the Holy Spirit showed me. What you do with it is entirely up to you.

If, for any reason, you don't think it's time to get real with yourself, then set this book down and ask yourself this question:

What are you afraid will happen *if you do* get real with yourself?

Okay friend, it is decision time. I assume you are ready. If so, go get a pen. I will wait here for you.

1. Why are you striving for acceptance?

_____

_____

_____

_____

_____

2. Who are you?

_____

_____

_____

_____

_____

3. Why are you so insecure?

_____

_____

_____

_____

_____

4. What is your purpose for living?

_____

_____

_____

_____

_____

_____

I, _____, accept The Challenge and hereby make a commitment to go deep within myself. I will seek what the *Truth* means to me, and I will finish strong, that I might find the *Hope* I seek.

_____   _____

             Signature   Date

ACCEPTING TRUTH, FINDING HOPE!

PART 1: ACCEPTANCE

Why Are You Striving for Acceptance?

Brokering Lies and Stealing Thrones

> Behold, I stand at the door and knock. If anyone hears my voice and opens the door, I will come in to him and eat with him, and he with me.
>
> Revelation 3:20 English Standard Version

How much will it cost if you believe the lie of all lies?

I know we don't know one another, and while I cannot hear your story through the pages of this book, I will tell you mine, so you can at least get to know me. Then, one day when we meet, you can tell me your story so I can get to know you, too.

Before I dive into the centric material of this book, I want to know if you paid attention to the verse at the top of this page. Maybe you glanced at it or maybe

> *How much will it cost if you believe the lie of all lies?*

you ran ahead like I tend to do and didn't even notice it. Maybe you rolled your eyes at it or maybe you have it memorized.

As you continue this journey, you will be presented with a verse at the top of the page at the beginning of each new chapter. Please don't make the mistake of passing it over. Read it each time and ponder it's meaning with each new chapter.

Ponder it with me right now.

Behold, I stand at the door and knock. If anyone hears my voice and opens the door, I will come in to him and eat with him, and he with me. Revelation 3:20 English Standard Version

Have you ever heard the knock that Jesus is referring to?

Do you know what Jesus means in this verse?

A theme in my writing style, and in my personality, is to ask a lot of questions. You will also notice I tend to answer questions with a question or three. Frustrating, I know. For the record, you won't be the first person to think this about me. As you get to know me in the pages ahead, you will begin to understand why I do this. For now, I will chalk it up to "I am just full of questions". Please don't confuse me for just being *full of sh***. But, if you do draw that conclusion, it's okay. I can handle it.

There are moments in this book, like above, where a *redacted curse word* will jump off the page. It could have easily been avoided, but I used it for effect because I needed this opportunity to explain that you will encounter redacted curse words periodically as we walk the halls of the museum of my past together. I don't use them excessively in the pages ahead, nor do I use them to sound tough, cool, or to offend you. And I don't change them to other "nice words" to sound religious or to be politically correct. As a Christ follower, I am real, I am raw, I am vulnerable about my past, and I am going to tell you my story as it happened. Thus, a curse word now and again. Hopefully, you can handle it.

With my Rated R disclaimer out of the way, I feel compelled to ask you a very important question.

How much will it cost if you believe the lie of all lies?

Do you know what I am talking about when I say, "lie of all lies"?

Let me illustrate it for you in the form of an exploratory question.

Why is it when you hear someone speak about how God performed a miracle for him or her, you pull a $100 dollar bill metaphorically out of your wallet and buy the lie?

"Wait a second Ricky, what lie are you talking about?", you may be asking me.

How many times have you looked at the person on your left or on your right and had no issue believing God's love, mercy, abundance, provision, and blood is and always will be available for them to receive from Him, but that it couldn't possibly be available to you? "Sure, God will bless others. He just won't do it for me. God will heal others. He just won't do it for me. I mean, how could He possibly even care about me? After all, look at the mess I have made of my life. If the neighbors knew what I really thought about in my most private moments, let alone all the things I have done, they would sell their house just to get away from me."

If that sounds remotely familiar, then you bought the lie of all lies.

Just in case you didn't notice what I am about to point out for yourself, and I bet you a copy of this book that you didn't, you will agree to buy a copy of this book for a friend, or even an enemy.

Ready? Here is the point I bet you missed. In the process of buying the lie, you placed yourself higher than God. Welcome to idolatry. The sin most of us think we never commit.

"Idolatry?"

When you buy this lie, this is what you say to Jesus.

"Jesus, the cross was good enough for everyone but me. You, Jesus, don't have the power to save me. I am above your grace. I am above your salvation. Your blood can't cover my sins. I am, in fact, so special that none of what you did or said applies to me."

You kick Him off His throne, you set up shop there, and you make idols out of your mess, out of your sin, out of everything you think He can't help you fix or restore.

At one point or another, my friend, we all do it. So, start shopping for a copy of this book to hand out, because someone you know needs it right now just as much as you do.

If this is where you are, or if you have ever been in this place of brokering lies and stealing thrones, I want to offer you a word of encouragement. Not too long ago, I came face-to-face with this reality myself. I didn't think God loved me. In fact, I was convinced He was angry at me. If you knew everything I have done, there is no way you would let me walk into your home, let alone speak into your life. And, as such, God could not possibly accept or love a man like me. I sincerely feared I was too far gone to be loved by Him. Part of this was bad theology, and part was sheer ignorance of the *Truth*. No one had shared the *Truth* with me on this subject, and I was saved. Yes, saved. Saved, yet utterly hopeless and struggling to survive each day in fear that I would be found out for the fraud that I thought I had become.

> I sincerely feared I was too far gone to be loved by Him. Part of this was bad theology, and part was sheer ignorance of the *Truth*.

So, I ask you one more time. How much will it cost if you believe the lie of all lies?

It will cost you everything in this life and in eternity!

There is hope for people like us. You're about to learn how to trade this lie in for the *Truth*. I promise, you are not too far gone to be loved by God. And, since you made a commitment and accepted The Challenge, I agree to keep my end of the bargain and I will lead you directly to the *Truth*, no matter how difficult the journey may be. The one thing I cannot do, however, is accept the *Truth* for you. That part will be up to you.

In a moment, I will share information about my journey and how I found the *Truth*. But right now, I want to ask you the one question we all get asked but rarely, if ever, answer correctly.

Who are you?

If you are tempted to tell me your name, your title, where you grew up, where you went to school, what degree you possess, who your parents are, or anything remotely similar, you have failed to answer the question.

Friend, this isn't a party, and we are not standing awkwardly together holding red Solo cups trying to get to know one another in a superficial way. In fact, I am not even asking this question so I can get to know you. I am asking you to ask yourself this question to see if you know who you are.

> *Who are you without your title or your career?*

Who are you without your title or your career?

Who are you without your degree, or your awards, or your trophies?

Who are you without your significant other, or your kids, or your friends, or your family?

Imagine if you woke up tomorrow and you had literally lost everything that defines who you are right now. Then, ask yourself this question again.

Without anything or anyone to define me, who am I really?

Most of you are shifting in your chairs because you realize you can't answer this question. In fact, you live every single day of your life in constant fear that you will be found out for the *fraud* you *think* you have become.

If this is you, then I know your kind well. My first name used to be Detective. Trust me friend, you are not alone.

For now, all I want you to do is agree not to buy any more lies or steal any more thrones as you consider these questions. But don't get too comfortable under this shade

> *My first name used to be Detective.*

tree of contemplation. We need to move on for the moment. Don't worry, we will come back to this.

"Follow me."

Gushing Fountains of Endless Life

Behold, I stand at the door and knock. If anyone hears my voice and opens the door, I will come in to him and eat with him, and he with me.

Revelation 3:20 English Standard Version

Why are you striving for acceptance?

Acceptance is a universal desire that every single human being craves from birth to grave. You spend nearly every waking minute seeking the acceptance of others. The concept of keeping up with the Jones' is evidence of this universal truism. In the digital age, this has been amplified through the advent of social media platforms that draw our faces away from our realities and into our augmented realities of the *small screen*.

You began your striving for acceptance with your focus aimed on your parents as a small child. Your friends and classmates became your focus somewhere around puberty, then your boy or girlfriends, your professors, and your employers. Somewhere along the way, if you go to church, regardless of your religious beliefs, you seek the acceptance of the church and its members, as well as the god of your religion.

You buy new possessions to impress or keep up with others (the proverbial Jones' in case the generational reference above was lost on you), and you cling to others and steal blessings in relationships to satisfy your own emotional needs. You present yourself as acceptable to the world on the worthiness-auction-blocks of social media through countless selfies and daily updates about your *wonderful life* in hopes you can exceed the number of replies and likes from the post before. Every day, you march to the beat of your own drum singing the battle cry of your life - Acceptance, Acceptance, Acceptance, please grant me your Acceptance. Yet, you end the day as empty as you began it, worn out from knocking on countless doors hoping others will let you in.

The irony of this is that acceptance possesses you, no matter how hard you try to possess it. No matter what, you just can't seem to fill the emptiness within you with all the glories you have received from others each and every day. As a result, some of you stuff this void with shopping, some with pornography, masturbation, or sex, some with alcohol or drugs, and some with isolation, self-loathing, or even self-harm. Regardless of the salve of addiction you apply, it never satisfies the craving deep in the void, does it?

Why is this true?

Why are you continually striving for acceptance?

Why do you act out with self-soothing salves of addiction when you don't get enough, or even when you get more than you wanted from others?

If you are honest with yourself, you will admit that you are striving for acceptance. In your heart of hearts, you want to be good enough, pretty enough, handsome enough, or smart enough. You want to be needed, desired, and wanted, and, in the end, you just really want to be loved.

Do you truly feel accepted, needed, desired, wanted, and loved?

Even with all your daily efforts to fill that void deep within, I bet your emotional cup is overflowing with unmet needs and expectations that important people in your life are not even trying to meet. As a result, your love quotient is extremely low. It's even possible your love quotient has flat lined. Yet, every day, you get back on the hamster wheel of insanity; back on the worthiness-auction-blocks of social media, striving harder than the day before, seeking what none of us can truly give you.

"Wait a minute, what did you say Ricky? What is it that no one can give me that I am truly seeking by striving for acceptance?", you might be asking me.

Hope!

None of us can give the other any sense of real hope.

Our promises of fidelity and forever are quickly broken, and our love tends to be conditional at best.

So, all your striving for acceptance is just an effort in futility. Solomon called it the vanity of vanities. When you do fill the void, it will be temporary. After all, those who let you in will also let you down.

"Where do I find hope, then?", you might be thinking.

Hope can only be found in the *Truth.*

In John Chapter 4 of the Bible, Jesus encounters a Samaritan woman at Jacob's well and He and she had this exact same

Hope can only be found in the *Truth.*

conversation you and I are having. I will present the Word to you first and then add commentary. I am using The Message translation, as it is far easier to read and comprehend than *thou* may be used to from the old King James.

The Woman at the Well

4 ¹⁻³ Jesus realized that the Pharisees were keeping count of the baptisms that he and John performed (although his disciples, not Jesus, did the actual baptizing). They had posted the score that Jesus was ahead, turning him and John into rivals in the eyes of the people. So, Jesus left the Judean countryside and went back to Galilee.

⁴⁻⁶ To get there, he had to pass through Samaria. He came into Sychar, a Samaritan village that bordered the field Jacob had given his son Joseph. Jacob's well was still there. Jesus, worn out by the trip, sat down at the well. It was noon.

⁷⁻⁸ A woman, a Samaritan, came to draw water. Jesus said, "Would you give me a drink of water?" (His disciples had gone to the village to buy food for lunch.)

⁹ The Samaritan woman, taken aback, asked, "How come you, a Jew, are asking me, a Samaritan woman, for a drink?" (Jews in those days wouldn't be caught dead talking to Samaritans.)

¹⁰ Jesus answered, "If you knew the generosity of God and who I am, you would be asking *me* for a drink, and I would give you fresh, living water."

¹¹⁻¹² The woman said, "Sir, you don't even have a bucket to draw with, and this well is deep. So how are you going to get this 'living water'? Are you a better man than our ancestor Jacob, who dug this well and drank from it, he and his sons and livestock, and passed it down to us?"

¹³⁻¹⁴ Jesus said, "Everyone who drinks this water will get thirsty again and again. Anyone who drinks the water I give will never thirst—not ever. The water I give will be an artesian spring within, gushing fountains of endless life."

¹⁵ The woman said, "Sir, give me this water so I won't ever get thirsty, won't ever have to come back to this well again."

---

¹³⁻¹⁴ *Jesus said, "Everyone who drinks this water will get thirsty again and again. Anyone who drinks the water I give will never thirst—not ever. The water I give will be an artesian spring within, gushing fountains of endless life."*

---

¹⁶ He said, "Go call your husband and then come back."

¹⁷⁻¹⁸ "I have no husband," she said.

"That's nicely put: 'I have no husband.' You've had five husbands, and the man you're living with now isn't even your husband. You spoke the truth there, sure enough."

¹⁹⁻²⁰ "Oh, so you're a prophet. Well, tell me this: Our ancestors worshiped God at this mountain, but you Jews insist that Jerusalem is the only place for worship, right?"

21-23 "Believe me, woman, the time is coming when you Samaritans will worship the Father neither here at this mountain nor there in Jerusalem. You worship guessing in the dark; we Jews worship in the clear light of day. God's way of salvation is made available through the Jews. But the time is coming—it has, in fact, come—when what you're called will not matter and where you go to worship will not matter.

23-24 "It's who you are and the way you live that count before God. Your worship must engage your spirit in the pursuit of truth. That's the kind of people the Father is out looking for: those who are simply and honestly *themselves* before him in their worship. God is sheer being itself—Spirit. Those who worship him must do it out of their very being, their spirits, their true selves, in adoration."

25 The woman said, "I don't know about that. I do know that the Messiah is coming. When he arrives, we'll get the whole story."

26 "I am he," said Jesus. "You don't have to wait any longer or look any further."

23-24 *"It's who you are and the way you live that count before God. Your worship must engage your spirit in the pursuit of truth. That's the kind of people the Father is out looking for: those who are simply and honestly themselves before him in their worship. God is sheer being itself—Spirit. Those who worship him must do it out of their very being, their spirits, their true selves, in adoration."*

27 Just then his disciples came back. They were shocked. They couldn't believe he was talking with that kind of a woman. No one said what they were all thinking, but their faces showed it.

28-30 The woman took the hint and left. In her confusion she left her water pot. Back in the village she told the people, "Come see a man who knew all about the things I did, who knows me inside and out. Do you think this could be the Messiah?" And they went out to see for themselves.

While this story appears to be about water and a well, it's really about *Acceptance* and *Hope*. The Samaritan woman was, well, a Samaritan, and, sociologically speaking, that made her an outcast all by itself. Jews hated

Samaritans in this day. They would be stepped over long before they would be ministered to.

She had been married and divorced five times. If you think this is shameful in our present day, think about the condemnation she would have encountered then. And, to top it off, she was living with a man who was not her husband. Once upon a time, this was shameful in our society, but today it seems to be commonplace.

Based on the facts presented in this story, it's obvious that she has been striving for acceptance by seeking to fill her "love bucket" with the "water of men". But that hasn't worked out so well for her and she seems to still be thirsty for love. While we don't know the details of her five marriages, or the terms of her five divorces, it doesn't take a genius to see that this woman is striving for acceptance.

The remarkable thing that strikes her immediately in this transaction is that Jesus is not only willing to talk to her, but He asks her for a drink.

So, why did He ask her for a drink?

You see, Jesus wasn't interested in her social status or in condemning her for her sinful living. He knew everything she had ever done, and He had compassion for her. He knew she was coming to that well, which is why He stopped there to rest. He went out of His way to make sure this woman knew there was a better way to live her life.

When He asked her for a drink, He was not interested in her drawing water up from Jacob's well. He simply wanted her to know that regardless of the shame she felt from the many men who had let her in, and then let her down, He wanted her to invite Him in so He may eat with her and she with Him. He wanted her to know that she would never be alone again; that once she accepted Him, she would never need to strive for acceptance again. He simply wanted her to surrender her love bucket at His feet.

Instead of condemnation for all that she had done wrong, Jesus offered her hope through a relationship with Him!

The emptiness you feel in the void in the middle of your chest cannot be satisfied with anything less than the artesian spring of hope that is Jesus Christ.

We all face trials and fall short of a perfect life. But, on the outside, we do a remarkable job of covering up our broken pieces so no one will know just how screwed up we truly are. Meanwhile, because we feel so alone and ashamed of our poor decisions, we are dying on the inside. We falsely think that we can pro-tect ourselves if we just keep it all a secret. That, my friend, is the sin of self-preservation.

The emptiness you feel in the void in the middle of your chest cannot be satisfied with anything less than the artesian spring of hope that is Jesus Christ.

I bet you can think of at least one wrong decision you have made in this life where, afterwards, you declared, "I will take this to my grave".

Am I right?

Now, I want you to imagine walking out on a stage. As the curtain opens, your grandmother, daughter, dad, or whoever is most important to you in this life is sitting in the front row. They wave and smile at you lovingly right before you hit play on the metaphorical videos of all your secret sins. Imagine showing the pictures of all your skeletons in the closet. Imagine telling them about your real motivations for why you did the things you have done.

No way, huh?

Okay, would you consider telling one person before you die? I know, it's daunting, isn't it? But why is it so daunting to be exposed like this? The answer to that question is simple.

You bought the lie of all lies.

Remember us discussing this earlier?

Well, make no mistake about it. You're not alone in this. Right now, someone you know is buying the lie, too. Which means they need to find freedom from the darkness and bondage of their sin just as much as you do. In fact, we all do. I believe this is why God called me to write this book.

So, my encouragement to you is this - find a friend that you can really do life with and get that toxic stuff out of you. Shine the light on your worst mistakes and your most disgusting sins. The *Truth* will set you free when you do.

I have done it, and I am going to do it again in this book. I can testify that it is beyond freeing to not have to hide from your sins. The disciple of Jesus named John confirms this for us in 1 John 1-10, taken from The Message translation.

1-2 From the very first day, we were there, taking it all in—we heard it with our own ears, saw it with our own eyes, verified it with our own hands. The Word of Life appeared right before our eyes; we saw it happen. And now we're telling you in most sober prose that what we witnessed was, incredibly, this: The infinite Life of God himself took shape before us.

3-4 We saw it, we heard it, and now we're telling you so you can experience it along with us, this experience of communion with the Father and his Son, Jesus Christ. Our motive for writing is simply this: We want you to enjoy this, too. Your joy will double our joy.

Walk in the Light

5 This, in essence, is the message we heard from Christ and are passing on to you: God is light, pure light; there's not a trace of darkness in him.

6-7 If we claim that we experience a shared life with him and continue to stumble around in the dark, we're obviously lying through our teeth—we're not *living* what we claim. But if we walk in the light, God himself being the light, we also experience a shared life with one another, as the sacrificed blood of Jesus, God's Son, purges all our sin.

[8-10] If we claim that we're free of sin, we're only fooling ourselves. A claim like that is errant nonsense. On the other hand, if we admit our sins—make a clean breast of them—he won't let us down; he'll be true to himself. He'll forgive our sins and purge us of all wrongdoing. If we claim that we've never sinned, we out-and-out contradict God—make a liar out of him. A claim like that only shows off our ignorance of God.

Do you understand this passage?

Jesus is the Word of Life. He has been from the beginning. Jesus was made manifest, meaning He became a man to testify to each of us that we can be in fellowship with Him and with one another.

You were not made to do life alone. He wants to do life and spend eternity with you. Jesus will forgive you of all your sins if you just confess them.

If you hang around any Christian for any length of time, you're going to be asked this question:

Are you saved?

Well, are you?

Most people respond in the same manner - "I think I am, but I am not really sure."

Do you know what it means to be saved?

To be saved means you believe that Jesus is the Son of God and that He was sent by the Father to die on a cross in your place. He received the death sentence that you and I deserve and paid our sin debt so we could spend eternity with Him. And here is the best news of all. If you had been the only one who needed forgiveness for sin, He would have laid down His life just for you. In fact, He *did* die for you.

Do you believe that?

In the Bible, God is sometimes referred to as Abba. Do you know what Abba means?

It means Daddy.

For most of you, God is a distant, angry, and/or absent figure, but He is not your Daddy or your friend. Quite possibly, you have never even tried to have a relationship with Him. If this describes you, then I want you to know that you have bought the lie, again. I used to believe this lie. I always wondered how God could possibly love me given all the things I willingly did wrong. Then, in 2008, He gave me a daughter. Later in the book, I will tell you her story, but for now I want to illustrate my point. I tell her all the time that there is nothing in this world that she could ever do to make me stop loving her. If she worshiped the devil, murdered children for sport, and said she hated the great state of Texas, I would still love her. I know my statement is hyperbole, but my love for her is unconditional. There is nothing I wouldn't do to keep her in relationship with me, including death. I would die for her. That's how much I love my child. While I will not go into their individual stories, I feel this same way about my second daughter and my son. Nothing can ever come between my love for them.

What more would the God of all creation do for His children?

John 3:16 English Standard Version (ESV)

For God So Loved the World

16 "For God so loved the world,[a] that he gave his only Son, that whoever believes in him should not perish but have eternal life.

God has already accepted you, broken mess, and all, and He has prepared a way for you to be with Him forever. The only thing you must do is choose. That is *The Challenge* He gives us in His book.

> *God has already accepted you, broken mess, and all, and He has prepared a way for you to be with Him forever.*

If you choose Him to be your Savior, at that very moment of belief in Him, you are saved. At the point of salvation, He wipes your slate clean, regardless of what you have done.

"Ricky, pardon my interruption, but what happens if I keep doing bad things after I am saved?", you may be asking me.

You're going to keep sinning no matter how hard you try not to. Your soul is your sin-center and you have been feeding it sin all your life. At birth, the Bible says we are born spiritually dead. When you accept Christ and become saved, your spirit is brought to life, thus, born again. Don't expect that becoming a Christian will somehow give your newborn baby spirit an edge on your mature soul. That's like hiring a newborn to babysit a rebellious teenager. Guess who will get their way every time? Your soul will. But as you starve your soul of the sin it craves and feed your spirit the Word, your spirit will mature. Eventually, your spirit will become more mature than your soul and your spirit will win the day most of the time. But no matter how mature your spirit becomes, your soul will continuously ask you to feed it the junk food it desperately craves. And guess what? You will give in at some point. Everyone does. So, don't beat yourself up if you are still struggling with sin after you are saved.

In Romans 8, Paul the Apostle of Christ reminds us that there is no condemnation for those of us who are in Christ Jesus. Don't get it twisted, though. We are not given a license to sin. We are, however, offered an endless supply of grace for all the times we choose sin over righteousness. That is precisely why Jesus told the Samaritan woman, "The water I give will be an artesian spring within, gushing fountains of endless life."

Did you know being saved is a three-part process?

The three parts are called Justification, Sanctification, and Glorification.

When the slate is wiped clean, this is called Justification. As you progress through life, you're going to continue to sin, as we discussed, and as you continue to confess your sins, Jesus continues to forgive you. Thus, Sanctification. When you die, you will be saved one last time, and that is called Glorification.

For most of my Christian walk, I vaguely understood what being saved meant, but I had no idea why we needed to be baptized.

There are two forms of baptism I am going to cover here. The first form is the baptism of the Holy Spirit. The moment you are saved, you are baptized into the Holy Spirit. This means you are placed in permanent union with Christ and with other believers in the body of Christ.

1 Corinthians 12:13 English Standard Version (ESV)

[13] For in one Spirit we were all baptized into one body—Jews or Greeks, slaves[a] or free—and all were made to drink of one Spirit.

While I am not planning on going into depth about this in this book, there is a second type of baptism by the Holy Spirit that is mentioned in scripture. In net effect, this second baptism of the Holy Spirit is soul-level. When you are saved, the Holy Spirit enters your spirit. That is the first of the two types in the first form. When you receive the gift of the Holy Spirit, this is when your soul is also filled with the Holy Spirit. Our souls contain our mind, will, and emotions. When our souls are filled with the Holy Spirit, this is what is meant by being "Spirit-filled". After the second, both your spirit and soul are filled with the Holy Spirit. I encourage you to dig into this on your own once you have dealt with salvation.

The second form is water baptism, the outward declaration of your acceptance of Christ.

Did you know that the great Exodus in the Bible is emblematic of salvation and baptism?

Have you ever heard about Moses leading the Israelites out of Egypt in the book of Exodus? It is literally the best word picture I can find in the Bible for salvation and baptism in one story. I continue to be blown away at how God orchestrated these events so we could see His plan in action for our good and His glory.

"Let my people go," Moses, demanded of Pharaoh. After some convincing by God, Pharaoh finally released the Israelites from their bonds of slavery.

When they got to the Red Sea, Moses and the Israelites didn't have a way to get across, and Pharaoh had a change of heart, deciding to hunt them down and kill them all. The word picture here is that Satan will not give up on wanting you to be a slave to your sin. He wants you to continually strive for acceptance. The Red Sea represents the reality that no one can save him or herself. It takes God's intervention of grace on our behalf and faith on our part. Moses heard God's instructions to place his stick in the water, and, by faith, he did. As a result of his act of faith, God granted the Israelites grace, parting the Red Sea so they may escape the enemy pursuing them. This is what it means to be saved by grace through faith.

Here is the parallel. In salvation, you're freed from your bondage and slavery to sin, and you willingly leave all the idols behind from your old life (Egypt). In baptism, when you go into the water and come back up, the water drowns the idols of your old life, the same way it drowned the Egyptians that had enslaved the Israelites.

Have you taken an inventory of the idols you are holding onto?

What will it take for you to let go of them?

Are you afraid of what others will think if you become a Christ follower?

Tell me friend, why are you still striving for acceptance?

Storms, Sandcastles and Secret Beaches

Behold, I stand at the door and knock. If anyone hears my voice and opens the door, I will come in to him and eat with him, and he with me.

Revelation 3:20 English Standard Version

Are you walking in the light?

Remember back at the beginning of the book when I said I would tell you, my story? Well, here is the first of many segments where I will stand in the light of vulnerability and share some of my journey with you. I am not doing this to glorify myself. In fact, what you will read will embarrass me long before it will bring me an ounce of glory. So, why on earth would I decide to do this? Simply put, God told me to. I believe He wants you to know you are not alone in your struggles.

Alright, here goes. I am jumping in headfirst to confess my sins to you, walking in the light, that I may have fellowship with you and that the blood of Jesus may continue to cleanse my sins through the sanctification process. I guarantee this is not going to be easy when you decide to do it, but I hope you will follow my lead. You don't need anything special to do this. All Moses had was a stick and a stuttering problem.

I have lived my life from a place of constant fear and foolish, idolatrous, pride striving for acceptance in every single relationship I have been in. I have stolen countless blessings from others out of fear that no one would meet my emotional needs, something I still struggle with today. As a result of a lot of neglect and abuse during my childhood, I bought the lie at an early age and wrongly assumed that if I wanted to be accepted, I had to take control of my own destiny. I became the god of my own life and created many personas, one for each group of people whose acceptance I was striving to receive. My emotional cup was overflowing from many wounds, and the expectations I set for others, which were nearly always unstated, were rarely, if ever, met by anyone other than myself. I felt the void in my chest and longed to fill it with happiness, but I didn't know how. I didn't realize that happiness is just an emotion, and it cannot, nor should it, begin to fill this void. To soothe my aching soul, I turned to several different vices to self-medicate. I became a master of disguise and learned to manipulate and lie to get my way or get myself out of trouble. While I never consumed any form of illegal drugs, I drank alcohol in excessive volumes beginning at the age of 13. I taught myself to dip, which quickly

> *In small doses, I would take shots of religion, but the high never really lasted or satisfied my ache.*

and horribly ended with me hugging a toilet. After this tobacco debacle, I taught myself to smoke cigarettes, smoking a pack a day at the age of 15. In small doses, I would take shots of religion, but the high never really lasted or satisfied my ache. In fact, none of these soothed my soul like my favorite sin of all.

Sexual Idolatry.

Sexual immorality is where it began, but it soon morphed into sexual idolatry. It became my refuge, my rock, and my source for everything good and evil in my life.

For more than 30 years, I had built the ultimate sandcastle with no cornerstone, and I fought tirelessly to keep it hidden on a secret beach of the island I called my life.

Let me take you back to the beginning. Around the age of eight years old, a hurricane that had been gathering strength for about four years just off the coast of my father's life finally made landfall. This storm destroyed my father personally, financially, and corporately, and it took my parent's marriage, our family, and my childhood along with it.

But there were some sunny days before the storm hit. When I was eight years old, I asked Jesus Christ to be my Lord and Savior, a memory that is still vivid in my mind's eye. I was a shy boy who stuttered when I spoke, but I was also highly intelligent and far more athletic than I would ever receive credit for. I had a mom, a dad, and a half-sister six years my senior. I also have a second half-sister and a half-brother with whom I was not raised. I had many friends in the neighborhood where we lived, a Mongoose bicycle with mag wheels, and an RC controlled racetrack covering our pool table that NASCAR would have been envious of. I thought I had a pretty good life at that point in time.

When the storm rolled in, it came with a series of furious blows. A female relative in her teenage years, who will not be identified, made a poor choice, and decided to coax me into allowing her to play with my penis. While naked in front of me, she told me that if I allowed her to do so, she would allow me to play with her vagina. I trusted her emphatically, so I reluctantly did as I was asked. When she was done fondling me, she abruptly covered her nudeness and told me to leave the house and go play. I had no idea what I had done wrong to warrant this response, but it shot a poisonous dart of betrayal and rejection into the deepest depths of my heart. I hung my head in shame as I put my pants back on. I went outside, jumped on my bike, and rode down my favorite dirt trail. While riding, I saw something in the tree line that would further change things for the worst - my first pornographic magazine. After memorizing the vivid images in my young mind, I hid the magazine under some brush so I could come back and enjoy the treasures I had found there.

I woke up one morning shortly after the molestation with a migraine and sudden, severe allergies to every tree, grass, and pollen, and more than 80 out of 100 things on an allergy test. In fact, when they ran the tests on my back, it swelled up so much they couldn't accurately read the results. Prior to this, I was not allergic to anything.

I ran a daily fever of at least 100 degrees with spikes as high as 106. My eyes would swell shut, I would sneeze for hours on end, and I could barely breathe due to my bronchial tubes inflaming to the point of occlusion. I went into respiratory distress many times, landing me in several emergency rooms throughout my childhood years. In addition, I had very painful stomach problems that caused more than 20 diarrheic bowel movements a day. This was my daily reality for the next 6-7 years of my life.

I saw more doctors than I care to mention. To the medical community, I was a bit of an enigma. They could not find anything that would treat my symptoms or explain my sudden illnesses. More than one specialist accused me of lying about my conditions and told my mother I was just stressed out. It was the very foods I ate every day that were making me so sick, but it wouldn't be discovered for another 37 years. At the age of 45, I was finally diagnosed correctly. I have a condition called Eosinophilic Esophagitis, which presents at the age of eight years old. In addition to environmental allergies, I am also allergic to dairy, eggs, corn, peanuts, potatoes, soy, baker and brewer's yeast, barley, oats, pineapple, and most fish.

Now, remember me saying a hurricane was brewing off the coast of my father's life? Around 1980, his construction company was financially destroyed when a man defrauded him of $90,000. That was a lot of money back then, and this unfortunately put him at a crossroads that would further change our lives forever. You see, he couldn't afford to pay his taxes *and* his employees, so he chose to pay his employees. He planned to pay the taxes he owed over time, justifying it by thinking the government would survive without this money. But his employees needed to be able to provide for their families.

The IRS disagreed, and without notice, they came and took everything from us over a $30k debt. They crushed us financially for many years to come and they took pride in doing so. They froze every asset, blocked every credit card, and garnished every paycheck my mom would later earn, even though she had nothing to do with my dad's business or his decision not to pay his taxes. They even saw fit to seize mine and my sister's savings accounts. Yep, the IRS seized $50 from me to protect the Republic.

As a result of extreme stress, guilt, and murderous thoughts, my dad would fly off the handle in fits of rage over the smallest of issues, destroying everything in our house and leaving the damage of a tornado behind him.

To say he was violent is an understatement. I remember a rare time I got into trouble; I was terrified of the man and typically did my best to stay far off his radar. As punishment, he told me to go get a belt. He always wore boots and had leather belts with large buckles. Some were ornate and had conchos or other metal decorations affixed to them. When I reached the closet, all the belt options sucked. So, I grabbed the one I thought would do the least amount of damage and I brought it back to him. He took the belt from me, bowed his head, and dropped the buckle towards the ground. With his grip firmly around the tail of the belt, he began to scream at the top of his lungs, "You think this won't f**king hurt?", repeatedly. As he slung the belt, the buckle began to crash off the walls and furniture. As wood splinters flew and pieces of sheetrock sailed, I seriously wondered if he was going to kill me.

When he lost his temper, his default was to throw things, including large pieces of furniture. And as vivid as those memories are to me, it was the insults he threw that did the most damage to my heart. He would call me "a p***y" and a "candy-a**" and tell me "To get the f**k out of his sight" because he didn't want to look at me.

I believe he did this because he couldn't see past the rage he had for this man who defrauded him, and he simply lost his way. He flirted with suicide and had thoughts of killing my mom, my sister, and me. One night after one of my baseball games, I found him under his truck with a gun to his head. According to my mother, he had planned to kill all of us, then himself.

During my dad's hurricane, we were all getting rained on so hard it felt like we were in hurricanes of our own. What I have learned since then is that God had a reason for allowing all of this to happen to us. I still don't know the "why", but I do know that He worked it all out for our good and for His glory. At the time, though, I just couldn't see it. I was blinded by fear. I was only able to see the sheer power of the torrential rains and straight-line winds that threatened my daily existence. And, like my father, I began to sink into a sea of despair.

Has this ever happened to you?

Did you know that it also happened to one of the disciples, Peter, while he was following Jesus?

Do you know this story?

I think of all the stories in the Bible, this one is my all-time favorite. I guess after hearing the first act of my childhood, this makes sense because I can relate to being in a bad storm.

Let me share what happened to Peter, and then I'll get back to telling you, my story. For the biblical record, you can also find this story in the gospels of Mark and John, but Matthew tells it best, going into more detail than the others. Let's listen to Matthew tell this story in Matthew 14:22-33 in The Message translation.

Walking on the Water

22-23 As soon as the meal was finished, he insisted that the disciples get in the boat and go on ahead to the other side while he dismissed the people. With the crowd dispersed, he climbed the mountain so he could be by himself and pray. He stayed there alone, late into the night.

24-26 Meanwhile, the boat was far out to sea when the wind came up against them and they were battered by the waves. At about four o'clock in the morning, Jesus came toward them walking on the water. They were scared out of their wits. "A ghost." they said, crying out in terror.

27 But Jesus was quick to comfort them. "Courage, it's me. Don't be afraid."

28 Peter, suddenly bold, said, "Master, if it's really you, call me to come to you on the water."

29-30 He said, "Come ahead."

Jumping out of the boat, Peter walked on the water to Jesus. But when he looked down at the waves churning beneath his feet, he lost his nerve and started to sink. He cried, "Master, save me."

[31] Jesus didn't hesitate. He reached down and grabbed his hand. Then he said, "Faint-heart, what got into you?"

[32-33] The two of them climbed into the boat, and the wind died down. The disciples in the boat, having watched the whole thing, worshiped Jesus, saying, "This is it. You are God's Son for sure."

It's truly amazing what we can do when we are in the will of God and when we have our eyes focused on Jesus. But when we start looking at how the mortgage is going to get paid or how hard we will have to strive and scheme to make ends meet, we sink into a sea of despair. Just like Peter did. Just like my dad did. Just like my mom did. Just like I did.

> *It's truly amazing what we can do when we are in the will of God and when we have our eyes focused on Jesus.*

At the age of 10, my parents officially divorced. I remember being excited when I first heard the news. No more domestic terrorism, hallelujah. However, the excitement left when I learned that me, my mom, and sister would be moving from our small country home on five acres in Ovilla, Texas into a two-bedroom apartment in Red Oak, Texas. I was informed that my mother would get one of the bedrooms, and since "my sister was a girl", she would get the other bedroom. This meant I had to either sleep with my mom or sleep on the couch. Either way, 99% of my toys, bedroom furniture, and other items were not coming with us. As for me, I slept on the couch for the next six years.

Newly divorced, my mom had to get a job to support us. She had previously been a stay-at-home-mom and babysat for other working moms to earn money to help my dad. Fortunately, the First City Bank in Lancaster, Texas hired her as a teller. She made a whopping $18,000 a year and had no clue how she was going to be able to afford the rent, much less feed us. On the day our first rent payment was due, the apartment complex manager called and asked if she could meet with her. Worried about not being able to pay, my mom walked to the management office, not knowing what she would say. But when she got there, rather than asking her for the payment, the manager asked my mom if she would work weekends in the leasing office. In exchange for her services, she would receive free rent. You see, though my mom couldn't see Him walking on the waters next to her, God had control of the wind and the waves of her financial storm.

Since they couldn't get immediate repayment from my dad, the IRS pursued my mom relentlessly for many years. They garnished her wages, and we routinely had no money to live on. I remember one IRS agent telling my mom, "Thanks to me, lady, you'll never have credit again." I was too young to fully understand the conversations I overheard, but I did know one thing - they made life for us much more miserable than it needed to be. With God's help, though, we made it through. We always had clothes, a roof over our head, and food to eat. Yes, corn dogs, SPAM, macaroni and cheese, corned beef hash, off-brand Spaghetti-O's, Fruit Round Ups (we couldn't afford Fruit Loops), and chicken nuggets do qualify as food when that's all you can afford to eat. Though we lived very modestly, God always met our needs.

As the days went by, my mother could barely keep her wits about her. She had no idea what to do with a kid like me. I was sick every day, and between the stress of barely making enough money to survive, my health issues and/ or injuries, and the IRS' daily threats and harassment, she didn't know how to respond to anything in a healthy way.

So, she resorted to the one thing she did know. Tough love. She began to tell me things like, "The world isn't going to stop spinning just because you are sick Ricky", and "You had better learn to get over it and live your life being sick." I even remember her telling people that, given the chance, she would "Trade me in for a different child who wasn't as sick as I was all the time."

Given her work schedule, she was rarely ever home. When she was, she was either lost in her own stress, arguing with my sister about taking her clothes without permission, or getting ready to go out dancing with her friends. Regardless, she didn't have time for me. I vividly remember one time when I was 10 years old taking a bold step and asking her to stay home and spend time with me. I really needed her, and since she wasn't volunteering to be with me any other time, I went out on a limb and tried to steal a blessing for my young, aching soul. She was getting ready to go out country dancing and drinking with her friends and she got angry with me and told me to "stop being so selfish". She needed time for herself.

After that rejection, I never again asked her to spend a single second with me. She didn't stop there, though. She routinely tore me down with her words, commonly referring to me as a momma's boy and telling me I needed to toughen up. If something hurt my feelings, she would ask me if I wanted a "suck-a-tit". I still don't know what that means, but I guess she thought she was helping me not be timid and shy. All it did was break my will and cause me to strive for acceptance in new and different ways. I went above and beyond to get good grades and be overly obedient to her, at least for a season. Little did I know, I would spend the next 30 years striving for her acceptance through various levels of performance. I thought if I could achieve the highest of worldly achievements, maybe she would show me love. It didn't work. No matter how much I obeyed, rebelled, or achieved, nothing changed my circumstances.

Through the years, as my dad re-married and divorced, he would make an obligatory cameo appearance, both rare and fruitless when he did. His only priority was his work, and sadly, it still is.

As you might imagine, I grew up physically and emotionally miserable. I did not understand why I had to be sick all the time, or why I was an orphan in my own home. I prayed for healing; to not be sick. I knew God heard me, but I did not understand why nothing changed.

> *I knew God heard me, but I did not understand why nothing changed.*

Naturally, I projected my parent's negative emotions toward me onto God and assumed He must be angry with me.

Have you projected similar emotions onto God because of your life circumstances?

How did it change the way you strive for acceptance?

As for me, I grew my hair out long and turned towards rebellion. I changed my clothes from boots and jeans to torn Levi's and heavy metal band t-shirts to fit in with the other kids in my apartment complex. I learned to fight, and I developed a reputation for myself with my new friends. I was a handsome young man, and had no problem attracting girls, something that quickly became an area of interest for me. At the age of 11, I discovered masturbation and it became my daily obsession. By the age of 12, I could talk the sexual talk, but I hadn't yet taken the sexual walk. My upstairs neighbor, who was nine years old at the time, would knock on my door at least once a week. I would let her in and, inevitably, she would sit on the couch, spread her legs open wide and ask me the same question each time: "Do you want to hump me?" I was a virgin and although I didn't want anyone else to know that about me, I would simply tell her she was too young for me, and she should go home. Sadly, many people used her at the tender age of nine years old. It broke my heart for her then, and it still does today.

At the age of 13, I began drinking. By 14, I would routinely get so drunk I would wake up in different clothes and places I had no memory of getting to. I spent most of my nights at the street races, and, one night, narrowly escaped being killed by a man who held a knife between my eyes during a robbery at a pawnshop in Oak Cliff, Texas. For some reason, he backed down. But, in self-defense, my sister's boyfriend killed one of the robbers in an alleyway, stabbing him in the back with a machete. I watched the whole thing.

By the age of 15, I was doing everything I could to have sex with as many girls as I could possibly get into my bed. I lied about my age and got my first job at a grocery store, working hard for little pay and supplementing my income by stealing cigarettes. I was spinning out of control, and I was 100% addicted to striving for acceptance.

Every day, I ran harder and faster than the day before on the hamster wheel of insanity, all to fill the void. But no matter how many girls I had sex with or how many times I masturbated, how much alcohol I drank, how many fights I won, or cigarettes I stole, nothing satisfied the void within me. Acceptance of applause, striving for love through sexual immorality, lying, cheating, and stealing all became the sinking sand of the island that I was building my life upon. And, no matter how many storms came and went, I just kept building my sandcastles on those secret beaches.

Are you living your life on an island?

How many sandcastles have you built?

How many secret beaches do you have that you hope no one ever discovers?

Storms are inevitable in this life. But, if you are building your life on the sinking sand of an island of acceptance, I want you to know there is hope for you. His name is Jesus Christ. He will come rescue you just like He did Peter. Just like He did me.

I will leave you with a question from the disciple named John, in Chapter 5, verse 44 of the Bible:

How can you believe? While accepting glory from one another, you don't seek the glory that comes from the only God.

Judge, Jury, and Executioner

Behold, I stand at the door and knock. If anyone hears my voice and opens the door, I will come in to him and eat with him, and he with me.

Revelation 3:20 English Standard Version

Have you reached a verdict?

The Book of Revelation describes our coming King and Judge with unmistakable clarity:

Revelation 19:11 English Standard Version

[11] Then I saw heaven opened, and behold, a white horse! The one sitting on it is called Faithful and True, and in righteousness he judges and makes war.

Jesus Christ is the one atop this white horse in the end of days. He is the King. He is the Judge.

So, if He is the Judge, why do you continuously place yourself in the Judge's seat? Or do you reject the notion that you do?

Have you ever questioned God?

I mean, if God is so loving, then answer these questions for me:

Why do young kids die from cancer?

Why do some men get away with raping women and children?

Why do some parents die in car crashes, leaving their children orphaned?

Why do the worst possible things always seem to happen to the best people?

Here are a few of mine that I have asked:

Why was I always sick, injured, and left to do life alone as a young kid?

Why did a man try to kidnap me while I was riding my bike when I was 9 years old?

Why did my best friend, Texas State Trooper Kurt D. Knapp, get killed in the line of duty when he was only 28 years old, leaving Jennifer, Makayla and Wyatt without a husband and father?

Why was my daughter born with four heart defects, a rare form of dwarfism, and given three weeks to live at birth, with no hope for survival?

These are just a few circumstances that have touched me personally. How many from your own life can you think of that you want answered by God?

Why do you think God allowed these things to happen if He is so loving and kind?

I think we can agree there are many times in life where we wish God would explain what He is thinking when bad things happen. But when we *question* (meaning judge in this context) God's motives and intentions for His creation, we are placing ourselves in a position of authority, either equal to or above God. We are saying, "You, sir, owe me an explanation for your actions." This is, once again, idolatry.

At the time of occurrence, I didn't understand why God allowed the things above to happen to me and my family, or to Kurt and his family. These events rocked my world and made me question my worth, God's love for me, and my faith in Him. But as time has passed, I can look back in the rearview mirror of my life and see what God did next. It is with this hindsight that I can say He knew what He was doing. I haven't always liked the circumstances, but I have a hard time arguing against His love when I see the results of His plan and His purposes for my life.

I encourage you to look at your circumstances through a different lens and ask yourself how God brought something good from something difficult.

Let me ask you another series of questions.

When was the last time you said you hated someone?

I haven't always liked the circumstances, but I have a hard time arguing against His love when I see the results of His plan and His purposes for my life.

When was the last time you said you wished you could get away with murder because you would kill someone for how they have treated you or for what they did to someone else?

I would like to be vulnerable and share a story with you from my days as a Criminal Investigator. Let me preface that I did not investigate the case I am going to reference. One of my colleagues at the Dallas County District Attorney's Office asked me and a few others to come to the courtroom as an extra layer of law enforcement presence while he presented the state's case against a man named Steven Lynn Long.

Steven Lynn Long was accused of raping, sodomizing, and murdering an 11-year-old girl named Kaitlyn Briana Smith. As I sat in the courtroom and heard the disgusting details of how this man murdered this precious little girl, I began to boil with anger. Wrath was all I could think about concerning this pathetic excuse of a man. When the case concluded and the verdict was being announced, I remember standing there staring a hole into the back of Steven Lynn Long's head. Kaitlyn's picture was still on the mantle of the judge's bench, and as I thought about what he had done to her and how cold-hearted and callous he was, I slid my hand under my jacket and onto the handle of my gun. I gripped that gun handle tightly and all I could think about was how I wanted to blow this man's head off for what he had done to her. I was beyond angry with him, and I wanted to see him hurt as much as he hurt Kaitlyn and her family.

In that moment, I wanted Steven to burn in Hell. I wanted to be the judge, jury, and executioner of Steven Lynn Long. I confess this sin to you, as I was wrong to sit in judgment of Steven. He is not a pathetic excuse of a man, regardless of how disgusting I considered his sin to be.

You see, Jesus died on the cross for Kaitlyn so she could be in Heaven with Him. But can you believe that while Jesus hung there in misery on that cross, He was also thinking about how much He loved Steven Lynn Long? Can you believe that God wanted to spend eternity in Heaven with him, too?

It's true. Jesus loves Steven just as much as He loved Kaitlyn. His grace is and was sufficient for both of them.

It's true. Jesus loves Steven just as much as He loved Kaitlyn. His grace is and was sufficient for both of them.

Have you ever been that angry with someone, like I was with Steven, that you wanted to see them rot in Hell?

Maybe just hearing this story makes you question how God could love a man like Steven Lynn Long just as much as He loved a precious little girl like Kaitlyn Briana Smith.

Well, since you, too, like to play judge, jury, and executioner of God and man, today, you get to be the "Judge".

Your Honor, The Judge

The matter before the court is this: how do we know Jesus really is who He says He is? What evidence proves it? *Is* there any evidence to prove it? Before you don your black robe and sit on the Judgment Seat, let me ask you a few pointed questions.

Do you believe that Jesus is the Son of God, the Messiah, the Lord of Hosts, the Holy One, and the Great I Am?

Have you ever seen with your own eyes any evidence to prove your case, either way? Or do you hold an opinion based on conjecture and/or abject ignorance?

Have you ever investigated the matter for yourself? Or do you listen to would-be-pundits who support your decidedly-so opinion on the subject without any direct examination of the evidence on your part?

In this chapter, you will weigh all the evidence in the case against Christ and determine whether Jesus is guilty of being God or He is not guilty by reason of being a liar. I will play the part of the investigator who has brought the case to a prosecutor. She and I will present the evidence and give testimony to the court in an effort to prove that Jesus is guilty of being God. A defense attorney will be present, and he will object to the evidence being presented in an effort to create reasonable doubt in your mind about Jesus' true identity. The Defense Attorney does not represent Jesus in this case; instead, he represents the opinion that Jesus is not God, and he scoffs at every shred of evidence that exists to prove otherwise. You might say he is a hater, and *haters are gonna hate, Proverbs 9:8.*

What is Your Evidence?

Before we go to trial, let me offer you a few details about the Criminal Justice system for context. I bet you have heard of eyewitness testimony, right? For eyewitness testimony to be a valid form of evidence in a case, the person identifying the defendant must be a credible witness; someone whose testimony is believable based on his or her experience, knowledge, training, and appearance of honesty and forthrightness.

But it takes more than a witness or two to hammer the metaphorical nail into the hands of the accused. That's where circumstantial and direct evidence come into play.

Circumstantial evidence is defined as evidence that tends to prove a fact by proving other events or circumstances, which afford a basis for a reasonable inference of the occurrence of the fact at issue.

Direct evidence can be any form of statement, such as an eyewitness' testimony, that is based on personal knowledge or observation and which, if true, directly proves or disproves an alleged or disputed fact without resorting to any assumption or inference.

You'll be hearing from eyewitnesses in this trial, and you will be presented with circumstantial and direct evidence.

The Facts of This Case

1. The Bible is an historical record of fact, not allegory, that will serve as business records for the case against Christ.
2. Over 2,000 credible eyewitnesses will be presented that positively identify Jesus Christ as God before He is crucified. These same eyewitnesses were recorded identifying Jesus in spontaneous utterances, and their recorded statements will serve as testimony about their personal knowledge of Him.
3. A Roman Centurion declares Jesus as the Son of God after Jesus dies on the cross in his presence.
4. Over 500 eyewitnesses saw Jesus alive after He was crucified on the cross.
5. Jesus confessed openly He is God on several occasions with many eyewitnesses on record.

All Rise, This Court Is Now in Session

Madam Prosecutor stands to her feet and addresses the court.

"Your honor, may I approach the bench?"

"Yes, you may.", you say to Madam Prosecutor.

"If it pleases the court, I would like to introduce Exhibit 1, quoted text from BibleInfo.com, for you to review before I call my first witness this morning."

Exhibit 1:

Who Wrote the Bible?[1]

Answer: 40 authors wrote the Bible over a period of 1,500 years. These Bible writers wrote as they were inspired by the Holy Spirit (see 2 Timothy 3:16-17). Moses was the first person to write portions of Scripture while John, the disciple of Jesus, was the last. Other famous people who wrote the Bible include David, Daniel, Peter, Paul, Jonah, Isaiah, and Solomon.

Diversity of Bible Writers

Those who wrote the Bible lived at different times, some separated by hundreds of years. In many cases they were complete strangers to one another. Some Bible writers were businessmen or traders; others were shepherds, fishermen, soldiers, physicians, preachers, kings—human beings from all walks of life. They served under different governments and lived within contrasting cultures and systems of philosophy.

All 66 Books of the Bible Agree

But here is the wonder of it all: When the 66 books of the Bible with their 1,189 chapters made up of 31,173 verses are brought together (KJV), we find perfect harmony in the message they convey. As the great scholar F. F. Bruce noted: "The Bible is not simply an anthology; there is a unity which binds the whole together."

Who Wrote the Bible: God or Man?

The Scripture says in II Peter 1:20-21, "You must understand that no prophecy of Scripture came about by the prophet's own interpretation. For prophecy never had its origin in the will of man, but men spoke from God as they were carried along by the Holy Spirit."

The Holy Spirit revealed to the prophets the messages of Scripture. The writers of the Bible wrote not according to their own will or whim, but only as they were moved, or controlled, by the Spirit of God. The Bible is God's own book.

II Timothy 3:16-17, "All Scripture is God-breathed and is useful for teaching, rebuking, correcting and training in righteousness, so that the man of God may be thoroughly equipped for every good work." The Holy Bible affects human beings so profoundly, because "all" the Bible is "God-breathed." It's more than a nice collection of moral principles. It's more than a great book. It's an inspired document, God's book. The prophets who wrote the Bible related what they saw and heard in human language, but their message came directly from God. – end quote from BibleInfo.com

You say, "I've reviewed the information about the authenticity of the Bible from BibleInfo.com, marked as Exhibit 1, and the information therein will be considered in my final deliberation."

Madam Prosecutor replies, "Thank you Your Honor. If it pleases the court, I would like to call Satan as my first witness."

The Defense Attorney stands to his feet and loudly proclaims, "Objection, your honor. This alleged witness is little more than a man-made carica-ture; a little red devil with horns and a pointy tail holding a pitchfork. Are you really going to entertain such ludicrous allegory based on a character named "Hot Stuff the Little Devil" from a comic book? Seriously Your Honor, should we expect Casper the Friendly Ghost to be the next wit-ness called?"

You reply, "Before I rule, do you have any evidence to prove the character of Satan, beyond the defense's assertion that he is a comic book character?"

"Yes, your honor. I submit the following business records from the Bible to the court which explains the being, character, and nature of Satan."

Exhibit 2:

Ezekiel 28:13-19 English Standard Version (ESV)

Here is some context for this chapter which is often misunderstood: Ezekiel 28:1-12 addresses the Prince of Tyre (the earthly king), while verses 13-19 address the King of Tyre – Lucifer, or Satan. Satan is the king of this world, the authority of which he received from Adam in Eve during the fall of man.

Ezekiel tells us the backstory of Satan through God's message of lament for the King of Tyre.

¹³ You were in Eden, the garden of God;
every precious stone was your covering,
sardius, topaz, and diamond,
beryl, onyx, and jasper,
sapphire,[a] emerald, and carbuncle;
and crafted in gold were your settings
and your engravings.[b]
On the day that you were created
they were prepared.
¹⁴ You were an anointed guardian cherub.
I placed you;[c] you were on the holy mountain of God;
in the midst of the stones of fire you walked.
¹⁵ You were blameless in your ways
from the day you were created,
till unrighteousness was found in you.
¹⁶ In the abundance of your trade
you were filled with violence in your midst, and you sinned;
so I cast you as a profane thing from the mountain of God,
and I destroyed you,[d] O guardian cherub,
from the midst of the stones of fire.
¹⁷ Your heart was proud because of your beauty;
you corrupted your wisdom for the sake of your splendor.
I cast you to the ground;
I exposed you before kings,
to feast their eyes on you.
¹⁸ By the multitude of your iniquities,
in the unrighteousness of your trade
you profaned your sanctuaries;
so I brought fire out from your midst;
it consumed you,
and I turned you to ashes on the earth
in the sight of all who saw you.
¹⁹ All who know you among the peoples
are appalled at you;
you have come to a dreadful end

and shall be no more forever."

Exhibit 3:

Isaiah 14:12-15 English Standard Version (ESV)

Regarding Satan
[12] "How you are fallen from heaven,
O Day Star, son of Dawn.
How you are cut down to the ground,
you who laid the nations low.
[13] You said in your heart,
'I will ascend to heaven;
above the stars of God
I will set my throne on high;
I will sit on the mount of assembly
in the far reaches of the north;[a]
[14] I will ascend above the heights of the clouds;
I will make myself like the Most High.'
[15] But you are brought down to Sheol,
to the far reaches of the pit.

Exhibit 4:

Job 1:6-12 English Standard Version (ESV)

Satan Allowed to Test Job
[6] Now there was a day when the sons of God came to present themselves before the Lord, and Satan[a] also came among them. [7] The Lord said to Satan, "From where have you come?" Satan answered the Lord and said, "From going to and fro on the earth, and from walking up and down on it." [8] And the Lord said to Satan, "Have you considered my servant Job, that there is none like him on the earth, a blameless and upright man, who fears God and turns away from evil?" [9] Then Satan answered the Lord and said, "Does Job fear God for no reason? [10] Have you not put a hedge around him and his house and all that he has, on every side? You have blessed the work of his hands, and his possessions have increased in the land. [11] But stretch out your hand and touch all that he has, and he will curse you to your face."

¹² And the Lord said to Satan, "Behold, all that he has is in your hand. Only against him do not stretch out your hand." So, Satan went out from the presence of the Lord.

Exhibit 5:

Revelation 12:9 English Standard Version (ESV)

Regarding Satan
⁹ And the great dragon was thrown down, that ancient serpent, who is called the devil and Satan, the deceiver of the whole world—he was thrown down to the earth, and his angels were thrown down with him.

Exhibit 6:

Luke 4 English Standard Version (ESV)

The Temptation of Jesus
4 And Jesus, full of the Holy Spirit, returned from the Jordan and was led by the Spirit in the wilderness ² for forty days, being tempted by the devil. And he ate nothing during those days. And when they were ended, he was hungry. ³ The devil said to him, "If you are the Son of God, command this stone to become bread." ⁴ And Jesus answered him, "It is written, 'Man shall not live by bread alone.'" ⁵ And the devil took him up and showed him all the kingdoms of the world in a moment of time, ⁶ and said to him, "To you I will give all this authority and their glory, for it has been delivered to me, and I give it to whom I will. ⁷ If you, then, will worship me, it will all be yours." ⁸ And Jesus answered him, "It is written,
"'You shall worship the Lord your God,
and him only shall you serve.'"
⁹ And he took him to Jerusalem and set him on the pinnacle of the temple and said to him, "If you are the Son of God, throw yourself down from here, ¹⁰ for it is written,
"'He will command his angels concerning you,
to guard you,'
¹¹ and
"'On their hands they will bear you up,
lest you strike your foot against a stone.'"

[12] And Jesus answered him, "It is said, 'You shall not put the Lord your God to the test.'"[13] And when the devil had ended every temptation, he departed from him until an opportune time.

After you review the exhibits, you say, "I'll allow the exhibits Madam Prosecutor in lieu of Satan personally appearing before the court. Objection is overruled."

Madam Prosecutor then calls Ricky Sluder to the witness stand.

"Mr. Sluder, will you please share the findings of your investigation against Christ with the court."

I reply in non-quoted text, which is consistent with my commentary as the author of this book.

The purpose of my investigation is to prove that Jesus Christ is God in the flesh, and while living in human form on the Earth, He possessed all manner of God's authority. Before I launch into the facts of my case, I cannot help but mention something I observed in Exhibit 6 above. Satan asked Jesus to offer him His acceptance, he attacked Jesus' identity more than once, he tested his security, and Satan tried to prevent Jesus from achieving His divine purpose, all of which we will touch on in the remaining chapters of this book.

For now, I'll stay on topic to avoid an objection from the defense.

Your honor, do you know why Satan asked the question, "If you are the Son of God, command this stone to become bread."?

You reply, "I am not able to testify in this case, so I cannot answer your question. But I would like for you to offer me your perspective for consideration in my final deliberation."

Satan challenged Jesus' identity, that much is clear. However, the less clear issue, but one that is at the heart of the matter for acceptance, is that Satan attempted to get Jesus to be his own provider and he wanted Jesus to strive for acceptance from Satan.

We all struggle with surrendering our will to the will of God and accepting Him as our provision in all matters. Jesus had the vested authority to do as He wished. After all, He is God manifest in human form. But here is a spiritual lesson I believe He wants all of us to learn. Jesus surrendered His will to the Father, was led by the Holy Spirit in the wilderness, and accepted that, while in human form, He would not be His own provision. Instead, the Father would be His provision. Jesus offered His acceptance to the Father.

In the New Testament, Jesus says repeatedly, "I am not here to do my own will, but that of my Father who sent me." He demonstrates for us how to surrender our will and how to accept the will of the Father who has also sent us into this world.

Let's examine Jesus' response to Satan's first question.

"It is written, 'Man shall not live by bread alone.'"

I believe that Jesus was saying we must learn to trust and rely on God's grace to sustain us. We must resist the temptation to become the provider when God alone is our provider.

Post crucifixion, Jesus tells Paul this very same thing.

2 Corinthians 12:9 English Standard Version (ESV)
⁹ But he said to me, "My grace is sufficient for you, for my power is made perfect in weakness." Therefore, I will boast all the more gladly of my weaknesses, so that the power of Christ may rest upon me.

Your honor, Jesus is saying, "Grace will be sufficient for me, Satan. I don't need to use my authority to turn this stone into bread. I accept the will of the Father over my own needs or desires, and I submit myself to Him. His will be done over my own. Furthermore, Satan, I don't have anything to prove to you, and I will not strive for your acceptance."

Let's examine the next thing Satan did when he couldn't get Jesus to strive for his acceptance. (Continuing in Luke 4:5-8)

⁵ And the devil took him up and showed him all the kingdoms of the world in a moment of time, ⁶ and said to him, "To you I will give all this authority and their glory, for it has been delivered to me, and I give it to whom I will. ⁷ If you, then, will worship me, it will all be yours."

Oh, this is so good Your Honor. Did you see what Satan did?

Satan said, "offer me your acceptance as the god of this world, and I will make sure you get all the glory."

Once again, Satan wanted Jesus to seek acceptance from him, and if Jesus would just bow down and worship him, He could receive all manner of authority and glory.

Why do you think Satan does this?

What does it mean when Satan says *"…for it has been delivered to me…"*?

Here is what I have learned about Satan in the biblical accounts I have read. Satan is a counterfeiter. He lacks originality and copies what the Father has put into order, but with his own twisted version. He knows that acceptance is for us to give to God, not receive from others; even he was responsible for offering God acceptance. But his pride got in the way, and it is my opinion and understanding that he thought he would be ruling with God, not Adam and Eve. When Satan realized that Adam and Eve, lower life forms than he as a Cherubim, were chosen to rule with God, he rebelled against this plan and refused to serve God and man as they ruled together. As such, in the Garden of Eden, Satan convinced Adam and Eve to choose to rule this present world with him, instead of with God. I believe that the fruit they ate was the lie he told them that they could be like God, and they could rule this present world without a need for God to be in it. It's my belief that in Satan's mind, if he couldn't rule with God, then God wouldn't get to rule with man as intended. Therefore, I believe, he tells Jesus that all the kingdoms of this world were *delivered* to him. Adam and Eve delivered this authority to him when they chose the fruit of the Tree of the Knowledge of Good and Evil (Satan) over the fruit from the Tree of Life (Jesus). So, Satan tried to get Jesus to accept him as God, the same way he convinced Adam and Eve – through deceitful promises of power and glory.

As a sidebar, I will cover more about the Garden of Eden in Part 3: Security.

Your Honor, when we command others to strive for acceptance from us, we place ourselves on a false throne; thus, mimicking Satan. We elevate ourselves to a false position of authority, and we take the glory that only God can receive from mankind. This is exactly what Adam and Eve did and it is why mankind "fell" and paradise was lost!

Jesus proves my point with His response to Satan in Luke 4:8 English Standard Version (ESV)

⁸ And Jesus answered him, "It is written,
"'You shall worship the Lord your God,
and him only shall you serve.'"

Not being one who gives up easily, Satan immediately counters Jesus with an identity attack meant to undermine Jesus' security in the promises of the Father by quoting scripture to him.

Continuing in Luke 4:9-12 English Standard Version (ESV)

⁹ And he took him to Jerusalem and set him on the pinnacle of the temple and said to him, "If you are the Son of God, throw yourself down from here, ¹⁰ for it is written,
"'He will command his angels concerning you,
to guard you,'
¹¹ and
"'On their hands they will bear you up, lest you strike your foot against a stone.'"
¹² And Jesus answered him, "It is said, 'You shall not put the Lord your God to the test.'

At the risk of oversimplification, Satan is trying to get Jesus to strive for acceptance from him, but this time he wants Jesus to prove that the Father really does love Him enough to protect Him, as the Father has promised. Jesus wisely rebukes Satan in verse 12 and reminds him that there is no need to test the promises of God. His Word stands, and that is enough.

Also, in case you missed it Your Honor, Jesus declares He is God, in this verse. Let me show you verse 12 again.

¹² And Jesus answered him, "It is said, 'You [Satan] shall not put the Lord *your* God to the test.'"

Satan was testing Jesus, who said, "do not put the Lord your God to the test." Thus, Jesus is saying here that He is, in fact, God.

If you will permit me some latitude here Your Honor, I am going to show you something I believe you need to see in this moment from this story.

If you look back at the verses, you will notice that this story is the primer for the framework of this entire book you are reading. Jesus lived every aspect of it!

1. Acceptance - Satan wanted Jesus to strive for his acceptance instead of offering it to the one true God.
2. Identity - Satan attacked and challenged Jesus' identity and tried to get Him to strive for acceptance from him in order to prove His own identity.
3. Security - Satan challenged Jesus about His security in the promises of God, which were tied to a second attack and challenge on Jesus' identity.
4. Purpose - Had Jesus given an inch, it would have upended Jesus' mission and kept Him from living from the place of His true purpose, which He goes on to do in the very next verse.

Continuing in Luke 4:14 English Standard Version (ESV)

Jesus Begins His Ministry

¹⁴ And Jesus returned in the power of the Spirit to Galilee, and a report about him went out through all the surrounding country. ¹⁵ And he taught in their synagogues, being glorified by all.

The defense attorney stands up and says, "Objection. Satan didn't definitively identify Jesus as the living God and therefore His testimony should be stricken from the record. Satan's testimony, at best, is circumstantial because it relies on Jesus to validate His own identity through striving works of acceptance."

Madam Prosecutor breaks in, "Your Honor, the next couple of witnesses are all associates of Satan, and they will not only corroborate Satan's testimony, but they will offer testimony that is direct evidence in identifying Jesus as God."

You say, "Objection overruled counselor. I want to hear this testimony from Satan's associates. Madam Prosecutor, this had better be good, or I will reverse my ruling."

Madam Prosecutor replies, "Understood Your Honor. If it pleases the court, Mr. Sluder will provide you with demon testimony from scriptures being placed into evidence. These are marked as Exhibits 7, 8 and 9 for your review. In the records provided, there are 2,000 eyewitnesses who positively identify Jesus as God in the presence of several witnesses. Mr. Sluder, will you please provide the court with the investigative findings from these exhibits?"

Exhibit 7:

Luke 4:31-37 English Standard Version (ESV)

Jesus Heals a Man with an Unclean Demon

[31] And he went down to Capernaum, a city of Galilee. And he was teaching them on the Sabbath, [32] and they were astonished at his teaching, for his word possessed authority. [33] And in the synagogue there was a man who had the spirit of an unclean demon, and he cried out with a loud voice,

[34] "Ha.[a] What have you to do with us, Jesus of Nazareth? Have you come to destroy us? I know who you are—the Holy One of God."

[35] But Jesus rebuked him, saying, "Be silent and come out of him." And when the demon had thrown him down in their midst, he came out of him, having done him no harm. [36] And they were all amazed and said to one another, "What is this word? For with authority and power he commands

the unclean spirits, and they come out." [37] And reports about him went out into every place in the surrounding region.

Exhibit 8:

Luke 4:38-41 English Standard Version (ESV)

Jesus Heals Many

[38] And he arose and left the synagogue and entered Simon's house. Now Simon's mother-in-law was ill with a high fever, and they appealed to him on her behalf. [39] And he stood over her and rebuked the fever, and it left her, and immediately she rose and began to serve them.

[40] Now when the sun was setting, all those who had any who were sick with various diseases brought them to him, and he laid his hands on every one of them and healed them.

[41] And demons also came out of many, crying, "You are the Son of God." But he rebuked them and would not allow them to speak, because they knew that he was the Christ.

Exhibit 9:

Mark 5 English Standard Version (ESV)

Jesus Heals a Man with a Demon

5 They came to the other side of the sea, to the country of the Gerasenes. [a] [2] And when Jesus[b] had stepped out of the boat, immediately there met him out of the tombs a man with an unclean spirit. [3] He lived among the tombs. And no one could bind him anymore, not even with a chain, [4] for he had often been bound with shackles and chains, but he wrenched the chains apart, and he broke the shackles in pieces. No one had the strength to subdue him. [5] Night and day among the tombs and on the mountains he was always crying out and cutting himself with stones. [6] And when he saw Jesus from afar, he ran and fell down before him.

[7] And crying out with a loud voice, he (the head-demon) said, "What have you to do with me, Jesus, Son of the Most High God? I adjure you by God, do not torment me."

[8] For he (Jesus) was saying to him, "Come out of the man, you unclean spirit." [9] And Jesus asked him, "What is your name?" He replied, "My name is Legion, for we are many."

[10] And he (the head-demon) begged him earnestly not to send them (about 2,000 demons in total) out of the country.

[11] Now a great herd of pigs was feeding there on the hillside,

[12] and they (about 2,000 demons) begged him, saying, "Send us to the pigs; let us enter them."

[13] So he gave them permission. And the unclean spirits came out and entered the pigs; and the herd, numbering about two thousand, rushed down the steep bank into the sea and drowned in the sea.

[14] The herdsmen fled and told it in the city and in the country. And people came to see what it was that had happened. [15] And they came to Jesus and saw the demon-possessed[c] man, the one who had had the legion, sitting there, clothed and in his right mind, and they were afraid. [16] And those who had seen it described to them what had happened to the demon-possessed man and to the pigs. [17] And they began to beg Jesus[d] to depart from their region.

[18] As he was getting into the boat, the man who had been possessed with demons begged him that he might be with him. [19] And he did not permit him but said to him, "Go home to your friends and tell them how much the Lord has done for you, and how he has had mercy on you." [20] And he went away and began to proclaim in the Decapolis how much Jesus had done for him, and everyone marveled.

After the reading of the investigative findings from scripture, Madam Prosecutor says, "Your honor, let the record reflect that the enemy of Jesus, Satan, and Satan's associates not only knew who He was, and is, but they made it known audibly in front of many witnesses that Jesus is the Lord God."

You say, "The record will reflect the testimony and I will consider it in my final deliberation of this case."

Madam Prosecutor says, "Mr. Sluder, will you please provide a summary to the court about our next witness, the Roman Centurion, since he is an unnamed witness in these proceedings?"

Your Honor, in the scripture this man was not identified by name, so please allow me some latitude as I describe him to the court. He was one of King Herod's top military men reporting to Pilate. He was more than just a Roman soldier, though. He was a high-ranking officer. This man was the Roman Military Commander, a Centurion, and as such he had more than 100 soldiers reporting to him. This man not only witnessed the brutal beatings of Jesus, but he was the man who ordered them. From the time Pilate accepted the plea of the crowd to crucify Jesus, this man was leading the charge of everything that happened to Jesus. From the repeated lashes with a cat-of-nine-tails and the robe of mockery, to the crown of thorns placed upon His head and the malicious beatings that took place all the way to Golgotha, where Jesus would be nailed to a cross. This man, Your Honor, was a seasoned veteran. He likely had presided over thousands of crucifixions in his career, and it is worthy to note that he likely had grown callous to the agony of the men he crucified. This Military Commander is mentioned in three of the four gospel accounts and his testimony is not only relevant to these proceedings, but it is extremely powerful.

Madam Prosecutor approaches the bench and says, "Your Honor, Mr. Sluder will be providing his investigative findings to you from scripture in Exhibits 10, 11 and 12 marked here for your review."

Exhibit 10:

Matthew 27:51-54 English Standard Version (ESV)

[51] And behold, the curtain of the temple was torn in two, from top to bottom. And the earth shook, and the rocks were split.

[52] The tombs also were opened. And many bodies of the saints who had fallen asleep were raised, [53] and coming out of the tombs after his resurrection they went into the holy city and appeared to many.

[54] When the centurion and those who were with him, keeping watch over Jesus, saw the earthquake and what took place, they were filled with awe and said, "Truly this was the Son[a] of God."

Your honor, I submit for your consideration that the Centurion was not alone in this admonition. The scripture says *they* were filled with awe, which implies more than one person. I submit for your consideration that even the four Roman soldiers who had earlier cast lots for Jesus' clothes realized that He was in fact the Son of God.

Now, if you will turn with me to Exhibits 11 and 12, I will share corroborating testimony of this Centurion's assertion that Jesus is God.

Exhibit 11:

Mark 15:33-41 English Standard Version (ESV)

The Death of Jesus
[33] At noon, darkness came over the whole land until three in the afternoon. [34] And at three in the afternoon Jesus cried out in a loud voice, "*Eloi, Eloi, lema sabachthani?*" (which means "My God, my God, why have you forsaken me?").[b]
[35] When some of those standing near heard this, they said, "Listen, he's calling Elijah."
[36] Someone ran, filled a sponge with wine vinegar, put it on a staff, and offered it to Jesus to drink. "Now leave him alone. Let's see if Elijah comes to take him down," he said.
[37] With a loud cry, Jesus breathed his last.

[38] The curtain of the temple was torn in two from top to bottom.

[39] And when the centurion, who stood there in front of Jesus, saw how he died,[c] he said, "Surely this man was the Son of God."

[40] Some women were watching from a distance. Among them were Mary Magdalene, Mary the mother of James the younger and of Joseph,[d] and Salome. [41] In Galilee these women had followed him and cared for his needs. Many other women who had come up with him to Jerusalem were also there.

Exhibit 12:

Luke 23:44-49 English Standard Version (ESV)

The Death of Jesus

[44] It was now about noon, and darkness came over the whole land until three in the afternoon, [45] for the sun stopped shining. And the curtain of the temple was torn in two. [46] Jesus called out with a loud voice, "Father, into your hands I commit my spirit."[e] When he had said this, he breathed his last.

[47] The centurion, seeing what had happened, praised God and said, "Surely this was a righteous man."

[48] When all the people who had gathered to witness this sight saw what took place, they beat their breasts and went away. [49] But all those who knew him, including the women who had followed him from Galilee, stood at a distance, watching these things.

As I finish my testimony from these exhibits, the Defense Attorney levels another objection. "Your honor, if all of this evidence is true, then why didn't the religious leaders of Jesus' day, the Pharisees, convict Him of being God? I'll tell you why they didn't, because they found Him not guilty of being God and they murdered Him for being a liar!"

Madam Prosecutor interjects, "Your honor, as providence would have it, I am entering into evidence Exhibit 13, and Mr. Sluder will provide you with testimony from Jesus Himself, as to why the religious leaders of His day arrived at the wrong verdict in their hearts about His true identity."

You say, "Alright, objection overruled. The exhibits will be reviewed and considered."

Exhibit 13:

John 5:39-44 English Standard Version (ESV)

[39] You search the Scriptures because you think that in them you have eternal life; and it is they that bear witness about me, [40] yet you refuse to come to me that you may have life. [41] I do not receive glory from people. [42] But I know that you do not have the love of God within you. [43] I have come in my Father's name, and you do not receive me. If another comes in his own name, you will receive him. [44] How can you believe, when you receive glory from one another and do not seek the glory that comes from the only God?

Your Honor, here is what I believe Jesus was saying to the Pharisees:

You search for the right words to quote to others from scripture so you can impress them with your biblical knowledge. You do this because you crave their acceptance; you want people to affirm you as religious men.

But you miss the point of the scriptures you read. It is a relationship with me that you should be seeking. Yet, you refuse to accept me for who I am. You proclaim for all to hear that you know my Father, because you have the very scriptures that have foretold of my coming memorized. Scripture memorization is pointless when it is kept for head-knowledge and not applied to your life and living within your heart.

It is true that you have the Law memorized, but you only do it so you can receive praise for your recitations. You love no one else as much as you love yourself. You can't possibly accept me as your God because you occupy your own throne as a self-aggrandizing god of your own life. Furthermore, you only want those who look and sound like you to be in your inner circle. How can you possibly believe what you claim you believe about my Father, when you would rather receive a worthless trophy from strangers, than the grace I offer you?

Madam Prosecutor says, "If it pleases the court, Your Honor, I will submit my two final Exhibits, 14 and 15. Mr. Sluder will testify to the fact that Exhibit 14 refutes the notion that after Jesus died, his friends took His body and hid it. Please let the record reflect that over 500 independent witnesses saw Jesus walking, heard Jesus talking, and they interacted with Him after He had resurrected. Mr. Sluder will testify to this fact in Exhibit 15, where Jesus declares His identity to the Pharisees."

Exhibit 14:

1 Corinthians 15 English Standard Version (ESV)

The Resurrection of Christ

15 Now I would remind you, brothers,[a] of the gospel I preached to you, which you received, in which you stand, [2] and by which you are being saved, if you hold fast to the word I preached to you—unless you believed in vain.

[3] For I delivered to you as of first importance what I also received: that Christ died for our sins in accordance with the Scriptures, [4] that he was buried, that he was raised on the third day in accordance with the Scriptures, [5] and that he appeared to Cephas (Peter), then to the twelve.

[6] Then he appeared to more than five hundred brothers at one time, most of whom are still alive, though some have fallen asleep.

[7] Then he appeared to James, then to all the apostles. [8] Last of all, as to one untimely born, he appeared also to me. [9] For I am the least of the apostles, unworthy to be called an apostle, because I persecuted the church of God. [10] But by the grace of God I am what I am, and his grace toward me was not in vain. On the contrary, I worked harder than any of them, though it was not I, but the grace of God that is with me. [11] Whether then it was I or they, so we preach and so you believed.

Exhibit 15:

John 8:48-58 English Standard Version (ESV)

Before Abraham Was, I Am

[48] The Jews answered him, "Are we not right in saying that you are a Samaritan and have a demon?" [49] Jesus answered, "I do not have a demon, but I honor my Father, and you dishonor me. [50] Yet I do not seek my own glory; there is One who seeks it, and he is the judge. [51] Truly, truly, I say

to you, if anyone keeps my word, he will never see death." [52] The Jews said to him, "Now we know that you have a demon. Abraham died, as did the prophets, yet you say, 'If anyone keeps my word, he will never taste death.' [53] Are you greater than our father Abraham, who died? And the prophets died. Who do you make yourself out to be?" [54] Jesus answered, "If I glorify myself, my glory is nothing. It is my Father who glorifies me, of whom you say, 'He is our God.' [a] [55] But you have not known him. I know him. If I were to say that I do not know him, I would be a liar like you, but I do know him and I keep his word. [56] Your father Abraham rejoiced that he would see my day. He saw it and was glad." [57] So the Jews said to him, "You are not yet fifty years old, and have you seen Abraham?" [b]

[58] Jesus said to them, "Truly, truly, I say to you, before Abraham was, I am."

Upon your review and the hearing of the exhibits read by Mr. Sluder, you say, "Based on the evidence I am seeing here, I am allowing all the evidence previously submitted to be considered in this case against Christ. Counselor, your objections are noted on the record, but remain overruled."

Madam Prosecutor stands to her feet, "Your honor, before I rest my case, I want to recap what I have presented to you today. First, I did not bring you testimonials of bias; anyone can parade the friends of Jesus in front of the court and clearly, they will say what we all expect them to say. He is God. We wouldn't expect anything less from His prophets, disciples, and apostles. However, I have presented the enemies of Jesus as witnesses on His behalf. The testimony and evidence I have presented to this court today is without relational bias and, therefore, the weight of this evidence is greater than the testimony of all of Jesus' friends. I implore you to consider the sources here as you weigh the evidence for your verdict."

The Defense Attorney rises to his feet and exclaims, "Your honor, I call for a mistrial. Madam Prosecutor has presented an argument that requires us to believe that the Bible is somehow an historical record. I ask the court to strike all of the evidence presented today because she failed to make a prima fascia case by citing everything from one unreliable book of allegory."

I interject from the witness stand, as I wasn't yet excused by the court.

Your honor, may I address the defense with a question? It will serve as further evidence in this case if I am permitted.

You say, "It's highly unprecedented Mr. Sluder for a witness to question a defense attorney, but I will allow it as I'm curious what you have to say."

Thank you, Your Honor.

Mr. Defense Attorney. Do you question the historical existence of Julius Caesar?

The Defense Attorney boldly exclaims, "Are you kidding me? Hell no. It is a well-documented fact that Julius Caesar lived and reigned."

I reply, Thank you sir, you just proved my point.

Your honor, may I explain the point that he just proved?

You say, "Yes, please, I am not sure I am tying the two ends together on this one Mr. Sluder."

Did you know that it is an historical fact that we have more sources citing the life of Jesus of Nazareth than we do for any other first century figure? There are at least 18 sources that historians are aware of and 12 of the 18 are non-Christian sources. In fact, Mr. Defense Attorney, there are more historical sources for the existence of Jesus than there are for the existence of Julius Caesar. Yet, you made it abundantly clear that Julius Caesar ruled and reigned. And before you object again, let me ask for the record to reflect that the Bible, as an historical record, has more surviving pages or fragments than any other body of work from antiquity. In fact, there are more than 5,800 Greek manuscripts and more than 8,000 Latin manuscripts. Your assertion, Mr. Defense Attorney, that the Bible is unreliable and that the life, death, and resurrection of Jesus Christ is allegorical, is intellectual dishonesty on your part. Because you choose not to accept Him, or the Word, does not make it untrue. I can claim that gravity is little more than scientific theory, Your Honor, but gravity will not lose its grip on me just because I choose not to accept its reality. The same is true of Jesus, His grip on your life and His love for you remain, regardless of your unbelief.

So, tell me Your Honor, is Jesus guilty of being God, or is He is not guilty by reason of being a liar?

Have you reached a verdict?

THE ROCK, THE VINE, AND WILD GRAPES

Behold, I stand at the door and knock. If anyone hears my voice and opens the door, I will come in to him and eat with him, and he with me.

Revelation 3:20 English Standard Version

What foundation are you building your life upon?

Do you see how my circumstances I shared with you in Storms, Sandcastles, and Secret Beaches shaped my perspective, which in turn, shaped the choices I made when selecting the foundation, I built my life on? I spent nearly 40 years striving for acceptance from nearly every person that entered my life. As a result, I created so many bad habits that each of them began to operate on autopilot in my subconscious mind. I found myself running in overdrive trying to prove my worth to anyone who would listen. Offering my resume verbally to impress people I just met or embellishing the truth about my upbringing, so I didn't sound like a charity case. I wanted to look, feel, and sound normal, but I had no idea what normal looked like. Truth be told, there is no such thing as normal. There is *Truth* and there are lies, but normal is something we manufacture and sell to one another based on our perception of reality within the culture we live.

It's entirely possible that you have wasted as much of your life as I have of mine chasing after the applause of mankind. Metaphorically waking up year after year, continuously sinking in the quicksand of your striving behavior. Suffering from your bad habits that have been formed by the very scar tissue of the wounds inflicted on your heart from the countless lies you have bought from family, friends, and strangers, alike.

So, tell me friend, have those wounds you have nursed year after year with the secret sedatives of your choosing impacted the choices you have made about the foundation of your life?

Of course, they have. The real question is, are you willing to admit it?

Fear and pride used to hold me back from admitting what I knew was true about me. I was so afraid I would shatter the "good reputation" I had built, and I was terrified I would lose everything I thought mattered in this life if I owned up to all my sins.

Does that ring true for you?

The problem with this fear-based mindset is it limits your ability to overcome your past and to deprogram those autopilot settings you keep repeating. Fear and pride are prison walls of the mind and heart that you cannot afford to hide behind anymore.

Fear and pride are prison walls of the mind and heart that you cannot afford to hide behind anymore.

Why do you justify those prison walls to yourself as a good thing, when you prevent yourself from ever finding the hope you seek by hiding behind them?

While you consider these questions, I am going to recite three different stories from the Bible to help you understand how acceptance frames your foundation for living and the consequences that stem from choosing the wrong foundation.

I have subtitled the stories to match the title of this chapter. Let's begin in the Old Testament with Wild Grapes and work our way into the New Testament with The Vine, as they are one story told from two different voices. Then, we will end with The Rock.

Wild Grapes:

Isaiah 5:1-10 English Standard Version

The Vineyard of the Lord Destroyed

⁵ Let me sing for my beloved
my love song concerning his vineyard:
My beloved had a vineyard
on a very fertile hill.
² He dug it and cleared it of stones,
and planted it with choice vines;
he built a watchtower in the midst of it,
and hewed out a wine vat in it;
and he looked for it to yield grapes,
but it yielded wild grapes.
³ And now, O inhabitants of Jerusalem
and men of Judah,
judge between me and my vineyard.
⁴ What more was there to do for my vineyard,
that I have not done in it?
When I looked for it to yield grapes,
why did it yield wild grapes?
⁵ And now I will tell you
what I will do to my vineyard.
I will remove its hedge,
and it shall be devoured;[a]
I will break down its wall,
and it shall be trampled down.
⁶ I will make it a waste;
it shall not be pruned or hoed,
and briers and thorns shall grow up;
I will also command the clouds
that they rain no rain upon it.
⁷ For the vineyard of the Lord of hosts
is the house of Israel,
and the men of Judah
are his pleasant planting;
and he looked for justice,
but behold, bloodshed;[b]
for righteousness,
but behold, an outcry.[c]

Woe to the Wicked
8 Woe to those who join house to house,
who add field to field,
until there is no more room,
and you are made to dwell alone
in the midst of the land.
9 The Lord of hosts has sworn in my hearing:
"Surely many houses shall be desolate,
large and beautiful houses, without inhabitant.
10 For ten acres[d] of vineyard shall yield but one bath,
and a homer of seed shall yield but an ephah."[e]

In Isaiah 5:1-10, entitled above as Wild Grapes, Isaiah is conveying a message of warning to the chosen people of God, the Israelites. Like a good Daddy would do, God did many wondrous things for His people. Like spoiled-rotten children would do, the Israelites (not unlike like you and me) chose to love other gods and turn their back on their one true Father. They pushed Him away, rejected His warnings, and chose disobedience over blessing. Because love is a choice, God let them have the things they chose over Him. It is not what He wanted then, nor does He want this for us now, but He refuses to force us to love Him. God refused to bless the life they chose, and He will not compromise His character for you. Thus, Isaiah wrote, "many houses shall be desolate". The people who reject God are the desolate houses. He is not within them, and their lives are empty. When you reject God, the fruit of your rejection leaves a sour taste in His mouth, the same way sour (*Wild*) grapes cause us to wince when we eat them.

The Vine:

Mark 12:1-12, English Standard translation.

The Parable of the Tenants

12 And he began to speak to them in parables. "A man planted a vineyard and put a fence around it and dug a pit for the winepress and built a tower, and leased it to tenants and went into another country.
2 When the season came, he sent a servant[a] to the tenants to get from them some of the fruit of the vineyard.

³ And they took him and beat him and sent him away empty-handed.
⁴ Again he sent to them another servant, and they struck him on the head and treated him shamefully.
⁵ And he sent another, and him they killed. And so, with many others: some they beat, and some they killed.
⁶ He had still one other, a beloved son. Finally, he sent him to them, saying, 'They will respect my son.'
⁷ But those tenants said to one another, 'This is the heir. Come, let us kill him, and the inheritance will be ours.'
⁸ And they took him and killed him and threw him out of the vineyard.
⁹ What will the owner of the vineyard do? He will come and destroy the tenants and give the vineyard to others.
¹⁰ Have you not read this Scripture:
"'The stone that the builders rejected
has become the cornerstone;[b]
11 this was the Lord's doing,
and it is marvelous in our eyes'?"
¹² And they were seeking to arrest him but feared the people, for they perceived that he had told the parable against them. So, they left him and went away.

Let's unpack Mark 12:1-9, entitled above as The Vine, but called The Parable of the Tenants in the Bible. I will begin with this outline so you can substitute the terms and follow what Jesus is conveying to the Pharisees. My hope is that this will help you form ways to interrogate the Word for yourself.

- The landowner represents God
- The vineyard represents God's Kingdom
- The tenants are the Pharisees with whom Jesus was speaking, but it also represents all people who reject Jesus
- The servants are God's prophets and faithful believers from the beginning to the end of time
- The beloved son is, none other than, Jesus Christ

God's Kingdom, the vineyard, has been planted on this earth. Just as it has been since the beginning, there are people who accept Him and people who reject Him. Jesus told this story to the Pharisees because they were angry with Him for entering the Temple and teaching things they disagreed with. You see, Jesus' declaration of being the Messiah and His message of grace, love, and forgiveness didn't align with the narrative the Pharisees had adopted as truth. Over many centuries, God sent prophets and ordinary men and women to share His message, and many of them were beaten and killed. So, He finally sent His Son into the world to share this message of hope. In this parable, God is trying to get our attention. He has an expectation that we won't waste our lives on worldly living (selfishness), and that we will tend to His *vine press* and produce *fruit* for His Kingdom.

The tenants were not interested in working for the landowner. They wanted the vineyard for themselves; they wanted to be God, not serve God. This is illustrated by the fact that they killed the servants, who represent the prophets of God.

While telling this parable, Jesus is looking into the eyes of the very men who were scheming to kill Him; the men who represented the tenants from the parable that killed the beloved Son. Talk about foreshadowing at its finest!

"Why would they want to kill Him?", you may ask?

Just like Adam and Eve before them, they wanted to steal His throne. They wanted to be God, not serve God.

Ironically, Isaiah was a prophet that the Pharisees likely quoted often. The fact that Jesus reiterated the warning Isaiah gave regarding *Wild Grapes* and the vineyard being destroyed should have resonated with them. Instead, they were blinded by their hatred of Jesus and their desire to be rulers of Rome rather than servant leaders of God.

Please allow me to paraphrase what Jesus says at the end of verse 9: You who refuse to answer My knock on your heart's door, when you reject Me, you reject the Kingdom, and you shall not enter it, and it will be by your own choosing.

Let's examine how this story ends in verses 10 and 11.

Mark 12:10-11

Have you not read this Scripture:
"'The stone that the builders rejected
has become the cornerstone;[b]
[11] this was the Lord's doing,
and it is marvelous in our eyes'?"

Paraphrase of *Have you not read this Scripture*:
Haven't you men memorized this verse, yet you stand here with no understanding of its meaning? You have waited for the Messiah, you read of His coming and you memorized the scriptures, yet you don't recognize me because you substituted religion for relationship. It's not a Messiah you seek, its Jewish rules and a reign over Rome that you really want.

Jesus quotes Psalm 118:22-23 in Mark 12:10-11 to remind the Pharisees what David spoke prophetically in the Old Testament about Himself, a verse the Pharisees more than likely had committed to memory. I hope you will look Psalms 118 up on your own and study it. It's worth the time investment and you'll see a lot of parallels from this book in that psalm. I want to take a quick minute to address one part of Psalm 118 with you. It is in verse 23, which is also verse 11 of Mark 12 above. Verse 10 of Mark 12 will be explained when you read The Rock.

[23] This is the Lord's doing;
it is marvelous in our eyes.

In case you are wondering what that means, it means CHOICE - free will. The ability to choose, which is given to each of us, is the Lord's doing and it is precious in God's sight. Love is a choice, my friend. God will not force Himself into your heart. He will just patiently knock on the door until you let Him in, or until your time expires and you enter eternity without ever accepting Him.

The Rock:

Matthew 7:24-27 English Standard Version
Build Your House on the Rock
[24] "Everyone then who hears these words of mine and does them will be like a wise man who built his house on the rock.
[25] And the rain fell, and the floods came, and the winds blew and beat on that house, but it did not fall, because it had been founded on the rock.
[26] And everyone who hears these words of mine and does not do them will be like a foolish man who built his house on the sand.
[27] And the rain fell, and the floods came, and the winds blew and beat against that house, and it fell, and great was the fall of it."

Did you see the explanation of Mark 12:10 above in Matthew 7:24-27? The cornerstone the builders rejected, is Jesus, and Jesus is *The Rock*.

I am going to take some poetic liberty and explain to you what I believe God is saying to you in Matthew 7:24-27.

Paraphrasing Jesus: In one of two ways you will establish a foundation for your life. You will either continue striving for acceptance from mankind or you will answer My knock and accept Me into your heart.

1. If you accept My invitation of grace, I will become your foundation. When you decide to open the door of your heart and let Me in, I will eat with you and you with Me. It means we will be in relationship together. It means you won't have to strive when the troubles of this life come (storms). It means when you feel beaten down in the eye of the hurricane and you feel like you have reached the end of your rope, you will always have Me to rely on. I will be your rock. I will be the cornerstone of your life. All builders know that you must have a cornerstone to erect a structure from a foundation, especially if you expect it to survive a storm. So, accept My invitation and allow your acceptance of Me to be the foundation of your life. Accept Me as your cornerstone and build your identity upon Me. Find your security in Me. Discover your many purposes through Me. And, in the end, you will not fall, regardless of how imperfect you live. You will have chosen wisely to accept Me, to receive Me,

to prepare a place in your heart for Me to dwell, and I will receive you into the Heavenly places where I will prepare a place for you to dwell with Me for all eternity.

2. However, if you reject My invitation of grace, you will have no real foundation at all. But in your foolishness, you will not even realize it. It means, we will not be in relationship together. It means you will ignore the knock and, instead, strive in your own strength and in your own ways to keep your head above the floodwaters when the storms of this life come. It means that when you feel beaten down in the eye of the hurricane and you feel like you have reached the end of your rope, you will have to rely on the fickle nature of mankind to sustain you, or upon yourself, upon your own strength. You will grow despondent when you realize you have no rock, no cornerstone. All builders know that you must have a cornerstone to erect a structure from a foundation, especially if you expect it to survive a storm. So, when you reject my invitation, your works, your "good deeds", will serve as your cornerstone for living. Reject Me as your cornerstone and you will choose to build your identity upon the sinking sand of others' applause. You will be your own security. You will define your own purposes. And, in the end, your fall will be great, for you will have wasted the grace and mercy I have freely given you. By your own choosing, your "good deeds" won't measure up to My standard at the Great White Throne Judgment and you will spend eternity apart from Me in Hell.

"Ricky, I need to ask a question. How can I trust that the Bible is really telling the truth, and how can I trust your interpretation of it?", you might be asking me.

The easy answer is, the Word validates itself. Did you not see that happen above with verse after verse validating itself? When you interrogate the Word, you will find the *Truth*. As previously noted, there were 40 authors who wrote 66 books over a 1,500-year period to create what we call the Holy Bible. Yet, as I have studied to write this book for your benefit, and mine, I have discovered that the four pillars of this book are iterated repeatedly throughout several books of the Bible. This message is weaved into the stories that make up the Word. Last, but certainly not least, Jesus Christ is the Word, which means it is true, for He is the *Truth* that I keep talking about. Once you accept Him, and begin a relationship with Him, then, and only then, does the Word come to life. For He is *The Way, The Truth, and The Life* (*John 14:6*). Therefore, the Word is true. It validates itself.

Sadly, my friend, many have and will continue to reject Jesus as the *Truth*. Judas Iscariot was one such *Wild Grape*. Judas was directly connected to *The Vine*. He walked with and talked to Jesus. He witnessed miracle after miracle, but he never intended to draw near and accept Him. He refused to answer the knock on his heart's door. Rather, he had his hand in the moneybag as the treasurer and was all about personal profit and selfish gain. Judas was one of many *Wild Grapes* mentioned by Isaiah in his version of the story about God and His vineyard.

As for trusting the Bible, you'll have to suspend your own disbelief long enough to interrogate the Word. No amount of evidence or miracles witnessed will change your mind if you don't. When you do choose to interrogate the Word for yourself, you'll find the answer to your question. My interpretations presented in this book are the fruit of my study. Maybe one day you will share some of the fruit of your study with me.

Let's put a bow on this chapter, shall we?

Acceptance is the foundation of your spiritual life, and Jesus is the cornerstone, *The Rock*, you need to build your life on. You were not created by God to build your foundation upon the sinking sand of mankind's applause or their acceptance of you. You were never intended to be *Wild Grapes*. You were intended to be connected to *The Vine*.

So, tell me friend, do you intend to keep striving for acceptance from men and women when you now know that Jesus Christ has accepted you just as you are?

Now answer for yourself, what foundation are you building your life upon?

Dressed in White, a Whore at Heart

Behold, I stand at the door and knock. If anyone hears my voice and opens the door, I will come in to him and eat with him, and he with me.

Revelation 3:20 English Standard Version

If God doesn't condemn you, then why do you condemn yourself?

Don't you just love the title God gave me for this chapter? Let me share with you how it came about. Sorry for the visual, but I was enjoying a nice hot bath one evening in my garden tub and when I stood up to dry off, I heard the Lord tell me, "She is a whore."

I paused and asked, "Who is a whore?"

"My bride, the Church.", He said.

Yep. God called me a whore. For the record, if you are saved, He called you a whore, too. If you're not saved, then you're a dirty whore. That's because you haven't been washed in the blood of the Lamb yet. That right there ain't your average preacher joke!

Does that offend you?

It doesn't offend me because I know He is right. I am a whore at heart. And so are you.

Like I did in the last chapter, I am going to share three different stories from the Bible with you to help you understand why God gave me this title and what it means to be a whore at heart.

I have subtitled the stories to align with the title of this chapter. Let's begin in the Old Testament with Married to a Whore and work our way into the New Testament with Standing Naked before God. Then, we will end with Going Back to My Old Way of Life.

Married to a Whore:

Hosea 1 The Message (MSG)

1 This is God's Message to Hosea son of Beeri. It came to him during the royal reigns of Judah's kings Uzziah, Jotham, Ahaz, and Hezekiah. This was also the time that Jeroboam son of Joash was king over Israel.

This Whole Country Has Become a Whorehouse

2 The first time God spoke to Hosea he said:
"Find a whore and marry her.
Make this whore the mother of your children.
And here's why: This whole country
has become a whorehouse, unfaithful to me, God."
3 Hosea did it. He picked Gomer daughter of Diblaim. She got pregnant and gave him a son.

4-5 Then God told him:
"Name him Jezreel. It won't be long now before
I'll make the people of Israel pay for the massacre at Jezreel.
I'm calling it quits on the kingdom of Israel.
Payday is coming. I'm going to chop Israel's bows and arrows
into kindling in the valley of Jezreel."

6-7 Gomer got pregnant again. This time she had a daughter. God told Hosea:
"Name this one No-Mercy. I'm fed up with Israel.
I've run out of mercy. There's no more forgiveness.
Judah's another story. I'll continue having mercy on them.

71

I'll save them. It will be their God who saves them,
Not their armaments and armies,
not their horsepower and manpower."

8-9 After Gomer had weaned No-Mercy, she got pregnant yet again and had a son. God said:
"Name him Nobody. You've become nobodies to me,
and I, God, am a nobody to you.

10-11 "But down the road the population of Israel is going to explode past counting, like sand on the ocean beaches. In the very place where they were once named Nobody, they will be named God's Somebody. Everybody in Judah and everybody in Israel will be assembled as one people. They'll choose a single leader. There'll be no stopping them—a great day in Jezreel."

In Chapter 1 of Hosea, God calls the entire nation of Israel a whorehouse. While preparing to write this section, I struggled with where to end scripture because Hosea is one of those books that is hard to summarize. The way God tells the story is just better than a man-made summary of it. Keep that in mind when you read what I have prepared for you below. It will be good, but you should seriously go find Hosea (one book after Daniel in the Old Testament) and read all 14 chapters. It's an easy read, and if you read it in the Message version, you likely won't have as many questions at the end. It's fairly direct and fairly obvious. I say "fairly", because not all the parallels are stated, but they are inferred.

With that said, let me dive into what I feel led to share.

Why does God call Israel a whorehouse?

Why did God tell the prophet Hosea, during their first conversation, to find and marry a whore?

Why would He tell Hosea to name his children Jezreel, No-Mercy, and Nobody?

Some of you may be scoffing and saying as you read these words, "there is no way God spoke to Hosea, and if by some chance He did speak, He didn't tell Hosea to marry a whore. That doesn't sound like something God would do."

I don't know about you, but I have a prophetic gifting, and I must admit, there are times I hear Him say things (not out loud, I am not insane) that make me question whether I heard Him correctly, and, more importantly, whether I am interpreting what I heard correctly.

Let me illustrate it by telling you what I heard during one of our conversations that occurred a few months before I went on Quest. I was 39 years old at the time of this conversation.

Our conversation went like this:

God: "Shut Up."

Me: "Did you just tell me to shut up?"

God: "Yes, shut up. You never shut up."

Me: "I really thought you would be more polite."

God: "Do you know why you can't hear me? It's because you won't be quiet. You never stop. You never shut up. Be still. Don't move. Don't think. Barely even breathe. Your body will breathe for you."

After what felt like 30 minutes of being completely still and completely quiet, God showed me a vision, and it was confirmed by another man at the house of prayer who also saw, for me, what I saw that night.

I saw a beautiful mountaintop with a white rock structure sitting on top of the mountain. As the image zoomed in (like a helicopter flying toward it), I could see vegetation growing on the top of this square, one room building with vines cascading about a quarter of the way down the walls. It had no roof, and as I flew over, I descended into the structure. The first thing I noticed was that there was an iron gate attached where I would imagine a door would be. It reminded me of a jail cell door. It was flung wide open, and I could see a path that led from this building down the lush green face of the mountain. Then, I saw a dank, gray, concrete floor with a giant male lion lying down on his right side, panting. He looked very content lying on the concrete, which seemed a little odd for a lion.

Within a split second, my mind engaged, and I began to have self-talk as the vision continued. I said to myself, "I could write a story about the symbolism of this lion and a man…" and then He cut me off.

God spoke up and said, "Yeah, yeah… you could write a story, I know. This lion is you!"

At that moment, my entire right side went cold. I could literally feel the concrete floor the lion was lying on.

Then, God spoke to me again. "I made you to be bold like a roaring lion, Ricky, and instead you lie here content in the middle of your sin. I have freed you from it, and you refuse to leave it."

I sat there in awe, staring at the iron gate that was flung open. My heart sank, and I confessed to Him that He was right. I was in love with my sin, and I didn't want to give it up.

You see, friend, I was fearful and insecure, striving to find love through the sin of sexual idolatry. It was my go-to; it was my security blanket.

And because He is loving and gracious, God met me right in the middle of my sin. After I confessed to Him, He said, "I've opened that door for you, Ricky. Anytime you want to get up and walk out, you can. It's your choice."

I am a whore at heart. But I finally got up off that dank, cold, gray, concrete floor and I found my inner lion. Since that day, I've been doing my best to boldly run the race He has set before me.

Over 30 years before this vision, I had accepted Jesus as my Lord and Savior. I had answered the knock, but I was just too dang scared to change my ways and live for Him. So, He pursued me, and I finally made the choice to let Him truly be the God of my life.

Hosea 3 The Message (MSG)

In Time They'll Come Back

3 Then God ordered me, "Start all over: Love your wife again,
your wife who's in bed with her latest boyfriend, your
cheating wife.
Love her the way I, God, love the Israelite people,
even as they flirt and party with every god that takes their fancy."
²⁻³ I did it. I paid good money to get her back.
It cost me the price of a slave.
Then I told her, "From now on you're living with me.
No more whoring, no more sleeping around.
You're living with me and I'm living with you."
⁴⁻⁵ The people of Israel are going to live a long time
stripped of security and protection,
without religion and comfort,
godless and prayerless.
But in time they'll come back, these Israelites,
come back looking for their God and their David-King.
They'll come back chastened to reverence
before God and his good gifts, ready for the End of the story of his love.

This is exactly what He is trying to show you through the story of Hosea
if you have made everything, except for Him, the God of your life. All He
wants you to do is surrender and allow Him to purchase you off the slave-
auction-block of sin. Give up the whoredom you are living in. Whatever
that sin may be, He has gone before you and is actively offering you a clean
slate. He is the God of unlimited chances and His death on the cross is
your ticket to redemption. He, Himself, was sold for 30 silver pieces, the
price of a slave, so He could take your place. You are not too far-gone. Your
sin is not too great for Him to cleanse. You are a "Somebody" in the heart
of God and He wants to wrap you up in His mercy and grace.

Standing Naked before God:

John 8 The Message (MSG)

To Throw the Stone

8 ¹⁻² Jesus went across to Mount Olives, but he was soon back in the Temple again. Swarms of people came to him. He sat down and taught them.
³⁻⁶ The religion scholars and Pharisees led in a woman who had been caught in an act of adultery. They stood her in plain sight of everyone and said, "Teacher, this woman was caught red-handed in the act of adultery. Moses, in the Law, gives orders to stone such persons. What do you say?" They were trying to trap him into saying something incriminating so they could bring charges against him.
⁶⁻⁸ Jesus bent down and wrote with his finger in the dirt. They kept at him, badgering him. He straightened up and said, "The sinless one among you, go first: Throw the stone." Bending down again, he wrote some more in the dirt.
⁹⁻¹⁰ Hearing that, they walked away, one after another, beginning with the oldest. The woman was left alone. Jesus stood up and spoke to her. "Woman, where are they? Does no one condemn you?"
¹¹ "No one, Master."
"Neither do I," said Jesus. "Go on your way. From now on, don't sin."

Can you imagine being in the throes of passionate sex and a bunch of "religious men" pop out of the closet, grab you, parade you through the streets buck-naked, and present you before God Himself?

I cannot imagine what was going through her mind, but I bet humiliation and shame were overflowing from the top of her emotional cup. If that happened to me, I would be mortified.

Stop reading for a second and imagine this is you. Try to feel what she must be feeling in this first part of the story. I bet this triggers an event where you were humiliated, and I bet you can feel some of that shame still today. Am I right?

Each time I read this story; I tend to take something new away from it. Here are a few of the questions I am left with that I know I will never have answered in this lifetime.

How did the Pharisees know these two people were going to have sex, at this hour, on this day?

Where exactly were the Pharisees hiding while this woman was having sex with an unidentified man?

Were they peeking in the window?

Were they hiding in the closet?

Were they sitting at the foot of the bed watching?

Before you accuse me of being crass, look at the verse of scripture that leads me to these questions:

3-6 The religion scholars and Pharisees led in a woman who had been caught in an act of adultery. They stood her in plain sight of everyone and said, "Teacher, this woman was caught red-handed in the act of adultery."

You don't typically walk down Main Street, trip over a bump in the sidewalk, and catch a woman red-handed in the act of adultery, do you?

So, how did this happen?

As a former investigator, this part of the story really boggles my mind.

Why didn't they bring the guy, too?

Isn't he just as guilty as she, according to the Law?

Is it possible that one of the religion scholars, or one of the Pharisees, was "the man" in question?

Maybe all of them were?

I can't tell you because the scripture doesn't let us in on the rest of the story, as Paul Harvey used to say.

But here is what I do know to be true.

According to their testimony, she was guilty. She didn't refute the allegations, so it seems she agrees she was guilty. I am guessing she was also standing there naked and sex-drenched, which might be why she just looked down at the ground. Having heard a few sermons on this story and having seen a few "Jesus movies", the woman is always clothed in these accounts. I am guessing it's because we like to "nice-things-up" for church, but why do we do that? The fact that we do is confounding to me because I can't imagine they were having sex fully clothed, can you?

So, unless someone can disprove my theory, I am sticking with "she was literally standing naked before God."

Now, that brings me to the next part of this story. Let's read what happens next together in verses 4-6 of John 8 The Message (MSG):

"Moses, in the Law, gives orders to stone such persons. What do you say?" They were trying to trap him into saying something incriminating so they could bring charges against him.

The depravity of man is well on display in this story, but maybe not in the manner that seems to be obvious.

Remember when I talked about being rained on and how I thought every storm I faced was my hurricane?

Well, I submit for your consideration that this woman was not caught in her own hurricane, but that of the religion scholars and Pharisees. The title of this story is Standing Naked before God. I chose this because, at first glance, it seems it's the *adulterous* woman who is the one standing naked before God. But I am going to show you another side of this story that wasn't obvious to me the first ~300 times I read it.

Okay, so ~300 is hyperbole.

That aside, I submit for your consideration that the religion scholars and the Pharisees are the ones who are being drenched by torrential rains of personal hurricanes. The depravity of these men is on display. They are the adulterers. They are the ones who are figuratively *Standing Naked before God*, yet they haven't figured this out yet in the story. That tends to happen to the best, and worst, of us.

Look at how calmly Jesus handled them during this display of depravity. He never showed anger. He never yelled at them. He didn't smite them, even though He could have. Frankly, most of us think He would do that to us because "He must be angry at me for my sin."

If you think that, my friend, you have another personal example of buying the lie of all lies.

Let's get back to the story in John 8:6-8 The Message (MSG).

6-8 Jesus bent down and wrote with his finger in the dirt. They kept at him, badgering him. He straightened up and said, "The sinless one among you, go first: Throw the stone." Bending down again, he wrote some more in the dirt.

What do you think Jesus wrote in the dirt?

Here is my theory. These men had many *Secret Beaches* that they didn't think anyone knew about. I believe Jesus began to name a few of these secret sins for each of the men so they would realize each of them deserved to be stoned just as much as she did.

We are all just like this woman, and yet at the same time, we are all just like these men. We are all guilty, aren't we?

Sometimes, we even do this same thing to others. We highlight someone else's flaws or sins because it makes us feel better about ourselves. Or so we think in the moment.

Who gives you the right to throw stones at another?

Are you without sin? If not, then why are you declaring yourself the *Judge, Jury and Executioner* of someone just as guilty as you?

Are others casting stones at you for your transgressions?

How does that make you feel when you are the one paraded into the streets, buck naked, caught red-handed in sin?

If only we were willing to treat each other the way Jesus handled this situation. Take a look with me.

[9-10] Hearing that (the words Jesus spoke – "The sinless one among you, go first: Throw the stone."), they walked away, one after another, beginning with the oldest.

The woman was left alone.

Jesus stood up and spoke to her.

"Woman, where are they? Does no one condemn you?"

[11] "No one, Master."

"Neither do I," said Jesus. "Go on your way. From now on, don't sin."

I have many "favorite passages" in the Bible, but this one is tied for number one for me. I am going to deconstruct what Jesus *didn't* say to her so we can highlight appropriately what He *did* say.

Jesus Didn't Say:

1. Woman, you need to go to church.
2. Woman, you need to repent of your sins so you can be forgiven.
3. Woman, you're forgiven this time, but next time you're going to pay for what you do.
4. Woman, you're a disgrace to the church and you're not welcome back here.

5. Woman, since you're a good person who helps others and gives to the needy and feeds orphans on occasion, I am going to let you off the hook.
6. Woman, you're lucky these men are scoundrels that I needed to teach a lesson.
7. Woman, clean up your act and get yourself right and then come see me.

No, friend, Jesus didn't say any of those things to her, and He doesn't say any of those things to you when you blow it like she did.

Here is what He did say:

"Woman, where are they? Does no one condemn you?"

She replies:
11 "No one, Master."

And here it is friend:
"Neither do I," said Jesus.

Now, what on earth does Jesus mean when He says the last part?
"Go on your way. From now on, don't sin."

Are any of us able to go and be perfect, sinless, creatures?

No.

So, why does Jesus say this to people repeatedly in the pages of the New Testament?

As simple as I can say it, I believe He is telling them, and us, the following:

My paraphrase of the meaning of these verses:
"Yeah, you're guilty of this sin. But I love you and I am not condemning you for it. My hope is that you will forgive yourself, and others, just as I am willing to forgive you before you ever ask me to. I am offering you grace and mercy. Offer it to others in return. As you walk through this life, I hope

you will remember what I have done for you, and I hope you will choose to change how you live your life. I want you to change your mind about your sins; to realize that I am not throwing rules at you to follow. Instead, I am trying to protect you from the consequence that *is* sin. I want you to accept me and draw near to me. And when you do, you won't want to sin anymore."

If Jesus doesn't condemn us, if He isn't condemning you, then why are you condemning others? Why are you condemning yourself?

Going Back to My Old Way of Life:

John 21 The Message (MSG)

[Gone] Fishing

21 ¹⁻³ After this, Jesus appeared again to the disciples, this time at the Tiberias Sea (the Sea of Galilee). This is how he did it: Simon Peter, Thomas (nicknamed "Twin"), Nathanael from Cana in Galilee, the brothers Zebedee, and two other disciples were together. Simon Peter announced, "I'm going fishing."
³⁻⁴ The rest of them replied, "We're going with you." They went out and got in the boat. They caught nothing that night. When the sun came up, Jesus was standing on the beach, but they didn't recognize him.
⁵ Jesus spoke to them: "Good morning. Did you catch anything for breakfast?" They answered, "No."
⁶ He said, "Throw the net off the right side of the boat and see what happens." They did what he said. All of a sudden there were so many fish in it, they weren't strong enough to pull it in.
⁷⁻⁹ Then the disciple Jesus loved said to Peter, "It's the Master." When Simon Peter realized that it was the Master, he threw on some clothes, for he was stripped for work, and dove into the sea. The other disciples came in by boat for they weren't far from land, a hundred yards or so, pulling along the net full of fish. When they got out of the boat, they saw a fire laid, with fish and bread cooking on it.
¹⁰⁻¹¹ Jesus said, "Bring some of the fish you've just caught." Simon Peter joined them and pulled the net to shore—153 big fish. And even with all those fish, the net didn't rip.

[12] Jesus said, "Breakfast is ready." Not one of the disciples dared ask, "Who are you?" They knew it was the Master.

[13-14] Jesus then took the bread and gave it to them. He did the same with the fish. This was now the third time Jesus had shown himself alive to the disciples since being raised from the dead.

Do You Love Me?

[15] After breakfast, Jesus said to Simon Peter, "Simon, son of John, do you love me more than these?"

"Yes, Master, you know I love you."

Jesus said, "Feed my lambs."

[16] He then asked a second time, "Simon, son of John, do you love me?"

"Yes, Master, you know I love you."

Jesus said, "Shepherd my sheep."

[17-19] Then he said it a third time: "Simon, son of John, do you love me?"

Peter was upset that he asked for the third time, "Do you love me?" so he answered, "Master, you know everything there is to know. You've got to know that I love you."

Jesus said, "Feed my sheep. I'm telling you the very truth now: When you were young you dressed yourself and went wherever you wished, but when you get old you'll have to stretch out your hands while someone else dresses you and takes you where you don't want to go." He said this to hint at the kind of death by which Peter would glorify God. And then he commanded, "Follow me."

[20-21] Turning his head, Peter noticed the disciple Jesus loved following right behind. When Peter noticed him, he asked Jesus, "Master, what's going to happen to *him?*"

[22-23] Jesus said, "If I want him to live until I come again, what's that to you? You—follow me." That is how the rumor got out among the brothers that this disciple wouldn't die. But that is not what Jesus said. He simply said, "If I want him to live until I come again, what's that to you?"

[24] This is the same disciple who was eyewitness to all these things and wrote them down. And we all know that his eyewitness account is reliable and accurate.

[25] There are so many other things Jesus did. If they were all written down, each of them, one by one, I can't imagine a world big enough to hold such a library of books.

Chapter 21 of John is like an *Oh, by the way* chapter added at the end of the book, and I am so glad it was included in the scriptures.

I am going to give you my interpretation of this chapter and what I strongly believe God has spoken to me about its meaning.

Peter and the rest of the men were fishermen. Blue-collar men that I strongly believe were rough around the edges and untrained in the Law. This fact gives me hope! Even today, He is still calling people like this to be the body of Christ.

When Peter says, "I am going fishing.", I interpret his words to be about identity. I truly believe that Peter, who was condemning himself for betraying Jesus, felt like he had given three years of his life to something, and it all ended when Jesus was crucified on that cross. I read Peter's words to say, "I am taking off my identity given to me by Jesus, and I am going back to my old way of living."

I am going to do my best to back up my theory using scripture.

In the early part of the Book of John, Jesus meets Peter for the first time in the text and He calls him by his given name – Simon, son of John. Then, Jesus does something interesting. He renames him. Take a quick look with me at the verse.

John 1:42 The Message (MSG)

[40-42] Andrew, Simon Peter's brother, was one of the two who heard John's witness and followed Jesus. The first thing he did after finding where Jesus lived was find his own brother, Simon, telling him, "We've found the Messiah" (that is, "Christ"). He immediately led him to Jesus.

Jesus took one look up and said, "You're John's son, Simon? From now on your name is Cephas" (or Peter, which means "Rock").

It's no mistake or coincidence that God led me to include this story at the end of Acceptance, which precedes Identity.

All through the rest of the gospels, Jesus only refers to Simon, son of John as Peter. Peter accepted his new identity, given to Him by Christ, when he boldly left his old life to follow Jesus.

Now, for the good part which I believe proves my theory.

[15] After breakfast, Jesus said to Simon Peter, "Simon, son of John, do you love me more than these?"

Let me jump in right here. Do you see it?

Simon, son of John…

Why didn't Jesus call him Peter?

I submit for your consideration that it is because Peter decided to shed his identity and go back to his old way of life. And since Jesus knows all, He went back to calling him by his "old-self" name.

Now, let's look at Peter's response:

"Yes, Master, you know I love you."

Alright, let me break down the meanings of love that are used in the Greek. When Jesus asks the question, He asks Peter if he (agape – unconditional love) loves Him. And for the first time, our impetuous friend who always answers Jesus with wild extremes gets honest. Peter replies to Jesus, "You know I (phileo – fondness or brotherly love) love you." Which is translated, "You know I am just *fond* of you."

Jesus goes on to ask Him this same question two more times, to both of which Peter answers honestly. I believe Jesus does this to allow Peter the opportunity to account for his sins of denying Jesus three times. Biblically speaking, to grieve the Holy Spirit, or to deny Jesus, is an unpardonable sin; unforgiveable, you will hear people say. But I say Jesus is willing to forgive you for this sin, and any other sin, as long as you still have breath in your lungs and are willing to admit where you went wrong.

I am a lot like Peter. I tend to live on the winds of wild extremes, and I am working hard daily to stop this nonsense. I want to be honest with God, with myself, and with those I love. I still get caught in the trap of striving for acceptance. In fact, I caught myself doing it this very week. None of us are exempt. None of us are going to ever figure it all out. None of us are going to be perfect.

But the good news, my friend, is that you don't have to be perfect.

If you have given up, thrown in the towel, *Gone Fishing*, and shed the grace and mercy that God has freely given you, then I ask that you just get honest with yourself and with God and come back home. Let go of religion and get a hold of relationship.

And if you're one of my readers who still hasn't accepted *Truth*, I pray you will.

With that said, I am going to leave you the same way I found you in this section.

You'll never get anywhere if you keep doing the same thing expecting a different result. If you truly want to find the *Hope* you so desperately seek, you will only find it in the *Truth*.

Revelation 3:20 English Standard Version

[20] Behold, I stand at the door and knock. If anyone hears my voice and opens the door, I will come in to him and eat with him, and he with me.

Will you choose Jesus to be the God of your life?

If not today, I hope you will soon.

Accepting Truth, Finding Hope!

Part 2: Identity

Who Are You?

Falling Apart, or Falling into Place?

But some people did accept him. They believed in him, and he gave them the right to become children of God.

John 1:12 Easy-to-Read Version

Is your life falling apart, or falling into place?

In a moment, I will share information about my journey and how I found the *Truth*. But right now, I want to ask you the one question we all get asked and rarely answer correctly.

Who are you?

If you are tempted to tell me your name, your title, where you grew up, where you went to school, what degree you possess, who your parents are, or anything remotely similar, you have failed to answer the question.

Think about this for a minute. Who are you without your title or career?

Who are you without your degree, your awards, or your trophies?

Who are you without your significant other, your kids, family, or friends?

Imagine if you woke up tomorrow and had literally lost everything that defines who you are right now. Then, ask yourself this question again.

Without anything or anyone to define me, who am I?

I asked you this question in Part 1: Acceptance, and I promised you that we would come back to it later. This is a very serious question that I hope you will really consider. If you can't answer it right now, that's okay. And if you are able, then that is great. This exercise is intended for you. But I want to share with you that I didn't receive an exemption from having to answer this question for myself. The difference is, you will get to see the struggle I went through when I was presented with this very question while writing this chapter. In fact, I have had the *privilege* of living every single one of these chapters, which has been anything but fun.

Without anything or anyone to define me, who am I?

Let me explain what I mean.

When I began writing this chapter, the date was June 23, 2019. I remember this vividly, because it was the day after my wedding day – June 22, 2019.

For context, I have been married and divorced twice previously. Both times I had private ceremonies instead of a formal wedding. Although I am a man's man with a lot of rough edges, I have always wanted to be celebrated on my wedding day and have longed for love that would result in having a formal wedding.

As I described to you in Part 1: Acceptance, I have strived for love all my life. Because I was so in love with the idea of being in love, I have made a lot of relationship mistakes. I have rushed into many serious relationships. Even when I knew I shouldn't be in a relationship with someone, I forced it anyway. I wanted what I wanted, and no one was going to tell me I couldn't have it. Not even God!

Do you force things simply because you want them so badly to be?

I honestly wish this wasn't my story! But more times than not in this life, I have found myself running a marathon in place on that hamster wheel of insanity. At the end of which, I was left feeling absolutely exhausted from the fruitless experience. Then when the guilt and shame kicked in from the decisions I made, I would get mad at God and blame Him for how things turned out.

Does that sound familiar to you?

To illustrate the lesson in this chapter, in the next few paragraphs you and I are going to hop in my "magic time machine", and we are going to visit specific days together from my past. As we arrive on the timeline of my past, we will "watch" what happens on that day together. Don't worry, we cannot mess up the space-time-continuum, so feel free to ask as many questions as you want if you don't understand what is happening.

Alright, buckle your seatbelt and let's take a trip back in time together. There are so many dates to choose from, but I think we need to visit June 22, 2019, first. Remember, I told you earlier that was my wedding day? Let's start there.

On June 22, 2019, I awoke that morning about 9:00 AM. I showered and did my usual routine of getting ready. After getting dressed, I spent time with the Lord. As I moved from my sitting area in the master bedroom to the eat-in-island in the kitchen, I received a text message from an ex-girlfriend inviting to me lunch. I replied to her and said I would meet her at her place in about an hour.

You backhand me on my shoulder and say, "Wait a minute, Ricky. It's your wedding day and you're gonna have lunch with an ex-girlfriend? Are you kidding me right me now?"

I reply with a wince and a smirk, Ouch. I get why you think I deserved that smack on the shoulder, but to fully understand why I agreed to meet her for lunch, we need to go further back on this timeline. Let's jump back in the magic time machine. I have set the first date, in a series of dates, to May 3, 2019. I think this will be far enough back to fill in the blanks. The time machine will then time-hop us to the next dates that I set for us to visit.

On May 3, 2019, my best friend Michael and his wife Ashley flew to Dallas to attend a very important gala with me and my fiancé. After an incredible evening, we decided to hit a few local hotspots in Dallas to enjoy some drinks and good company.

To make a very long story short, at about 3:00 AM on the morning of May 4, 2019, my fiancé looked me dead in the eyes and said, "We don't mesh."

She handed me the engagement ring and walked away. As I stood there embarrassed and shocked, Michael and Ashley came along beside me and consoled my broken heart. Later that same morning, I began the process of cancelling the wedding and honeymoon. In the process of untying all the financial knots that go into a commitment like marriage, I lost over $70,000. I wish that were a type-o, but it's not. I was not a wealthy man at this stage of my life, so that kind of financial loss just added insult to injury.

The next six days that followed the breakup and cancellation of the wedding were some of my hardest and darkest days. To compound it, each morning when I journaled with God, He barely spoke to me. When He did, it was a sentence at best.

On May 9, 2019, I called into a conference call with my new boss. When I heard the beep that she had joined the line, I put on my "happy voice" in an effort to hide my pain from losing my fiancé and the majority of my life savings.

"Hey Ricky, how are you?"

"Hi Lalithya, I am hanging in there", I said.

"Ricky, I have HR on the line, your role is being eliminated effective tomorrow."

So, let me recap for you. On Sunday, I lost my fiancé. From Monday to Thursday the snowball of financial losses crested the $70k mark. On Friday I lost my job and the only source of income I had to provide for me and my daughter.

Well, I cannot speak for you friend, but I have reached my limit on reliving that week. Do you now understand why I agreed to have lunch with an ex-girlfriend, on what *would have been* my wedding day? She and I had remained close friends after our breakup over a year earlier and to tell you the truth, I didn't want to be alone that day. I needed to be around people who cared about me and who would offer me encouragement, so that is why I went. Can you relate to that feeling? Come on, let's jump back in the magic time machine and go back to the future where I will explain my mental, spiritual, and emotional response to all of this.

The easiest way to describe what I was feeling is to say that I felt like my life was falling apart. I felt so alone, so foolish, and so absolutely lost. I found myself in a great big storm and instead of focusing my eyes on Jesus, I stared directly at the waves that were crashing down on top of me. I was overwhelmed by the magnitude of this storm, and I sank into another sea of despair. As I fell into the raging sea, I cried out to the Lord.

"God, why are doing this *to* me? Why did you strip me bare? What did I do wrong to deserve all of this?"

As I reflect on the timing, I can't help but chuckle. I began putting words on paper for this chapter on June 23, 2019. I honestly had no clue what I was going to title this chapter,

> *"God, why are doing this to me? Why did you strip me bare? What did I do wrong to deserve all of this?"*

or what I was going to write about beyond something to do with identity. But I did know how I was going to start it. I was going to ask you to answer this question:

Imagine if you woke up tomorrow and you had literally lost everything that defines who you are right now. Then, ask yourself this question again.

Without anything or anyone to define me, who am I?

You know something friend, I never imagined God would have me answer that question at the same time I planned to ask you to answer it! It's easy to answer it when all is right in the world. But what about when you're in the midst of a personal hurricane like I was?

Tell you what, let's take one more trip in the magic time machine together. I think you will benefit from what I was feeling about my own identity as my world was *seemingly* crashing down around me.

We will end this chapter together reviewing what I wrote on that fateful day. Here is what God led me to write to you on June 23, 2019, during one of the worst storms of my life:

Who am I?

Intellectually and spiritually, I know I am a son - meaning a child of the living God. My life verse was given to me by God in a very peculiar way, which I will explain to you shortly. But I must tell you, friend, that when the proverbial bottom fell out of my life in May of 2019, I didn't handle it well at all.

Deep breath. As of this writing, I am still not handling it well.

I haven't been acting like a person who has *Hope*, or even one who knows *the Truth*.

I have been choosing, instead, to act like an orphan.

Do you know what that means?

My life has been riddled with one abandonment after another, and as a result, I struggle with abandonment issues. I project this insecurity on God. Let me say it more accurately: I don't just project it, I projectile vomit it all over Him.

Great word picture for you, huh?

Presently, I am madder than hell at God for *playing games with my life* and I don't understand why any of this is happening *to* me.

Answer this question for me friend. Why did He do this *to me?*

I have sunk deep into depression, and while I have admitted this to no one, I have daily thoughts of suicide. They are brief thoughts that I would never seriously act upon, but I must admit they enter my mind frequently.

Doubt has become my daily companion and my faith in a *Good Daddy* has seemingly taken a backseat to what feels like the *absent father of my youth*.

I mean, what will I do if I don't recover financially?

What will I do if I lose my house that I have invested in so heavily?

What about my career? Who will hire me?

Or is God removing me from this line of work completely, just as He once told me He would eventually do?

What will I do when the little bit of money I have left runs out?

Oh, what a difference a day makes in your life. I went from being on top of the world to being stepped over like a bum on the street.

Do you know this feeling I am experiencing?

Are you in this same boat with me?

Has doubt ever overshadowed your faith?

Or is this what you have come to expect from God?

After all, if it wasn't for bad luck, I wouldn't have any luck at all, right?

Isn't this the kind of punishment we expect God to levy upon the *wicked*?

Yet, I am writing a book to honor His name, and to somehow convince you to trust Him and accept Him as a loving Father. And this is how He treats me?

You may not be writing a book, but I bet you have been a *good person* who has lived a *decent life*. And yet you find yourself in a position that is completely *unfair and unwarranted*, am I right?

What kind of *loving* God would do this *to* us?

You know, as I type these words on the page, I am struck by something that I need to ask you and me.

Have you ever been really pissed off at God, like I am, only to wake up several years later and thank Him for the very thing you once cursed at Him about?

I am reminded of a verse of scripture that just spoke to me and I really think, if you will ponder it in light of your circumstances and your present understanding (or in my case, lack thereof), it will speak to you, too.

Isaiah 55:8-11 The Message (MSG)

8-11 "I don't think the way you think.
The way you work isn't the way I work."
God's Decree.
"For as the sky soars high above earth,
  so the way I work surpasses the way you work,
  and the way I think is beyond the way you think.
Just as rain and snow descend from the skies
  and don't go back until they've watered the earth,
  Doing their work of making things grow and blossom,
  producing seed for farmers and food for the hungry,
So will the words that come out of my mouth
  not come back empty-handed.
They'll do the work I sent them to do,
  they'll complete the assignment I gave them.

So, if Isaiah is right and God's ways are not our ways, then maybe we are looking at our circumstances all wrong.

As such, I must pose another question to us both.

What if God isn't doing this *to* us? Rather, what if God is doing this *for our good?*

What if our present pain is part of His greater plan that will one day benefit us and bring glory to His name?

What if our present circumstances just look like our lives are falling apart, but maybe, just maybe, instead of falling apart, our lives are actually falling into place?

> *What if God isn't doing this to us? Rather, what if God is doing this for our good?*

What if taking my fiancé, career, and money away was a gift *from* God *to* me, *because* He loves me?

What if instead of abandoning me, He has been attempting to purify me in the fires of refinement?

What if all that is needed from me is to let go of the things that are holding me back from becoming more like Him?

As I continue to process all the heartache of my world with you in the pages of this book, I am reminded of another verse of scripture that I need to share with you.

Malachi 3:3 English Standard Version (ESV)

³ He will sit as a refiner and purifier of silver, and he will purify the sons of Levi and refine them like gold and silver, and they will bring offerings in righteousness to the Lord.

What if what we are going through right now is just as it is described above?

Do you understand the meaning of this verse?

Let me explain, just so we are on the same sheet of music.

In the text, we read that God will sit as a refiner and purifier of silver. Like the sons of Levi, you and I are the silver. When it says they will bring offerings of righteousness to the Lord, it means they will belong to the Lord.

At the beginning of this chapter, I snuck a new verse in. It will be the verse that you see at the beginning of every chapter in Part 2 Identity.

Did you see it?

John 1:12 Easy-to-Read Version

¹² But some people did accept him. They believed in him, and he gave them the right to become children of God.

Do you see how this verse ties Part 1: Acceptance to Part 2: Identity?

When we accept Him, He gives us *the right to become* children of God. This verse is powerful when you truly consider its meaning in light of our conversation here.

Think about it for a moment.

We have the right to *become* children of God.

Doesn't this imply we have to *do* something to be His children?

Let's explore this together. To do so, we must go all the way back to the very beginning.

Genesis 1:26 English Standard Version (ESV)

²⁶ Then God said, "Let us make man in our image, after our likeness. And let them have dominion over the fish of the sea and over the birds of the heavens and over the livestock and over all the earth and over every creeping thing that creeps on the earth."

From God's perspective, I have never *not* been a son. While that may be terrible grammar, it's some of the best news I can declare.

So, if that has always been true, then why does it say I have the right to become a child of God?

Isn't that a contradiction?

No, it is not a contradiction, and I will explain why in the simplest of terms. Let me go back to the wedding I have longed for as an example. Two people stand before an officiant in the wedding ceremony who have the *right to become* husband and wife by a declaration of their decision to be joined to one another. When you say, "I do", at the altar, you are saying, "I choose to be in relationship with you." As I previously mentioned in Part 1: Acceptance, love is a choice. When God decided to make man in His image, He chose us to be His children. In that moment, He said, "I do", to you. Then He gave us the free will to choose or reject Him as our Heavenly Father. Each of us metaphorically stand at the altar with Him, and it is our turn to give an answer. You either choose to say, "I do", or you choose to say, "I don't".

So, what does any of this have to do with our present circumstances or the refinement of silver verse that I cited for you above?

Well, it has everything to do with both. Let me show you.

There is a story about a woman who goes to a silversmith to watch the process of refining silver while studying this same verse we discussed in Malachi 3. She wanted to understand what it means.

Here is how the story goes:

The Refiner's Fire

As she watched the silversmith, he held a piece of silver over the fire and let it heat up. He explained that in refining silver, one needed to hold the silver in the middle of the fire where the flames were hottest as to burn away all the impurities. The woman thought about God holding us in such a hot spot. Then, she thought again about the verse that says: "He sits as a refiner and purifier of silver." (Malachi 3:3)

She asked the silversmith if it was true that he had to sit there in front of the fire the whole time the silver was being refined. The man answered, "yes." He not only had to sit there holding the silver, but he had to keep his eyes on the silver the entire time it was in the fire.

If the silver was left a moment too long in the flames, it would be destroyed. The woman was silent for a moment. Then she asked the silversmith, "How do you know when the silver is fully refined?" He smiled at her and answered, "Oh, that's easy — when I see my image in it."

You see, friend, God made us in His image when He created man. Then, He allowed us to either choose Him or reject Him. As we walk through this life, He does everything He can to purify us from the sin-saturated life we are all born into as a result of the fall of man.

He doesn't do this *to* us. Rather, He does this *for* us so He can see His likeness *in* us.

As He exposes us to the fiery flames of adversity, He is trying to purify us to get us to let go of the slag or dross that needs to be removed from our lives. Slag is the stony waste material that is separated from metals during the smelting or refining process. Dross is foreign matter, dregs, or mineral waste (in particular, scum) formed on the surface of molten metal.

We all have slag or dross in our lives and God is hoping we will allow the fires of purification to smelt them off us so His likeness can take its place in our lives.

However, not all of us are willing to let go of the slag or dross we cling to. Not all of us want His likeness to take the place of the scum in our lives.

Jeremiah 6 The Message (MSG)

God gave me this task:
"I have made you the examiner of my people,
   to examine and weigh their lives.
They're a thickheaded, hard-nosed bunch,
   rotten to the core, the lot of them.

Refining fires are cranked up to white heat,
but the ore stays a lump, unchanged.
It's useless to keep trying any longer.
Nothing can refine evil out of them.
Men will give up and call them 'slag,'
thrown on the slag heap by me, their God."

It is not God's desire that one of us be thrown on the slag heap. God's desire is, as He places us in the fiery flames of refinement, we let go of the slag and allow Him to take the place of the slag; that He may see His image in us.

As for me, I confess to you, my doubts. In the midst of this raging storm that surrounds me, like Peter, I have moments where I walk on water and moments where I give the wind and the waves my full attention. I take my eyes off Christ, and I sink into a sea of despair.

Friend, that is exactly where I was when I began this chapter.

So, why do I do this? Why do you do this?

Simply put, I fail to place my full trust in Him when the trials of life come. I fail to recognize that when He strips me bare, He is removing slag from me so He can see His image in me. I fail to remember that He is Creator, and I am creation.

But when I review the record of His promises, I am reminded that I have, yet again, bought the lie of all lies and have failed to trust the Holy God of Heaven with my life.

If He is for me, then who can be against me?

My prayer for me:

"Forgive me, Father, for my unbelief and for my sinful-tantrums of falsely accusing you of hurting me. Forgive me for attempting to cling to the very dross that you are removing from my life with your fiery furnace of adversity. Let me not cling to that which causes me to remain an unchanged lump of ore, rendering your refinement process useless. As hard as it is to request, I want you to leave me in the furnace as long as it takes to change me, Lord, so you can see your image clearly in me."

For you:

He calls you son or daughter.

In His eyes, you have always been His child.

On the cross of Calvary, He shouted, "I do", when He said, "It is finished", and He gave Himself up that you may have the choice to say, "I do", back to Him.

Regardless of your gender, friend, He stands at the altar an eager Bridegroom awaiting you, His Bride, hoping you will commit your life to Him. Maybe, just maybe, today could be your wedding day. My prayer for you is that you will accept Him; that you will say, "I do."

If you have already said, "I do", but, like me, you are struggling with letting go of the dross of your life, I hope you will seek the Lord in the same manner I did in the prayer above.

So, regardless of whether your life is falling apart or falling into place, I will leave you with this question.

Without anything or anyone to define you, who are you?

Striving to Belong and Prove 'em all Wrong

But some people did accept him. They believed in him, and he gave them the right to become children of God.

John 1:12 Easy-to-Read Version

Will I find the happiness I seek when I prove 'em all wrong?

In Storms, Sandcastles and Secret Beaches, I found a stopping place for my story at the age of 15 years old. In this new chapter we are now in, I am going to pick up where I left off and, as the Holy Spirit leads, I will share my journey. I want to emphasize again, that I am not seeking glory, or pity, for anything I share with you. Rather, I am leading the way for you to share your journey with someone else. The number one lie the enemy tells us is that we are all alone and if we tell anyone what we have done or what we are struggling with, we will be mocked, laughed at, or worse yet, be destroyed and lose everything and everyone that matters to us. Please do not buy that lie. If you have already purchased that lie, Jesus Christ stands ready to exchange it for a *Hope* that only He can provide.

Remember my friend, you're not alone...and neither am I.

In 1992, I was 16 years old, and I met my first love working at the small grocery store in my hometown of Red Oak, TX. We fell in love fast and were honestly good for one another at that period of our lives. As our relationship grew, I found myself spending more and more time with her at her house. Her parents were nothing like my own. Her father spoke to me like

I was a son. He was interested in me and made a point to try and teach me things. To be honest, I didn't even realize it at the time, but looking back I can see how he was trying to prepare me to be a man. Her mother was equally great to me. They routinely made me supper and we would all sit at a table and eat together. For the first time in my young life, I felt like I had a family. I felt like I belonged.

Her mom and dad talked to me about college and encouraged me to go. My sister was the first person to graduate from high school in my family, so talking to my mother about this subject was difficult. She made it appear that she supported me going, until we drove down to San Marcos, TX to tour the campus of Texas State University. My first love's family was there, and we all toured the campus together. I had a blast and couldn't believe that attending college could be my reality. On the way home, my mother gave me an ear-full about how snobbish her parents were, how she couldn't afford to send me to college, and how I was putting her in a bad position by asking to go. I went from excited and on top of the world to feeling defeated and hopeless after that three-hour drive. You might say she took out a large needle and burst the balloon of my college dream.

While college is a major milestone in any high school graduate's life, it just seemed unreachable for me. It had nothing to do with my grades. Rather, it had everything to do with my social status. I knew how poor we were, and I worried I wouldn't be able to go to college because I couldn't possibly afford the housing and tuition – just as my mother continuously reminded me when I brought the subject up. Not to mention, I was told I didn't fit the mold of a typical college student. My high school counselor made sure I knew that was true when I approached him asking questions on how to apply. I will never forget the conversation I had with him in his office.

Counselor: "Come in."

Me: "Hi, my name is Ricky Sluder and I wanted to know if you could help me understand what I need to do to attend college. You see, I don't have anyone at home I can ask."

Counselor: (After looking at my long stringy hair, torn clothes and generally thuggish appearance) "Ricky, you're really not the college type. You really shouldn't be on the college track. In fact, I am going to remove you and put you on the early release from school-work program. This way you can work more hours at your job."

Me: "Okay, that will help me in the here and now, but why can't I go to college?"

Counselor: (Looking over my file, proud he found something to justify his biased opinion of me) "Well, you never took Chemistry. That class alone will keep you from college admittance in the state of Texas. Ricky, I think you should consider another option."

Me: "Like what, sir?"

Counselor: "Where do you work now?"

Me: "I work in a small warehouse making hard wood floors. I used to work at a grocery store, but I got an offer to make $5 per hour and I took it."

Counselor: "Well, that job won't qualify for our early release program, so we will need to work something out. As for what you should consider, well, I think you should consider Automotive Technician school."

Me: "Automotive Technician school? Okay, I will take a look around and see what I can find out about it. Thank you for your time."

Counselor: (Smiles proudly at his sage advice)

Me: (Walking down the hall dejected and talking to myself) "Automotive Technician school... F**k you. I am going to college. Just hide and watch me."

In May of 1994, I graduated from Red Oak High School. Instead of learning how to work on cars like my counselor advised me (not that there is anything at all wrong with that, it just wasn't for me, and I knew it), I enrolled in Emergency Medical Technician (EMT) school. I graduated at the top of my class with my state license as an EMT right before I stepped onto the campus of Texas State University as an incoming freshman. Chemistry course requirement be damned.

I declared my major as Respiratory Therapy, even though in my heart of hearts, I really wanted to be a police officer. When I received my acceptance letter a few months earlier, I remembered my mother asking me what I had planned to study. I told her I had always wanted to help people and I felt I could do that best in law enforcement. She told me that going to college to become a cop was a total waste of time and money. In my mother's back-handed complimentary way, she reminded me that I was too smart to be a police officer and I should be a doctor instead.

So, as I pointed out in Acceptance, I set out to please her, striving for her acceptance of me. I walked to the medical side of campus and met with my advisor. He told me that to be accepted into the Respiratory Therapy program at the last minute, I would have to take Pharmacology as an incoming freshman. If you're not familiar with this course, it is the study of drugs and their effect on the human body. It's one of the harder courses I have ever taken, and when I planned my freshman year, I told myself that a "C" was every bit as good as an "A". Well, when you make such decisions, you should really investigate the grade point standard for the classes you are taking. You see, on the medical side, an 84-75 was a "C", whereas in my other courses, a 79-70 was a "C".

My first love and our crew of friends met a lot of new friends that first semester living in the dorms together on campus. As a result, I had some of the best times of my young life. As a crew, we made partying our daily pastime. When I say we partied, I mean we partied! Somehow, despite all the alcohol I consumed the night before or how late I stayed up, I always made it to class on time. Studying, however, was a social construct that I didn't seem to think was very important.

By the time December came around, we were all kicked out of the dorms for Christmas break. My high school sweetheart had broken up with me. My roommate had failed-out and his parents would not allow him to return. And, I had made the wrong Dean's List.

My GPA my first semester was a 1.8 out of 4.0. My letter from the Dean indicated I had been placed on Academic Probation and failure to improve my GPA would result in the loss of my financial aid and immediate expulsion from Texas State University.

The three-hour commute to my mother and new stepfather's house was one of the longest drives I remember making. I was heartbroken and ashamed of myself. I didn't want to face my mother or sister because I feared what they would say to me. All I wanted to do was to go to college and make something out of my life. I wanted to prove everyone who said I couldn't do it, wrong, and I wanted to find the happiness I had always dreamed of finding.

Instead, I failed.

Maybe, my counselor was right.
Maybe, I wasn't college material.
Maybe, my mom was right.
Maybe, I wasn't good enough to run with the college kids.

The anger I had suppressed from years of neglect and verbal abuse began to swell within me, but I told myself I had to hold it in. So, I smoked a pack of cigarettes on that drive home, trying to figure out what I would do to salvage the situation. My new quest became figuring out how I could manipulate the situation so I could come out on top.

When I got home and confessed how I had done the first semester, I was met with the "I told you so" responses I expected from my mother. And before my brain could process the response, my mouth told my brain, "Shush, I got this one."

So, I said what any *logical* college-aged kid who was on Academic Probation would say in response to such hurtful statements.

Me: "I am gonna graduate with honors."
My mother: "Ricky, you can't pass your first semester. How do you think you are going to graduate with honors?"

When she said it, she had a grin of satisfaction on her face which I knew meant she didn't think I could do it. This pissed me off to a level I am not sure I had reached prior, and I knew what I had to do. I had to strive harder than I had ever strived before.

Me: "I am gonna make a 4.0 every semester until I graduate."

My mother: "There is no way you can do that."

Her words cut me like a knife. So, I told myself, *go back to college, work harder, bring up those grades, and do everything possible to keep striving to belong and prove 'em all wrong. Then, I will find the happiness I seek, and they will have no choice but to admit I am worthy and offer me love.*

I went back to college, changed my major to Criminal Justice, made a new set of friends, a new best friend (Kurt David Knapp), worked full time, went to school full time, attended every summer session, and I did exactly what I said I would do. I made the Dean's List with a 4.0 GPA every semester, except for one 3.8 GPA during a summer session. I graduated in exactly four years with a 3.98 GPA in my major and a 3.39 GPA overall.

I did it!

But you know something? At graduation, as I sat there in the auditorium with my honors cords around my neck (wishing I could choke my high school counselor with them), I still didn't feel a sense of accomplishment that was lasting. My mother came to my graduation applauding my success and offering what I thought then was fake smiles. But she never said she was sorry for not believing in me. She only focused on what I was going to do next.

Texas State Trooper – Class A98.

I was hired on my first application by the Texas Department of Public Safety and was recruited among the Top 10 percent of my class of about 160 cadets. To say I was proud was an understatement, and I did it just to prove everyone wrong about me.

This chip I had on my shoulder was growing larger each day and its weight was becoming harder and harder to carry around.

I began to dream of being a Texas Ranger. The Rangers are an elite law enforcement division of the Texas Department of Public Safety, and I couldn't wait to be the first from my class to wear that Ranger badge. But first, I had to pass the DPS Academy which has a rich legacy of being the toughest police academy in the state. And let me tell you, the rumors are true!

My pride continued to swell, and I finally felt like my striving had paid off. After all, I had graduated in the Top 10 percent of the nation among Criminal Justice graduates, was selected in the Top 10 percent of my DPS Academy Class and was told in a special ceremony that we (the Top 15 Cadets of A98) were the *BEST* of the *BEST*.

I metaphorically raised my middle finger in a burst of pride toward my high school counselor, my mother, my father, my sister, and everyone else who never truly believed in me. As Toby Keith would later sing, "How do you like me now?"

That was the condition of my heart when I entered the DPS Academy, and I knew I had to step up my striving a notch or two higher. I now had more to prove. I needed to be the best Trooper-Trainee to ever graduate from the academy. My best friend, Kurt, was attending B-98, and I had to set the precedent. I had to be the best.

But something else was happening that I didn't understand. In that moment of standing on the mountain top shouting my arrogance at all who told me I couldn't, it was then that God knocked me off my pedestal. He did it with one very loud word that repeated over and over in my mind.

RESIGN.

As I sat through class after class, this singular word rang in my head. I couldn't begin to understand why, so after a particular class ended, instead of getting into formation for lunch, I stayed in the room and fell up against a wall. I looked up to Heaven and had the following conversation:

Me: "Am I really supposed to resign?"

God: "Yes, I never intended this for you."

Me: "Then, why did you let me have this?"

God: "Because I never would have heard the end of it from you if I didn't. I needed you to see if for yourself. This isn't for you, and you know it."

Me: "You're right. And although I prayed for this, I must admit this isn't what I really want."

God: "Resign."

So, I resigned my position and walked the "walk of shame". I packed up all my stuff in the presence of my fellow cadets and I left Texas DPS. I remember making the drive from Austin to Red Oak with a singular line of thought running through my mind.

How would I make that call to Kurt to tell him I quit? What will he think of me when he hears this news?

Cell phones were around in 1998, but we didn't use them the way we do today. So, I didn't call anyone. Instead, I just showed up at my mother and stepfather's house. They had expected me to come home that weekend anyway as we had to leave the academy on Friday and come back Sunday night. However, they weren't prepared for me to tell them I had resigned.

Have you ever done something you knew you needed to do, but had no idea how to answer the question, "Why did you do that?"

I didn't know how to articulate my reasons and I didn't think I could say, "God told me to." People would think I was crazy. Instead, I stuck to one answer:

"I didn't think Texas DPS was the right fit for me."

I chose a lie over the truth.

Why do we do this? Why do we tend to choose a lie over the truth? Why can't the truth be enough for us or for other people in our life?

I find it interesting that every time I choose a lie over the truth, I am literally choosing something over *The Truth*; I am choosing something over God.

After all, Jesus is *The Truth, The Way, and The Life*. And the same book that tells me this, also reminds me that Satan is the *Father of Lies*.

So, when I accept a lie over truth, I am literally accepting Satan over Jesus.

When presented this way, it sounds so terrible. But when we wrap our justifications around why we choose a lie over truth, it seems to dull the *terrible* connotation and the lie becomes something more believable than the truth.

And that, my friend, is yet another example of how we continue to buy the lie of all lies.

If resigning from the top law enforcement agency in the great sate of Texas wasn't bad enough, I found myself living at my mother and stepfather's home, unemployed, and sharing a bedroom with my 15-year-old stepbrother, Ryan.

This is not how life was supposed to turn out for me. I was so depressed, and I only got more depressed with each law enforcement agency that rejected my application. I found myself at rock bottom and I ran to God for help.

I want to level-set that I was a believer at this point in my life. But my theology was built around religion, not relationship. I had a works mentality, not a grace mindset.

With that as the backdrop, I began to study the Bible, listen to Christian radio, and I spent countless hours watching TV preachers and listening to sermons. I figured if I *proved* to God that I was a *REAL* Christian, He would bless me. My intent was to strive for His acceptance in the same manner I had strived for acceptance from mankind.

But as I delved deep into His word, I continued to be rejected by law enforcement agencies and rejection poked a hole in my heart that let despair in. What I realize now that I wish I had seen back then, was that God already made it clear He didn't want me in law enforcement. So, why was I so hell-bent on re-entering the very career He just took away from me?

Easy answer - I wanted my will to be done and I demanded that God bless it.

Here is where the story takes an interesting turn. As I said, no one would hire me, so I took the one job that didn't turn me down.

Security Guard.

Can you say humility check?

Yes sir, I went from Texas State Trooper-Trainee with hopes of being a Texas Ranger, to Security Guard making $7.38 per hour at a pager (beeper) company. I didn't think my life could get any worse.

What is interesting is how God began to work on my identity during this time. My stepbrother, Ryan, was a 15-year-old boy who had moved in with his dad because he was running with the wrong crowd at his mother's house. He and I were seven years apart in age, but I had already lived the path he was walking. Since we shared a bedroom, we also shared a lot of deep conversations. One of those conversations centered around salvation, and I had the pleasure of leading my brother to Christ.

Maybe that was the point of God telling me to resign.

Maybe it was *coincidental* that we ended up in the same bedroom together and he accepted Christ as his savior.

I don't personally believe in coincidences, but I also don't know all the reasons God told me to resign. I do believe Him gaining Ryan's acceptance was just one part of His plan.

God chose this point in my life to teach me about trust. I didn't have a clue how to answer the question I asked you in the last chapter (*Who am I?*), but I wanted so badly to be able to. I wanted to know my purpose and I had no idea that in the midst of this chaos, God was teaching me lessons on both.

One day driving home from work, I heard a sermon on Malachi 3:10. Traditionally speaking, it's a sermon on tithing, or giving 10% of what you earn to God. These sorts of messages were a big turn-off for me. I never understood why preachers asked you for money and then made it sound like God expected it from you and you were a horrible person if you didn't give it, as commanded.

I mean, why does the Creator of the universe need my money?

Didn't He create the money I have?

Doesn't He have cattle on a thousand hills?

What could He possibly need my money for?

I mean, I was already *broke* with the net income I made. Take away an additional 10% and I was seriously not going to eat. Why would God want me to starve?

All great questions I pondered, and I am sure you have, too. But something was said that caused me to respond in a surprising way.

The preacher said, "This is the only place in the Bible where God tells you to test Him in this."

Malachi 3:10 New International Version (NIV)

[10] Bring the whole tithe into the storehouse, that there may be food in my house. Test me in this," says the Lord Almighty, "and see if I will not throw open the floodgates of heaven and pour out so much blessing that there will not be room enough to store it.

I had always heard you are not supposed to test God. If you think back to Luke 4, Jesus told Satan he wasn't supposed to put the Lord God to the test. Remember? So, doesn't that make all this fuzzy stuff that doesn't line up just right in the Bible all the more questionable?

Sometimes it seems that way, but when you think about God as a Daddy who loves you, who wants you to trust Him like a child trusts a loving parent, it makes perfect sense why He would allow you the opportunity to *test* His faithfulness.

As for me, I had $400.05 to my name, in cash. My checking account was empty, which matched my savings account. If it wasn't for the grace of my mother and stepfather to allow me to stay in their home, I would have been homeless. I was at rock bottom, and I couldn't begin to understand how my life ended up there, given where I was just a few months earlier.

Anyway, when I heard this sermon, I had to face something head on and admit I did not trust God with my money.

So, I took the words *"test me in this"* literally. I drove home and placed the $400 inside a plain white envelope. Then, I drove to a church I visited a few times when I was a kid. I walked inside, handed the envelope to a lady, and I walked out to my car. Not one word spoken. As I sped away, making sure no one caught up to me to ask who I was or what the money was for (as if they would), I realized I still had that dang nickel in my pocket.

I started to cry, and I said out loud, "I just gave you all the money I have, minus this nickel, so I don't have any choice but to trust you now."

Feeling somewhere between unsettled and at peace, I drove back to my mother and stepfather's house. Everyone was still at work, so I hadn't told anyone what I had done. Within a few minutes of walking into the house, the phone rang.

Me: "Hello?"

Dad: "Hey son, how are you?"

Me: (Shocked my biological father called me, but played it cool and lied through my teeth) "I am good, how are you?"

Dad: "I am good. Hey, I got a question for you. Do you still have that shotgun? My place got robbed and I need a gun in case they come back again."

Me: "Yes sir, I still have it."

Dad: "I want to buy it from you. I am gonna come over and give you $500 for it this evening. Will that be, okay?"

Me: "What? Dad, it's not worth $500. You don't have to pay me; I will just give it to you."

Dad: "No, son. I am gonna pay you for it and I am gonna give you $500."

When I hung up the phone from this conversation, I could hardly believe what just took place. The fact that my dad called me was a minor miracle in and of itself. But what blew me away was that God just gave me back ALL my money, plus $100.

I hope you will take into consideration that when I did this, I was not a super religious person. I hadn't memorized a lot of scripture and I wasn't pious. I simply approached God the same way I would approach a loving parent. And remember, friend, a loving parent wasn't something I had ever experienced before. I stepped out in faith and figured the worst thing that could happen was that I would lose $400.

I took the risk. I put God to the test, and just as His word commands, He did not return void. He proved Himself faithful and He got my attention, at least for a little while.

During this season of my life, time seemed to stand still. I was in a great big hurry to be powerful, wealthy, and successful. But God was not interested in those things at this point in my journey. He was more interested in shaping me, humbling me, and smoothing the rough edges of that chip I had on my shoulder.

I went to work each day as a Security Guard wearing a uniform I despised and sat alone at a duty station for hours-on-end with nothing but my thoughts to keep me company. It was in the stillness and the quiet that God began to speak to me, and while I really didn't understand what I was experiencing, I know now He was working on my heart.

Poetic verses began to fill my thoughts and poems flowed from me that had wisdom and eloquence I knew were not from me. I replaced country music entirely with Christian radio, and while it bored me to tears, I was drawn to it and rarely changed the channel. As a result, I discovered gifted Bible teachers, and the messages they taught became seeds scattered in the garden of my mind.

Conversely, in my private moments, I sought love through sex in online chatrooms and various dating sites, as well as bars. I had more one-night-stands than I can even count, and I constantly looked for love in all the wrong places. I had a void in my chest that I wanted so badly to fill, but I wasn't sure exactly what was needed to fill it. In my mind, I thought I needed to find love, get married, establish myself in a career, and be successful. If I could just connect all those dots in just the right way, I would find happiness. But no matter what door-of-acceptance I knocked on and no matter how much acceptance I received, I was always let down, and that void continued to ache in the depths of my inner being. Happiness just never seemed to last.

Are you struggling with finding happiness and filling that void within you?

Friend, here is what I learned the hard way. Happiness is like helium, and we are the balloon. When we are full of happiness, we float around, lighter than air. But eventually, the helium dissipates, and gravity pulls that balloon back to the surface. Like helium, happiness fades and circumstances always bring us back down to earth. Some circumstances can even take us below sea level where we feel like we are drowning in a sea of despair. Happiness can never fill this void, just like a balloon cannot be filled with helium forever. It always dissipates, leaving us feeling empty inside.

Logic tells us that before we can fill any void, we should take the time to understand its shape. We learn this as children assembling puzzles, but as adults most of us don't take the time to evaluate the space we are trying to fill. Instead, we assume that happiness is the missing puzzle piece, and we fill this void with anything we think will give us the happiness-high we seek. For a while we float, but eventually the happiness fades.

So, what are we to do? What can possibly fill this void?

Do you remember the verse I shared with you in Part 1: Acceptance, Revelation 3:20?

When you open your heart's door and let Jesus in, He will fill your void with *Truth* and *Hope*! Jesus is the missing puzzle piece of your life, and He is the only thing that can fill that void completely.

Unfortunately, at this point in my story that I began telling you above, and maybe this is where you find yourself, I hadn't heard this message in this way. I had no idea that a relationship with Jesus could truly change my life. I just thought being a Christian meant I had to get up early for church every Sunday, stop saying the *F-word*, stop drinking alcohol, stop having casual sex, and "clean up my life and act right". But *Truth* isn't relative, and *Hope* isn't based on our works.

Let me illustrate my final point above, and in this chapter, to you with a Bible story.

> *But Truth isn't relative, and Hope isn't based on our works.*

Luke 23 English Standard Version (ESV)

The Crucifixion

[26] And as they led him away, they seized one Simon of Cyrene, who was coming in from the country, and laid on him the cross, to carry it behind Jesus. [27] And there followed him a great multitude of the people and of women who were mourning and lamenting for him. [28] But turning to them Jesus said, "Daughters of Jerusalem, do not weep for me, but weep for yourselves and for your children. [29] For behold, the days are coming when they will say, 'Blessed are the barren and the wombs that never bore and the breasts that never nursed.' [30] Then they will begin to say to the mountains, 'Fall on us,' and to the hills, 'Cover us.' [31] For if they do these things when the wood is green, what will happen when it is dry?"

[32] Two others, who were criminals, were led away to be put to death with him. [33] And when they came to the place that is called The Skull, there they crucified him, and the criminals, one on his right and one on his left. [34] And Jesus said, "Father, forgive them, for they know not what they do." And they cast lots to divide his garments. [35] And the people stood by, watching, but the rulers scoffed at him, saying, "He saved others; let him save himself, if he is the Christ of God, his Chosen One." [36] The soldiers also mocked him, coming up and offering him sour wine [37] and saying, "If you are the King of the Jews, save yourself." [38] There was also an inscription over him,[c] "This is the King of the Jews."

[39] One of the criminals who were hanged railed at him, saying, "Are you not the Christ? Save yourself and us." [40] But the other rebuked him, saying, "Do you not fear God, since you are under the same sentence of condemnation?

⁴¹ And we indeed justly, for we are receiving the due reward of our deeds; but this man has done nothing wrong." ⁴² And he said, "Jesus, remember me when you come into your kingdom." ⁴³ And he said to him, "Truly, I say to you, today you will be with me in paradise."

Let me explain the part of this story I am focusing on in verses 39-43.

As Jesus hangs on the cross, He is accompanied by two thieves who are being put to death for their crimes.

One thief rails on Jesus and mocks Him. He even challenges Jesus' identity as the Christ and demands Jesus save Himself and them. But the other thief, having humbled himself by acknowledging his sin-debts before all who witnessed their execution in the making and discerning Jesus' true identity, simply made a request from a heart filled with hope.
"Jesus, remember me when you come into your Kingdom."

And what does Jesus say to him?

Did He tell him to say five hail Mary's?
Did He tell him he should have gone to church more often?
Did He demand that he clean up his act before he could be in the presence of almighty God?
Did He tell him it was just too late for a person like him to be saved?

No.

Jesus didn't ask Him *to do* anything.

You might as well be hanging on a cross next to Jesus because you cannot correct what you have done wrong.

Hanging on a cross just hours away from death, there was nothing this man could have done to atone for his sin, if works were required of him. And that, my friend, is the point of the entire gospel message. You might as well be hanging on a cross next to Jesus because you cannot correct what you have done wrong.

This man, this thief, as we call him, set the example for every one of us who are striving to belong and prove 'em all wrong.

Do you know what that is?

To be crucified with Christ.

When you choose to be crucified with Christ, Jesus will say to you what He said to the thief:

"Truly, I say to you, today you will be with me in paradise."

My friend, happiness is a fleeting emotion, and no amount of striving will ever fill that void in the center of your chest. So-what if you never prove 'em all wrong, and so-what if you do. It doesn't matter either way. Your relationships, your titles, and your trophies don't define you. Whether you have conquered your demons or whether you are still fighting them, neither outcome defines you. Your identity can only come from one place, and you must be willing to die to yourself to find it.

In Galatians 2:20 English Standard Version (ESV), Paul, the man who once murdered Christians for sport, shares the same revelation the thief and I are trying to communicate to you.

[20] I have been crucified with Christ. It is no longer I who live, but Christ who lives in me. And the life I now live in the flesh I live by faith in the Son of God, who loved me and gave himself for me.

Hope is what you really want, not happiness. *Truth* is what you desperately need, not striving to belong and proving 'em all wrong.

When Jesus said, "Follow me", He meant all the way to the cross.

Why the cross, you may ask?

Because your *true identity* awaits you there!

I Once Was Lost, but Now I'm Found!

> But some people did accept him. They believed in him, and he gave them the right to become children of God.
>
> John 1:12 Easy-to-Read Version

I blew it big time, now what do I do?

Let's pick up where I left off with my story from the previous chapter. If you remember, I found myself in a place where I felt lost and utterly hopeless. I had big dreams that shattered, and I felt like God had allowed me to be tossed into a pit and left for dead. Because of horrible theology (works-based religion), I thought God was punishing me for all the wrong things I had done. I believed I deserved my negative circumstances.

Have you ever felt that way?

Are you constantly waiting for the other shoe to drop and for God to swing down His wrath upon you for all the wrong things you have done?

> *Sin is its own consequence and God is not waiting to punish you.*

If so, relax. God doesn't work that way. Sin is its own consequence and God is not waiting to punish you.

Some of you may be scoffing at that statement. You may even be thinking that if that were true then there would be no need for Hell. After all, isn't an eternity in Hell the ultimate God-ordained punishment?

Before I answer this question about Hell being a God-ordained punishment, let's address some facts about Hell. Hell is a very real place. The Bible talks more about Hell than it does Heaven. In fact, Jesus taught that more people would go to Hell than would go to Heaven. Check out this verse of scripture where Jesus is teaching this to the disciples:

Matthew 7:13-14 New International Version

The Narrow and Wide Gates
[13] "Enter through the narrow gate. For wide is the gate and broad is the road that leads to destruction, and many enter through it. [14] But small is the gate and narrow the road that leads to life, and only a few find it.

Now, I will answer the question for you. God has no desire for anyone to go to Hell. *Sending* people to Heaven or Hell isn't something He does. Remember, love is a choice. The road to Heaven and Hell ends with an abrupt stop, like a T-intersection on a back-country road. The decision you make to turn left and go to Hell or turn right and go to Heaven has absolutely nothing to do with how much God loves you.

As we have discussed in previous chapters, God has already accepted you. So, the decision between Heaven and Hell rests solely on your shoulders. You can reject Him and His grace for your sin and spend eternity apart from Him (Hell), or you can accept Him and His grace and be in relationship with Him for all eternity (Heaven).

As for me, I chose to say, '*I do*' to Him. I hope you will too.

Please hear me, friend. God is not interested in punishing you. Instead, He is allowing you to be placed into the refining fires of adversity, in hopes you will let go of the dross and slag that prevents you from reflecting His image.

Before I continue with how I found out '*Who I am*', I want to share a couple other stories with you that will properly set the stage for me to tell you, my story.

From Pit to Palace

Way back in Genesis 37, you will find the longest story told from this book of the Bible. As such, I am not going to quote scripture to you. Rather, I am going to summarize the story and tell you about the high points in hopes you will go read the full text for yourself.

It is the story of a man named Joseph. Joseph was the 11th son of Jacob, but first born to Jacob's favorite wife, Rachel. Like many doting fathers, Jacob allowed himself to be passive with all his sons, and foolishly he showed unequivocal favoritism to Joseph.

As you might imagine, knowing that their father loved them less than Joseph wounded the 10 older boys emotionally. They, in-turn, wounded Joseph mentally, physically, and emotionally. As a result of wounding Joseph, they also wounded their father, Jacob.

You see, Joseph had a prophetic gifting and could interpret dreams. In one of his dreams that he shared with his brothers, he told them how they would all bow down to him one day.

When Joseph was about 17 years of age, his brothers decided they had put up with him and the favoritism he received long enough. So, they devised a scheme to kill him. One of his brothers, Judah, stepped in and said, "Let's not kill him. Instead, let's throw him in a pit, take that coat dad made for him, and tell dad he was killed by an animal. Then, we can sell him into slavery and be rid of him forever."

And so, they did as Judah suggested!

Ironically, the brothers' plan to gain dad's acceptance through this foolish act of striving backfired.

When they told Jacob the lie about Joseph being dead, they broke Jacob's heart. Jacob then turned his attention and favoritism toward his youngest son Benjamin. Ben was the second born son of his favorite wife Rachel, who sadly died giving birth to Ben.

Joseph went from being the favored son of 17 years, to being a slave sold on the auction block after being sold to slave-traders by his brothers. And if being a slave to a powerful man named Potiphar wasn't bad enough, Potiphar's wife falsely accused Joseph of rape when he refused to have sex with her, an accusation that landed him in prison. For 13 years straight, Joseph faced severe adversity.

I bet you anything, if we could go back in time and hangout with Joseph in the prison during that period of his life, we would undoubtedly think God was punishing him for something.

Why else would all of this happen to him?

Isn't that why young children get diagnosed with cancer?

Isn't that why we suffer a job loss and financial ruin?

Isn't that why spouses cheat on one another?

Isn't that why parents become raging alcoholics?

I mean, isn't that why you are facing so many trials and tribulations, like those mentioned above, in your own life?

God must be punishing you. After all, there is no possible way He could ever love a person like you. Right?

Is that what you think?

If you do think this about Joseph, or yourself, you could not be further from the truth.

God loves you, and He has a very specific plan and purpose for your life.

"Ricky, how can you be so sure of that?", you may be asking me.

Well, for starters, Jesus formed you in your mother's womb. He created you so uniquely that there is only one you that will ever exist. If you don't believe me, you can read that for yourself in Psalm 139:13-18. God also tells you He knows the plans He has made for you. Those plans were designed by God to prosper you and never harm you. God said He was giving you a hope and a future (see Jeremiah 29:11).

We can also look at what happens in Joseph's life. Remember, his brothers threw him into a pit at age 17, pronounced him dead to friends and family, sold him into slavery, and then he spent the next 13 years alone in a foreign land living as a slave and imprisoned for a crime he didn't commit. But then God did something that only God could have done. One night, Pharaoh had a dream he could not understand, and he told one of his servants about it. It just so happened, three years earlier Pharaoh had thrown this same servant into prison and Joseph accurately interpreted this man's dream. After hearing of Pharaoh's desire to have his dream interpreted, this servant of Pharaoh remembered Joseph. At once, Pharaoh requested that Joseph be brought before him to interpret his dream. After Joseph told Pharaoh the meaning of his dream, Pharaoh promoted him from prisoner to Prime Minister of all the land of Egypt.

Who do you think gave Pharaoh that dream?

The same God who had been purifying the heart of Joseph through extreme fires of adversity, in preparation for Joseph to step into one of his many purposes.

I wonder, friend, is it possible that God has placed you in the extreme fires of adversity, in preparation for you to step into one of your many purposes?

Your adversity is not in vain. God has a plan designed just for you. Your very existence, coupled with the trials and tribulations you experience in this life, is the evidence of that promised plan.

Lost Son, Loving Father
Did you know God created you to glorify Him through a personal relationship with Him? He is not a mean cosmic killjoy. Rather, He is a loving Daddy who wants quality time with his children. As a daddy to two daughters and a son, I can say that spending quality time with my children is one of the greatest treasures of my life. God absolutely adores you, and He

simply wants you to be in an eternal relationship with Him. Let me prove it to you with our next story, which I am calling Lost Son, Loving Father.

In Hebrew culture, when a father died, he left an inheritance to each of his living sons. The inheritance could only be received after the father died. What you are going to read below is a story of a selfish younger son demanding his inheritance while his father still lives, which meant he would rather his father be dead for the sake of money. What isn't apparent in the story but is true of the culture of the time, was that this father would have also given the older son his inheritance, too. Both boys received their inheritance in full.

Luke 15:11-32 The Message (MSG)

The Story of the Lost Son

¹¹⁻¹² Then he said, "There was once a man who had two sons. The younger said to his father, 'Father, I want right now what's coming to me.'

¹²⁻¹⁶ "So the father divided the property between them. It wasn't long before the younger son packed his bags and left for a distant country. There, undisciplined and dissipated, he wasted everything he had. After he had gone through all his money, there was a bad famine all through that country and he began to hurt. He signed on with a citizen there who assigned him to his fields to slop the pigs. He was so hungry he would have eaten the corncobs in the pig slop, but no one would give him any.

¹⁷⁻²⁰ "That brought him to his senses. He said, 'All those farmhands working for my father sit down to three meals a day, and here I am starving to death. I'm going back to my father. I'll say to him, Father, I've sinned against God, I've sinned before you; I don't deserve to be called your son. Take me on as a hired hand.' He got right up and went home to his father.

²⁰⁻²¹ "When he was still a long way off, his father saw him. His heart pounding, he ran out, embraced him, and kissed him. The son started his speech: 'Father, I've sinned against God, I've sinned before you; I don't deserve to be called your son ever again.'

²²⁻²⁴ "But the father wasn't listening. He was calling to the servants, 'Quick. Bring a clean set of clothes and dress him. Put the family ring on his finger and sandals on his feet. Then get a grain-fed heifer and roast it. We're going to feast! We're going to have a wonderful time! My son is here—given up

for dead and now alive! Given up for lost and now found!' And they began to have a wonderful time.

²⁵⁻²⁷ "All this time his older son was out in the field. When the day's work was done he came in. As he approached the house, he heard the music and dancing. Calling over one of the houseboys, he asked what was going on. He told him, 'Your brother came home. Your father has ordered a feast—barbecued beef!—because he has him home safe and sound.'

²⁸⁻³⁰ "The older brother stalked off in an angry sulk and refused to join in. His father came out and tried to talk to him, but he wouldn't listen. The son said, 'Look how many years I've stayed here serving you, never giving you one moment of grief, but have you ever thrown a party for me and my friends? Then this son of yours who has thrown away your money on whores shows up and you go all out with a feast!'

³¹⁻³² "His father said, 'Son, you don't understand. You're with me all the time, and everything that is mine is yours—but this is a wonderful time, and we had to celebrate. This brother of yours was dead, and he's alive! He was lost, and he's found!'"

Remember what I said about the cultural significance of demanding an inheritance while the father still lived?

Do you get the symbolism of what it means that both sons received their inheritance in full, and only the wayward son truly wanted to be a part of his father's house?

In case you missed it, let me explain.

The father in this story represents God.

The older son represents the religious crowd that really isn't interested in a relationship with his younger brother, nor his father. The older brother represents those who want to keep the rules, for rules sake, but won't offer anyone an ounce of grace if they go against the established religion. For the older brother, religion is his god.

The younger son represents broken people in search of hope. People like you and me who have blown it! The younger son squandered his inheritance, and when he found himself at the end of his rope, he merely wanted to be a servant in his father's house.

Did you know that every person ever born has received an inheritance from God? And just like the prodigal son, we have squandered it. Do you know what inheritance I am talking about?

I am not talking about the trust-fund that the prodigal son blew through in the far country on sex, drugs, and rock-n-roll. Rather, I am talking about the inheritance of grace you and I received into our *Hope-account* when Jesus died on Calvary's cross.

While I am not sure of the details of your story as it relates to this paradigm, I would like to share mine with you.

I have lived my life in the same way the prodigal son lived his. I invested in the wrong things and found myself living in the slop of the mess I had made out of my life. When I finally stopped and evaluated what I knew about my Daddy (God), I knew I couldn't keep living as though I were the god of my own life! I felt so ashamed of how I treated the inheritance of grace He freely gave so I could become His child. I realized that, while I had treated myself to nearly every vice possible, none of it satisfied me. I was still thirsty, and I just wanted a drink of His living water. In that moment, I wanted to be a slave in Heaven over being a ruler in Hell.

I told myself it was time to go back home to my Daddy and tell Him how sorry I was; how I would gladly be a slave, believing I had forfeited my right to sonship. But something wonderful and unexpected happened to me in that very moment. It is the same thing that happened to the *Lost Son*, and it is the same outcome you should expect from God when you get tired of wallowing in the mess you have made.

For context, I am going to interpret the rest of this story in the first person, and I want you to accept that this is the outcome you will receive when your acceptance of God informs your identity as His child.

God saw me while I was still far off. To my surprise, He ran to meet me! I poured out my heart-felt apologies for my idolatrous lifestyle, expecting

Him to rebuke me. I expected Him to tell me I had crossed the line for the last time. But that is not what happened at all. Instead, He called me His son, embraced me, and kissed me. He wasn't interested in my apologies and wasn't interested in me being a slave. He was too busy calling upon the Angels of Heaven to prepare for a celebration because I came home to be in relationship with Him!

Friend, listen to me. All God wants is for you to be in relationship with Him. If you are still in the far country debating what you should do, let me encourage you to get up and run into the arms of a God who loves you unconditionally. Don't listen to those religious people, the older brother from this story, who will tell you that you need to clean your act up first, because you simply don't need to.

Why not, you may ask?

His grace is sufficient for you.

So, instead of running further away or quitting outright, run to the living God. He is waiting for you to come home, and when you do, there will be a party in your honor in Heaven.

I once was lost. But thank God, now I am found!

Salt in the Oats and Thirsty for Surrender

But some people did accept him. They believed in him, and he gave them the right to become children of God.

John 1:12

WILL I EVER GIVE UP THIS BUCKET, EVEN THOUGH ITS WATERS DON'T QUENCH MY THIRST?

An Officer and a Husband:

In 1999, after being promoted to Account Manager and then Operations Manager at the security company where I worked, I left that organization and became a Texas Child Support Enforcement Officer for the Office of the Attorney General.

While working for the Attorney General, I was applying to every police department in the Dallas-Fort Worth Metroplex. In hindsight, I am not sure why I continued to pursue law enforcement after God allowed me to have the position I originally wanted, only to ask me to give it up because it wasn't for me.

In 2000, I got a call from the UT Southwestern at Dallas Police Department inviting me to attend the University of Texas System Police Academy as a Police Cadet. Half of me was thrilled and the other half of me was embarrassed to admit to anyone that I was going to be a "Campus Cop".

I packed my bags and moved to Austin, TX for six months while I attended the police academy full time. I did exceedingly well, graduating number three in my class and being bestowed with the *Overall Outstanding Cadet Award*.

When I got back to Dallas, I began my 16 weeks of field training. My first four weeks were on "Deep Nights" where I worked from 11 PM to 7 AM each day and had Mondays and Tuesdays off.

Admittedly, I knew very little about the department that hired me and even less about the university where I was employed. But that, my friend, would change very quickly. In short, UT Southwestern is a world-renowned medical school and research facility. With inpatient hospitals, Ambulatory Surgical Centers, and outpatient clinics, it is located on about 230 acres of land in one of the 'roughest' and 'notorious' areas of Dallas, TX. In addition, the campus has outlying facilities that spread across more than 16 counties. The main portion of the campus is located on Harry Hines Boulevard with a Texas Department of Criminal Justice Halfway House for felons located directly across the street. I think I was on duty for approximately four hours before my Field Training Officer (FTO) and I had to draw our weapons on a suspect. Thankfully, I didn't have to pull the trigger on my first shift, but we came close.

I advanced quickly through my field training and was released early to be on my own as a patrol officer. I ended up working "Days" and stayed very busy with calls for service. If I remember correctly, as a department, we handled more than 100,000 calls for service each year. While assigned to the Patrol Division, I had my fair share of "shagging reports", foot pursuits, car accidents, arrests, fights, high-risk search warrants, and I even received the Meritorious Conduct Award. My Sergeant and I sacrificed our safety to save the life of another during a suicide attempt on a freeway overpass.

I was having the time of my life, and it all fed into my identity issues that had plagued me since boyhood. I was finally able to prove I was the man I had strived so hard to become.

So, all that ridicule I suffered at the hands of my parents would finally 'wash off of me', right? Not exactly.

Within six months of graduating the academy, I was laterally transferred from Officer to Detective. I was a great writer, I had good instincts, and the Dallas County District Attorney's Office accepted 100% of my cases without a Detective having to re-write them for me, which is what precipitated my move from the Patrol Division to the Criminal Investigations Division.

I loved being a Detective and before I knew it, I no longer had a first name. All of my colleagues called me Detective, which is how it goes in law enforcement. In addition, all of my friends were cops, so I was either "Detective", or "Corporal", or "Sluder" when someone said my name.

Right before my lateral transfer, I met my first wife, Amber. I was coming out of a horrible situation that cannot even be called a relationship. Rather, it was more akin to a Lifetime Channel drama where, literally, an older woman was pretending to be a younger woman online and, on the phone, yet I was meeting a younger woman in person who was controlled by the older woman. In short, it was a mess of a situation that I eventually had to turn into a criminal investigation. As such, Amber seemed perfect in contrast. We were fast friends and shared a love for one another.

After six months of dating, we decided on a whim to get married. We drove from Arlington, TX to Las Vegas, NV and found The Chapel of Your Dreams. Honestly, it was not as the name implied. In fact, the minister called me Robert twice during the ceremony and Amber and I have joked for over 20 years now that she really married someone named Robert as opposed to Ricky.

When we got back from Las Vegas I was so excited to be married and, being a romantic, I was trying to make sure Amber knew exactly how much I loved her. However, we missed one another's love languages by about three country miles and I interpreted this as rejection. As a result, I sank deeper and deeper into the despair I had always known. I tried to fake it and put on a happy face, but inside, I was miserable.

We both talked about wanting children, but her doctor assured us we couldn't conceive together. So, I poured myself further into my career and tried to ignore the storm that was raging inside of me.

Life outside my marriage was not much different. I made a point to be present at all the obligatory visits to family events like Thanksgiving and Christmas, but I seethed with anger and resentment under the smile I forced upon my face. I chalked it up, at the time, to being a cynical cop. But truth be told, I had so much unresolved hurt and anger toward my family and perceived *loveless* marriage that my emotional cup was constantly filled to overflowing. With each new year came more catty comments from my mother, more broken promises from my father, and more perceived rejection in my marriage. And the longer I did nothing about it, the more I acted out to soothe my aching soul.

Friend, I was miserable!

Have you ever felt this way?

Do you feel this way right now?

How did it, or is it, impacting your heart?

What did you do, or are you going to do, about it?

Are you striving in all the wrong ways like we discussed in Part 1: Acceptance?

I know I sure did. In fact, I still do more often than I wish I did. Old habits can be hard to break, and perfection is unattainable, so do yourself a favor and offer yourself grace for every time you blow it. Then, do something about it. Remember me telling you if you put it in the light, healing will come? I know it can be scary to open the door on that closet full of skeletons, but I promise you it will be worth it when you finally do.

Where was I in my story? Oh yeah, still angry about my childhood, unhappy in my marriage, pretending I wanted to be around my family, and striving to belong and prove 'em all wrong everyday by being a police officer. It's exhausting just telling you about it, much less having lived it.

Still Striving:
One of my many coping mechanisms was to achieve a higher status in my career. So, I turned the speed dial up on my proverbial hamster wheel of insanity.

Here are a few highlights:

I was the youngest Detective in my Advanced Homicide class.

I became certified as a Special Investigator for Sex Crimes and became a Rape Aggression Defense Instructor.

I joined our Special Response and Tactics (SRT) Team - another way of saying SWAT Team.

I became a Hostage Negotiator.

I worked Internal Affairs.

I worked Crimes Against Persons (CAPERS), Property Crimes, Auto Theft Task Force, and White-Collar Crime.

I don't think my identity could have been more wrapped up in my badge if I tried.

For the most part, I was keeping it together. I was still miserable, but my career allowed me to channel that anger in a *pseudo-healthy* way. I still repressed my emotions and I still refused to deal with any of the wounds that I had experienced, so I wasn't any better for the channeling that I did.

Then, it happened.

We say in law enforcement that any day can be your day to go home to the Lord. We mentally prepare each day to take a life, and we mentally prepare each day to give our life up, but we don't usually prepare to lose a friend.

On May 8, 2004, my best friend from college, Texas State Trooper Kurt David Knapp, was killed in the line of duty in Comfort, TX. He was 28 years old.

For the first time, I verbally told God I was mad at Him.

You see, Kurt had it made. He had a mother who adored him and a father who loved him. He and his wife Jennifer had met in the 6th grade and were an amazing couple. To make his "untimely death" worse, they had two young kids, Makayla, and Wyatt.

I sincerely wished God had taken me home instead of Kurt. Part of it was me being selfish and wanting to escape the pain of this life. The other part was because Kurt was deeply loved by so many, including me!

I was so heartbroken and had no idea how to cope with the loss. So, I reverted to old habits. I shoved it on top of everything else I had been pushing deep, deep down within me.

I wish I could tell you I went to counseling or that I used this opportunity to heal from the many wounds I had, but I didn't. Instead, I watched more pornography, had extramarital affairs, and tortured myself emotionally.

First Round Draft Pick:
In the summer of 2005, I received a case that would change everything for me professionally. It was a White-Collar Crime case that involved a prominent figure and I knocked it out of the park. I filed my First-Degree Felony case with the Specialized Crime Division of the Dallas County District Attorney's Office and moved on to solve the next crime. While sitting at my desk one day, my direct line rang. The Deputy Chief Prosecutor of the Specialized Crime Division had called to tell me that the Chief Prosecutor, Dick Zadina, wanted to meet with me as soon as possible. So, I saddled up my unmarked Crown Victoria and headed to the DA's Office.

I remember walking into the Specialized Crime Division that day. I had filed other White-Collar Crime cases, so this wasn't my first rodeo, but this case was my magnum opus and I really hoped they had good news for me.

Charlotte, the unit secretary, checked me in and let Mr. Zadina know I was there. I sat nervously waiting. Dick Zadina, in case you aren't familiar, had a reputation in Dallas County as being a seriously tough prosecutor with a lot of 'case law' to his name. I had never had the pleasure of meeting him, and I wasn't sure what to think when he asked to meet with me. I automatically assumed I had done something wrong, and he wanted to yell at me for screwing up an otherwise great case.

I digress.

Charlotte: "Detective Sluder, Mr. Zadina will see you now."
Me: (Standing up) "Okay, thank you."

I walked to the door of his office, knocked out of respect as I walked in, and I think I gulped out loud when I saw him stand up from his desk. I don't often feel short at 6 feet 2 inches tall, nor intimidated by another man's stature. But Dick stands flatfooted at 6 feet 10 inches tall and his deep, bounding voice matches his stature.

He shook my hand, thanked me for coming, and asked me to sit down. As if I had been called to meet the principal or something, I sat down so fast I kind of bounced off the arm of the chair. Physical grace was lacking due to my nervousness.

Dick sat back in his chair for a minute and just stared at me. I could see my case sitting on his desk, prominently displayed in the four five-inch three-ring binders it took to contain my work papers.

Dick: "Is this your case?"

Me: "Yes, sir."

Dick: "Who helped you assemble this case?"

Me: "No one, sir. I did it on my own. I mean, I had collateral help of course with each search warrant I executed, but I prepared the case on my own."

Dick: (Flips open one of the binders and turns to one of the search warrants I authored.) "Did you write this search warrant?"

Me: "Yes sir, I wrote all seven of them. Is there something wrong with how I styled that one?"

Dick: "Who taught you how to style it this way?"

Me: "I did. I just applied two different parts of the Code of Criminal Procedure in a way that I thought was creative..."

Dick: (Cutting me off.) "So, no one told you to do this? You just figured it out on your own?"

Me: "Yes sir. Should I not have done that?"

Dick: (Sits back in his chair, again, staring at me.) "You're my number one draft pick!"

Me: (Turning around to see who was standing behind me and then looking back at Dick.) "Are you talking to me, sir?"

Dick: "I want you to come work for me. Is there any way I can steal you away from your department? I need this kind of talent in my division. What you did in your search warrant was simply brilliant and I've never seen that done before. You had the defense attorney so screwed up in our pre-trial hearing today, and the Judge was singing your praises, son. What do you say? Do you want to come down here and work in Specialized Crime?"

Me: (Before my brain could stop my mouth.) "Hell yeah!"

Just like that, the pendulum swung for me in a direction that I had always hoped would happen. I went from being Detective (Corporal) Sluder of the UT Southwestern Police Department, to Special Criminal Investigator III (Lieutenant) Sluder of the Dallas County District Attorney's Office Specialized Crime Division.

Within a few weeks of joining, I was asked to serve full time on the FBI's Healthcare and White-Collar Crime Task Force. Detectives from every police department in Dallas County, including Texas Rangers, were asking me to help them solve their cases. One very memorable day, the Securities Exchange Commission (SEC) dropped off 30+ boxes of records in our office and said they couldn't figure out whether a crime had been committed or not. Within 30 days I had unraveled one of the most complicated Mortgage Fraud scams in Dallas County history.

In short, I finally felt like I had made it. I finally felt like all my striving had paid off. I was 30 years old, and I had reached the summit of the very mountain I had manufactured. While tired from all my striving and wounded from the many storms of life, I lapped up the waters of prideful self-attainment from my bucket, but it never seemed to satisfy my thirst.

"Who cares what my family thought of me?"

"Who cares that I didn't feel loved?"

While tired from all my striving and wounded from the many storms of life, I lapped up the waters of prideful self-attainment from my bucket, but it never seemed to satisfy my thirst.

"Who cares that my marriage was crumbling around me?"

"Who cares that I still felt like that shy little boy who just wanted to be loved and respected?"

I'll tell you who. Me!

I cared far deeper than I wanted to admit. While the cool winds of flying high had helped mask the sting of the pain that lingered deep within, I was still hurting and making terrible coping decisions.

Surprise:
In the fall of 2007, Amber and I had a heart-to-heart. We both finally admitted to one another that we were not happy in our marriage. A great friendship, and even love for one another, does not make a marriage when neither party is truly committed to it. So, we agreed that divorce would be the best option for us both.

From the outside looking in, everyone told us what a great couple we were; that they wished they had a marriage like ours. Little did they know, we were both just great actors! We knew we had a lot of explaining to do to the people who were closest to us and decided to take one final road trip as *husband and wife* to Carlsbad, NM before we delivered the atom bomb of divorce.

Because we were great friends, we had a wonderful time in the caverns. To top it all off, we figured we should have sex one last time before we call it quits. I will spare you any further details.

A couple weeks later, Amber called me while I was driving home after a long day of crime fighting. She hadn't been feeling well and decided to go to the doctor.

Amber: "Hey, I went to the doctor, and he told me I have a sinus infection, (something else I cannot remember), and I am pregnant."

Me: "I am sorry, what was that third thing again?"

Amber: "I am pregnant."

Me: "I didn't think that was possible."

Amber: "Yeah, well, I didn't either."

I have had a lot of 'scary' moments in my life, but this one just about made me wreck my truck.

For the rest of the drive home, I talked to God. At first, I was pissed off at Him for allowing this to happen just as we decided to get divorced. I didn't want my child to grow up in the same circumstances I grew up in. All I could think was how I was about to relive my terrible childhood by becoming just like my parents.

As I processed all this the best way I knew how, I remembered something from scripture.

Psalm 139:13-16 The Message (MSG)

13-16 Oh yes, you shaped me first inside, then out;
you formed me in my mother's womb.
I thank you, High God—you're breathtaking!
Body and soul, I am marvelously made!
I worship in adoration—what a creation!
You know me inside and out,
you know every bone in my body;
You know exactly how I was made, bit by bit,
how I was sculpted from nothing into something.
Like an open book, you watched me grow from conception to birth;
all the stages of my life were spread out before you,
The days of my life all prepared
before I'd even lived one day.

In that moment, I had a realization. God is the creator of all life. So, if He chose to give me a child, then it couldn't be a bad thing at all. In fact, I wasn't reliving my childhood and I hadn't become like my parents. I had a choice to make, and ultimately, I decided to be the daddy I always wanted. I turned my attention back to Heaven and said:

"You gave me this child, God, and I dedicate it back to you. Do with this child as you see fit. This child belongs to you. I am sorry for being mad at you."

I didn't know much, but I knew I wanted this child to know the Lord in a way I had never truly known Him. I wanted this child to be loved, and I figured the first act of love I could do as a daddy-to-be was to willingly dedicate this child back to God.

As the weeks sailed by and my eldest daughter grew in the womb, I often wondered what life would be like when this baby came. Amber and I were not growing fonder. We were, instead, growing further apart. We revisited our conversation on divorce and jointly decided that once the baby was born, we would file.

Week 17-18:

If you have ever been pregnant, or gotten someone pregnant, you likely know this milestone marks the point at which you can typically learn the gender of your child. We went to visit Amber's OB/GYN for a sonogram. As Amber lay there, pregnant belly exposed, a less-than-excitable nurse worked the sonogram wand and stared intently at the black and white screen. Being the smart aleck I am, I did everything possible to make her smile or laugh, and I can safely tell you I failed at both. After about 30 minutes of poking Amber and pushing on her stomach, she asked her and I to get up and go walk around the building as she needed the baby to move to a new position. We did as we were asked and returned to the room. After another 10 minutes or so, the nurse stopped what she was doing and said:

"The head, arms, and legs are not growing properly. There are two heart defects, and you are having a girl. I am sorry, but we can't see your kind at this office, so I will send the doctor in to give you a referral to a specialist."

She stood up and abruptly walked out, shutting the door behind her. I literally sat straight down. Thankfully, there was a chair under me. We both sat in silence, trying to process what we had just heard.

When the doctor came in, he was so kind and gentle. He apologized profusely for what we were going through. He told us he would refer us to the best specialist in Fort Worth and that we would be in great hands.

Week 19-20:

We drove to the Fort Worth Medical District and checked in with our new doctor's staff. After a lot of paperwork and a small wait, we were greeted and asked to come back to an exam room. I remember it being dimly lit and designed for everyone in the room to be able to view what was happening on a monitor. We met our new doctor who ended up performing another sonogram. He measured the head circumference, chest circumference, arm length, leg length, and he showed us where our daughter was missing both her atrial and ventricular septum. In common terms, my daughter's heart was missing the walls that separated the top two and bottom two chambers of the heart. He said it was too early to know what condition we were dealing with, but we would come back each week for the same routine. As he left the room, a nurse said one more group wanted to meet with us. We walked to another room and met with what I now realize was some sort of social worker. Here is where it gets interesting.

We were told that when we came back for our next appointment, we needed to let them know our decision. Confused, I asked them what decision they meant. The lady said since our next appointment would be in the 20th week of the pregnancy and our child would likely not be viable, they would need to know at the beginning of the appointment whether we planned to terminate the pregnancy or not.

I am not sure if I was more in shock that I had to decide between life and abortion or that she said my child would likely not be viable.

My heart sank. All my life I had said I was Pro-Life; that there was no way I could ever abort a child. Now, I had a week to make the decision in real-time based on very little information. To say it was intense is an understatement.

Much of that week is still lost in a fog. But here is what I do remember:

When Amber and I got home from meeting the specialist, she went out on the back porch and sat there alone while I went to my office. My mind was filled with so much chaos I could hardly think straight. Then, as I contemplated the decision I needed to make, a very clear memory floated to the surface and drowned out all the noise.

In 1999, God had given me a poem called "Dear Mom". I pulled the poem up on my computer screen and I read these words a twenty-three-year-old version of me had written:

Dear Mom

I guess I will never know,
But what if I had been given the chance?
To run and play in summer fields of green…
To make angels in the winter snow…
To admire the colors of autumn's scene…
To smell the spring in winds that blow…

Do you ever wonder,
What I might have been?
A preacher to save the lost...
A writer to place words to pen...
A soldier to pay the ultimate cost...
Or maybe just a sinner,
To be forgiven of sin.

You can never know the love you missed!
I would have cried at night and played all day,
Noodle pasted pictures and hand molds of clay.
I would have made you proud with all I had done,
You would have been my Hero, and I, your son.

But for you I was just a choice,
And you did what you thought was right.
But I wish you could have heard my voice,
Before you aborted me last night.

If I could have only formed the words,
To somehow make you see...
But my quill will never write,
For this author will never be.

by Ricky D. Sluder

Copyright ©2003 **Ricky Dale Sluder**

I often wonder why God gave me a poem on abortion. I struggled with what to do with it. I eventually published it and then left it alone on my computer, thinking someday God would show me the purpose.

And friend, did He ever!

I cried as I contemplated those words and I knew I had to give this child, my daughter, her best chance. I knew God didn't make a mistake, so there was no way this pregnancy could be terminated. I got up and walked outside and talked to Amber and we both agreed, we were keeping our baby.

For the next 19 weeks, we had the precious opportunity to watch our baby grow in the womb in real time. Every week, we got a new sonogram and the more our daughter matured in the womb, the more we laughed at the funny things she was doing when the camera was on her. One time she was sucking her thumb, another she was literally holding her foot with her leg pointing straight up. And each time, the reality of her heart condition seemed to get heavier. I still close my eyes sometimes and see that tiny heart on the monitor with blood swooshing back and forth in blue and red colors. Without a heart wall (septum) to stop the blood, it would sweep across each chamber before disappearing with the next beat.

Week 36-37:
Our doctor told us he thought he finally had our daughter's diagnosis figured out. Ellis-van Creveld Syndrome (EVC). He explained that this was one of the rarest forms of dwarfism, which would explain the smaller head circumference, arm and leg lengths, and heart defects. You see, 1 in every 60,000 to 200,000 live births of children born with EVC presents with either an Atrial Septal Defect, Ventricular Septal Defect, or both.

While it was exciting to finally understand what was wrong with our daughter, the internet painted a very grim picture for us of this condition.

Now that we knew the condition, it was time to tell our families what we had learned. I invited my mom over to our house and explained that we were having a girl and that she had two heart defects. I went on to explain that her heart defects were part of another condition called EVC, which meant she would also be born with a rare form of dwarfism. My mom looked a little puzzled. Her eyebrows furrowed a bit and she said, "You know the only place I think I have ever seen a midget was at the circus."

I took about a breath-and-a-half and then fired back:

"If you ever refer to my daughter as a midget again, I will choke the f**king life out of you."

As if *she* were offended by *my* comment, she said:
"Huh? I didn't mean anything by it. You just don't see… people… like that all the time."

Once again, when I needed my mother to just be kind, offer support, and love me, she chose to be cruel instead.

Monday March 17, 2008:
Our doctor scheduled a cesarean section for delivery on Monday March 17, 2008, and at 7:33 AM, Kylie Taylor Sluder was born. She came into this world with six fingers on each hand, lungs full of air, and a head full of hair. Amber and I got to see her for a brief minute while they cleaned her up, and then doctors rushed her off to the Neonatal Intensive Care Unit (NICU).

They sewed Amber back up and took her to her room at one end of the hospital while Kylie was at the other end. I gathered up our stuff from the Labor and Delivery Department and I made my way to the waiting room to let our families know that Amber had been admitted and Kylie was in the NICU.

Whenever I entered the NICU, I had to scrub-in and wear a gown and other protective equipment to make sure I didn't bring anything in that would harm the precious but fragile children. Kylie was in a plexiglass tub and was breathing on her own. I marveled at the sight of my daughter and had the opportunity to reach inside and touch her. I, of course, took full advantage of it. She grabbed my finger with her little hand, smiled (probably from gas, but I choose to believe she knew her daddy was there) and, right then and there, I fell so deeply in love with that child it literally hurt!

It felt like I spent an hour with her, but I am sure it was far less. Before I left the unit, I was met by the Cardiologist who was taking care of her in the NICU.

Doctor: "Mr. Sluder, your daughter doesn't have two heart defects."

Me: (About to comment because he left this one hanging out there as though he were done talking.)

Doctor: "She has four heart defects."

Me: (Shocked.) "Okay, so what are the other two?"

Doctor: "She has a membrane occluding her Pulmonary Vein and her Mitral Valve is prolapsed."

Me: "Okay, so what is the prognosis with all of that?"

Doctor: "At three-weeks old, she will go into Congestive Heart Failure, and she will die. There is nothing we can do for her."

I couldn't believe what I had just heard! My eyes began to tear up. In an effort not to cry, I took a few pictures of Kylie so I could show Amber what she looked like. Then, I walked out of the NICU and into the waiting room.

I sat down by my dad and stepmom and explained to everyone what the doctor just told me. As you might expect, they all sat there in silence, likely not knowing what to say. I told them I had to go break the news to Amber and I would be back later.

My heart was beyond heavy, sitting somewhere between angry and numb. I was trying so hard to stay strong and keep it all together because I thought I had to. Not to mention, I didn't have a family that would help me process everything in a normal, healthy way.

When I broke the news to Amber, we sat and cried together. I apologized to her repeatedly. I didn't know what else to say.

I walked back down to the waiting room hoping to find some form of compassion from my family for my aching soul. But when I got there, they were gone. I sat in their now empty section of chairs and cried alone.

As I sat there, I remember thinking to myself, "F**k it, I'll do this alone, too."

But I wasn't alone!

No, my family wasn't there for me. At least, not beyond the obligatory hospital visit. But God was right there with me the whole time, and you know what? I missed it. I was so caught up in myself that I failed to realize His word never returns void.

Do you know what I mean when I say this?

In the Bible there are at least 18 different verses I can think of that tell us something profound we really need to get ahold of. Here is the central theme of these verses:

"I will never leave you, nor forsake you!"

Think about this, friend. God promises His children repeatedly throughout the Bible that He will never leave us. He is for us. He has a plan for us, and believe it or not, while we cannot always see Him or understand His plan, He and His plan are always present and in action.

In the midst of this storm, I starred directly at the wind and the waves, and failed to see Jesus standing on the water next to me. I bet if you are hurting right now, you probably feel totally alone, too. I promise you; you are not alone. Call upon the Lord and I guarantee you He will already be there next to you.

When I was done feeling sorry for myself, I got up and went back into the NICU to spend time with my daughter. Fortunately, I arrived just in time to get to feed her. I spent all day at the hospital, either feeding Kylie, checking on Amber, or visiting with doctors about one or both. Before I realized it, it was midnight.

> *In the midst of this storm, I starred directly at the wind and the waves, and failed to see Jesus standing on the water next to me.*

"The dogs!"

At home, we had two large dogs. They were very well behaved, but every creature has its limits when it cannot go to the bathroom for 20 hours. So, I ran to my vehicle and drove home to let them out. When I got there, I was mentally, physically, and emotionally exhausted. I walked out onto the back porch, lit a cigarette, and sat in my patio chair. As I smoked that cigarette, I kept thinking one immutable fact over and over in my mind.

"I cannot control my way out of this one!"

I took a drag off my cigarette, blew out the smoke, and raised my arms toward Heaven and crossed them in an X pattern saying:

"Kings-X Lord. You got me! I cannot control my way out of this mess I am in. So, here is where I am at. If you give me this child for a day, a week, or a year, I will praise you still. No matter what you decide, you are my God. Your will be done, not mine."

And for the first time in my life, I can say I truly meant every word I said. The weight of the stress somehow fell off me. I didn't feel better, but I felt lighter. I knew, no matter what, God would handle it all and I surrendered it all to Him.

I let the dogs back in and I went back to the hospital.

Tuesday March 18, 2008:
I don't remember much about this day, but I remember the Cardiologist doing a sonogram on Kylie's heart. I remember watching the monitor as the blood swooshed back and forth in her common chambers, just like it did for nineteen weeks when she was in utero.

I remember checking on Amber and feeding Kylie at every feeding, basically walking from one side of the hospital to the other all day long. Around midnight, I went back home to let the dogs out. I smoked my cigarette on the back porch and then went right back to the hospital.

Wednesday March 19, 2008:
If this were a shampoo bottle, it would say *Wash, Rinse, and Repeat,* because it seemed like I was living in the movie Groundhog's Day. With one remarkable exception.

Imagine I hit fast-forward on the video of this day, skipping through the sonograms, checks on Amber, and Kylie's feedings.

After the last feeding, I decided to go home early and let the dogs out. It may have been 6 or 7 PM, but for me it was super early. When I came back, I scrubbed-in and walked back to Kylie's plexiglass tub and it was empty.

Her cute nameplate the nurses made for her was gone. Her pacifier and blanket were gone. Everything was gone!

My heart sank to the bottom of my feet. All I could imagine was that she had died, and I wasn't there for her. I panicked! I began to look in every plexiglass tub and incubator searching for my daughter. Finally, a nurse came in and asked me if I needed help.

Me: (Tears welling up in my eyes) "Yes, I cannot find my daughter, Kylie. Do you know where she is?" (Fearing the worst)

Nurse: "Oh yeah, she is in the other room now. Go through that door and you will find her."

I almost tripped over myself getting there and when I walked into the room, I saw cribs and rocking chairs. A nurse was holding a baby swaddled in a blanket, about to feed it, when she said.

Nurse: "Would you like to feed her dad?"

Me: "Yeah, I would love to."

We switched positions, and I asked.

Me: "Why is she in here now?"

Nurse: "Did the doctor not tell you?

Me: "Tell me what?"

Nurse: "Well, I cannot tell you. The doctor has to tell you."

Puzzled, I sat down in the rocking chair and slowly rocked with Kylie while I fed her. It makes me want to cry just reliving this moment.

A short while later, I was intercepted by the Cardiologist who was very frazzled. He asked me to come with him to an office in the NICU. When I walked in, there were X-rays of Kylie's hips, legs, and other such things all over the pre-lit wall, allowing him to review patients' X-rays and MRIs and such.

While I scanned the wall, he was pacing like a lion at the zoo.

Cardiologist: "What I am about to tell you is physiologically impossible, and I am still trying to figure out how this happened."

Me: "Okay..."

Cardiologist: "Do you remember seeing the sonograms I performed and how the blood flowed freely because there wasn't a septum in between her ventricles or atria?"

Me: "Yes sir. I've seen it for nineteen weeks in utero, too."

Cardiologist: "Well, that's the thing. I re-did the sonogram this evening and there is a perfect septum separating her ventricles. And that membrane that was occluding her Pulmonary Vein... it's like it never existed. It's gone!"

Me: (Shocked and becoming elated.) "So, what does this mean?"

Cardiologist: "I don't know...I can't explain it. I guess my machine was glitching on the prior tests, because none of this makes any sense."

Me: "It's not your machine. I know what I saw. Like you said, there is no physiological explanation for this, so it has to be a miracle."

Cardiologist: "I don't believe in those."

Me: "Well, I do! So, what does this mean for Kylie's prognosis?"

Cardiologist: "You can take her home on Friday. I will have the staff prepare the room in the NICU for you to stay in tonight and tomorrow so you can get the hang of caring for her before you transition home."

Still frazzled, he left the room.

As for me, I was in total shock. God just healed my baby girl.

"I gotta tell Amber!"

I didn't run to the other side of the hospital, I sprinted to her room. When I got there, she informed me she was being discharged Thursday morning. Once I caught my breath, I explained the miraculous news to her; that God had healed our daughter. The timing of her discharge was perfect, making it possible for both of us to stay in the NICU and care for Kylie Thursday night, together.

What I didn't realize until after I got home and dressed Kylie in her first Easter dress, was that God healed her on the third day of her life and orchestrated everything in such a way that I got to take Kylie home on Friday March 21, 2008.

AKA – "Good Friday"

Tell me, friend. Do you believe in miracles?

Do you believe God healed my daughter on the third day of her life and then sent her home on Good Friday?

Or do you believe, like the doctor, that it was a glitching machine and a coincidence that all of this aligned with Good Friday and Easter?

At the very beginning of the book, do you remember me saying this at the end of the first chapter?

While you haven't heard my story yet, I'll confess up front that I am very stubborn. So, why would a stubborn control freak like me give up during this battle when I had refused to give up so many times before?

Have you ever heard the adage, "you can lead a horse to water, but you can't make him drink"?

For now, let's just say, Daddy put some salt in the oats, and I was thirsty for surrender.

As for me friend, I know God used this extreme circumstance as *salt in the oats* to make me thirsty for surrender. And I am so glad He did!

Survival Mode:
I wish I could tell you it was all sunshine and rainbows after God miraculously healed Kylie, but it wasn't anything close. More storm clouds came, and different winds blew, and the storms of life raged on for me and Amber.

Although Kylie received an amazing gift of healing that saved her life, two of the four heart defects were still left un-healed. She lacked a septum between her atria and her mitral valve was leaking like a sieve, as they say.

As such, Kylie was very susceptible to infection and her doctors told us daycare was not an option for her. Amber gave up her career and became a full-time stay-at-home mother. I began working 'off-duty' jobs on nights and weekends to make up for the lost salary. We still weren't in a great place marriage-wise, but I made her a promise I had planned to keep. I told her that, while I hadn't been a great husband up to this point, I would make sure she was taken care of financially. It was the least I could do!

At work, I had co-founded the Texas Mortgage Fraud Task Force, and I was at the top of my game. But something was missing. I wasn't fulfilled and I couldn't figure out if it was because of my home circumstances, the PTSD from my childhood, or dealing with people who hated me because of the badge I wore. I was under unbelievable stress, and I had a hard time seeing my forest for the trees.

How about you? Do you know what I am talking about?

Have you felt this way before?

What I didn't understand was how I could have exactly what I wanted in my career and still not be happy.

When I came home from fighting crime in a suit, I would change into my SWAT-style uniform. You see, I had a night and weekend job at a grocery store.

"A grocery store?", you might be asking.

Yep, a grocery store in a bad neighborhood!

Sadly, this grocery store had to pay police officers to work there to keep the employees and customers safe from the "bad guys" who would eventually show up to commit their crimes. I wish I could tell you my uniform and presence were enough to keep them away, but I would be lying.

I got into a lot of fights with people who just wanted to fight a cop. And for every person who chose to hit me with their fists, there were at least five more waiting to cut me with their words. I have been called everything but a "white boy from Red Oak". I honestly never in my wildest dreams thought I would experience racism to the degree that I have but hate and ignorance are real.

Why do you think that is?

Why do you think we find reasons to hate someone because of the color of their skin or the culture they represent?

I am not writing this book to debate racism and its root causes. But I will say that when we buy the lie of all lies, a wound is formed. When the wound is formed, a stronghold begins to grow that cripples our thinking.

Why is that true?

In short form, once wounded by the lie, you form a belief that leads to an action. The people who tormented me night after night with their insults were speaking from a place of woundedness. I don't think for one second that I was their real problem. I was just a convenient target for them to projectile vomit on. They, like me, were broken and hurt and in desperate need of *Hope*.

If you happen to be one of those people, I want you to know I forgive you. If I could, I would give you a big hug right now and offer to listen to your hurts. I sincerely hope this book finds its way to at least one of you.

Coming Full Circle:
While driving to work at 7:30 AM on July 13, 2009, I prayed a unique prayer. Something in me needed to come out and I chose this morning to discuss it with the Lord.

"Father, I have always said I would do anything you wanted me to do, as long as it meant I got to be a Detective. I've always said you made me to be an investigator, but I am not so sure that is true. I don't know what to do. I am very confused with my life. If you never meant this for me and you don't want me in law enforcement, make it so clear to me that I can't screw it up."

When I got to work, it was business as usual. I chatted with my fellow investigators before heading to my office to start working on a case that had a link to terrorism. While reading through the documents and trying to figure out if I had jurisdiction on this case or not, my phone rang. It was my Deputy Chief asking me to come and talk to the Chief.

In my world, this was a common occurrence, so I thought little of it.

Me: "Hey Chief, you wanted to see me."

Chief: "Yeah, come on in and sit down."

Me: "Sure, what's up?"

Chief: "I got a phone call this morning and I was told to tell you to resign."

Me: "What? Who told you to tell me to resign?"

Chief: "I was just told to tell you to resign."

Me: "Tony, I have never done anything wrong. I've always worn the white hat. I don't get it."

Chief: "Ricky, I was just told to tell you. If you don't resign, then you will be let go."

I sat there in disbelief. My law enforcement career had just come to an abrupt halt. I wrote and signed my resignation letter, packed up my office, and exited the building for the last time at 1:30 PM. As I sat in my truck, it hit me. God had answered my prayer from that morning, and He did so within five hours.

What on earth was He up to?

Over the next few days, I began feverishly applying for jobs in the private sector. After almost 30 days, my phone still wasn't ringing. I wasn't sure what I was going to do. Then, something interesting happened. At the time, I had no perspective on this, but I certainly do now, and I think God was testing me in a few different ways.

I received a phone call one day from the Deputy Director for the University of Texas System Police. He told me most of the commissioned police officers of the University of Texas at Dallas Police Department, including the Chief, had been indicted on various criminal charges and that he was taking over as the interim Chief of Police. As such, he needed a Detective to help him sort through things and I came highly recommended. He told me the salary, and it was about half of what I needed. But, since I didn't have any other prospects, I told him I would take it.

As I processed the call, all I could think about was how grateful I was that I was going to have an income and health insurance again. You know, those *tangibles of life* that usually take precedence in our thinking. As I thought about it, I realized an *intangible* that was truly ironic. Ten years earlier, I was embarrassed by the idea of being a "Campus Cop". But I had been humbled since then, and if God wanted me in that role now, I would serve that department to the best of my ability.

I apologized to God for getting a big head when I was at Dallas County. A shift had taken place within me, and I was now more interested in my title as "Kylie's daddy" than I was about being a big-shot Detective.

When I was asked to share my testimony at our church's Men's Group, I told everyone who was listening how I had let my identity become my title. Once it was taken away from me, I realized I still had an identity and a purpose that was far greater than my career. I just had no idea what that identity and purpose were.

I believe this act of humility was what God was trying to achieve in me. I was finally willing to let go of this idol in my life.

Let me ask you, friend. What idol(s) do you need to surrender?

Without titles, money, or family, who are you?

The Calm Before the Storm:
I spent a literal 30 days as a Detective for the UT Dallas Police Department before I left to investigate Healthcare Fraud for a Centers for Medicare and Medicaid Services Zone Program Integrity Contractor. God took me on an amazing journey, growing me in ways I didn't realize were even possible. Within three years, I was earning six figures working for IBM as a Global Fraud Subject Matter Expert.

Amber and I decided to live separately, and I took care of the financials so she could take care of our daughter full-time.

While I was soaring again in my career, I was spiraling in my private life. Although still married, I began dating again.

"Why on earth would I do that?", you might ask.

I was striving for acceptance. I was desperately wanting someone to love me, even if for just a little while. I was trying everything I could within my arsenal of striving to replace the identity idol I had given up. The problem was that my identity idol couldn't hold a candle to the power of the largest idol in my life.

Sexual idolatry.

I wish that were a type-o and I wish I didn't have to confess this to the world, but that is the truth.

It had been a god in my life for longer than I can remember. Everything I did was to satisfy this idol. No matter how far I went in my quest to satisfy this thirst, nothing seemed to work. I always ended up feeling less whole than before.

What is your most powerful idol?

How far do you go to satisfy it?

Does your thirst ever really get quenched, or do you keep going back for more in hopes it will eventually be quenched?

Remember the story of the woman at the well (Gushing Fountains of Endless Life)? What was true for her is true for you and me. No matter what you fill your bucket with, it will never satisfy your thirst. The only hope we have of satisfying this thirst is to accept Jesus Christ's offer to drink from his endless supply of living water!

The problem is we place our emphasis on the idol, the bucket, instead of the source of the living water. I am not sure what your bucket is, but I know you do.

So, tell me friend, how is that idol shaping your identity?

What are you going to do about it?

Are you willing to leave your bucket at the well in exchange for the living water?

The Unthinkable Happens:
In March of 2012, Kylie turned four years of age, and though I was a train wreck on the inside, I was totally smitten with my little girl. She was smart, curious, loving, and her health seemed to be getting better instead of worse. In December of 2012, we went to a cardiology appointment that included the usual battery of tests. This time, however, we were asked to meet with another doctor, a colleague of our cardiologist. He turned out to be a heart surgeon and he didn't have the best news for us. He said Kylie's mitral valve was leaking worse and he was scheduling her for heart surgery on Monday

morning. He was going to have to create a septum to place between her atria before repairing her prolapsed mitral valve. This news hit me like a ton of bricks. I hiccupped for 72 hours straight due to the stress.

All I could think about was, "What will I do if she doesn't survive this open-heart surgery?"

Amber and I didn't have a lot of time to prepare, but we put together a photo shoot with Kylie so we would have those pictures, just in case. I cannot begin to tell you how difficult it was to mentally prepare to lose my child for the second time. Of course, I was hoping for the best, but I had to prepare myself for the worst.

Monday morning came and Kylie was taken back for the surgery. Several hours later, we were told that everything had gone as planned and she was in recovery. From recovery, she was transferred to the Pediatric Intensive Care Unit (PICU) where we spent several days with her there. After removing all her tubes and wires, they told us we were being transferred to the Cardiac Rehabilitation floor where we would soon go home.

But Kylie went from alert and talking to just staring at things with a very delayed response. As it turned out, when the tubes and pacer wire were pulled out of her heart, a small tear was left behind. Her heart was leaking blood into her pericardial sac. Fortunately, we caught it before it killed her. But because she was on a blood thinner, the internal bleeding was not going to stop on its own. The medical team had to release the blood that was trapped around her heart and give her a full blood transfusion.

On December 23, 2012, Kylie was finally well enough to come home with me. Because of the heart tear and new blood, they couldn't reintroduce the same blood thinners, making her at risk for a stroke. But that didn't seem to be in the forecast. She was doing well, and I was excited to get to spend Christmas with her at home.

On December 30, 2012, when I woke Kylie up that morning, it seemed like any other morning with one exception. Kylie wouldn't speak. I thought maybe she was just being an obstinate four-year-old. She was moving and seemed fine, but she would just shake her head "no" every time I spoke to her.

It wasn't until she dropped a mirror in my bathroom, and it shattered on the floor that it hit me.

"She is having a stroke!"

I picked her up and carried her to the living room. I grabbed her milk cup and I asked her to take a drink. The milk streamed down her face and my heart sank. I put her in her car seat and raced to the Emergency Room. When we arrived, her left pupil had blown, her face was drooping on the right side, and she had no use of the right side of her body.

Once they brought her back from the brain scan, I met with a neurologist.

Neurologist: "Mr. Sluder, your daughter didn't just have a stroke. She had five."

Me: "Okay. So, what is the damage?"

Neurologist: "Well, the epicenter of the primary stroke hit right here. See all the white area? That brain tissue is now dead. In the middle of this part of the tissue is her speech center. It has been destroyed. I don't think she will ever speak again, but I am also not in charge of those outcomes. The other clots you see hit across the brain, and the extent of the damage from those are just now being noticed. I am not sure if she will recover from the paralysis. We will have to wait to see what happens."

Kylie was transferred back to the same PICU we had just left seven days earlier. I remember sitting in a chair watching her sleep at about 1:00 AM when this thought occurred to me, and I began to talk to God.

"I said a day, a week, or a year, didn't I? I should have asked for more time. If this is what you want for her, then I accept it. I want your will to be done, not mine. But you also tell us to tell you the desires of our hearts, and my desire is to have my daughter back better than she was before."

It was a short prayer but one I genuinely meant. I cringed at the idea that I would never hear her precious voice call me daddy ever again. I cannot begin to tell you how broken-hearted I was. I felt like the world had stopped turning and I didn't understand why any of this was happening.

Then, on the third day of our PICU journey, Kylie suddenly received all her fine and gross motor skills back. The paralysis was completely gone. She began to say words, and while it took three months in total, she eventually had the expressive language ability of a seven-year-old at the age of four.

God had miraculously healed her again!

I cannot explain why my daughter received three miraculous healings (one of these was not shared in this book, you will have to wait for the movie to come out), when so many other children are left debilitated or even die from such events.

Nor can I tell you why God chose to put me through so much adversity, a mere fraction of which I have shared with you in this book.

But I bet you can relate to these hardships in your own ways. While our stories are not the same, I bet you have been exposed to that fire of refinement at least once in your life.

Maybe you are in it right now.

Do you blame God for your present circumstances?

Are you angry with Him?

I want you to know it is okay if you say "yes" to both questions.

I know that is not the religious answer, but you won't ever get that from me.

Here is why I know God is okay with you being mad at Him:

Remember me telling you the story about how Peter went fishing and finally got honest with God? Well, it was in that honest moment that God saw Peter's true heart, and I believe He waits patiently to see ours, too.

As I wrap up this chapter, I want to leave you with this. Life is hard. Somedays it just plain sucks. But it's always worth living! Whether you know it or not, you are a child of the living God, and He wants you to offer Him some of your time. He wants you to be in relationship with Him. So, if you are still hanging on to the dross, clinging to that dang bucket of yours, trade it in for the *Truth* and discover who you truly are in Christ.

In the next chapter, I will walk you through how I discovered the *Truth* of who I am. Hopefully, my story will illuminate a path for you to do the same.

In case you are wondering whether I still struggle with wanting that bucket to cling to, even after I traded it in; yes, I do!

But buckets be damned, my friend, as that is not what defines you or me. Thanks to the salt in the oats that made me thirsty for surrender, I now know who I am.

Do you taste some salt in your oats?

Tell me friend, are you thirsty for surrender?

Discovering the Truth of Who I Am

But some people did accept him. They believed in him,
and he gave them the right to become children of God.

John 1:12 Easy-to-Read Version

Lord, who do you say I am?

As promised, I am going to tell you how I learned the truth about my
identity after decades of living in a false identity. I have been building
up to this moment and hopefully what I have shared from the Bible, and
from my life, has helped you see how adversity and striving for acceptance
can shape your identity. My prayer for you is that you come to know who
you truly are. That way, you can answer that important question, "*Who are
you?*", from a place of true confidence!

In 2013, God woke me up on an airplane. That's important to note because
I don't usually sleep on airplanes. It is part of my PTSD from childhood,
with additional layers from being a cop. I struggle with trust issues, and
because I typically don't trust people, I am usually not able to relax enough
to sleep in public. This particular day was an exception to my rule, you
might say. And if I am being honest with you, it pissed me off that He
woke me up.

God: "Wake up!"

Me: "Seriously, I just fell asleep?"

God: "Everything that was, will have nothing to do with that which is to come."

Me: "What? Why do you talk to me in riddles? I seriously have no idea what that means."

I will paraphrase the conversation from here. In short, He told me I would be with the company I had just joined in 2013 until I turned 42 years old. He also told me I would go on to write books, movies, and that I would teach and preach. To be honest with you, I seriously thought I was losing my mind. I knew what I heard was not from me, because it came from a second voice from within me that was identical to voice that told me to resign from Texas DPS.

For context, when this took place, I was 37 years old. I was roughly six months removed from divorcing wife number one after 11 years of marriage (seven years together and four years legally separated), and about two months away from marrying wife number two.

Up to this point, I hadn't really had a God conversation where He told me something that profound. Nothing amazing happened over the next few months, but I could not shake what I was told.

In October of 2013, I got married for the second time and, in case you were wondering, we did not have a wedding. She had already had her wedding, so I was told that the Justice of the Peace would have to suffice. We had a nice honeymoon in Antigua though, so I pretended that was enough for me.

Three months into my second marriage, I brought up our need for better communication. She decided that hitting me in the face would be the appropriate response. I'd love to tell you this was the first red flag of a bad relationship decision, but I would be lying to you. This was a relationship built on passion and nothing else. Well, at least for me, that is. I won't speak for her.

I came very close to divorcing her after she hit me, but she begged me to stay, and I eventually caved to her request. We received a flyer in the mail from a church hosting a marriage seminar and marriage re-dedication ceremony. She felt like this was a sign from God for us to reconcile, and at the time, I agreed.

I never recovered from the assault or the other betrayals that occurred early in our relationship and into our marriage. For the record, she didn't cheat on me. In fact, I technically cheated on her during our talks of divorce. I share this with you to let you know it was a two-way street of brokenness. She was not the only person at fault, and I am not a victim. Rather, I was complicit with her in burning our marriage to the ground.

We ended up attending the marriage classes, we participated in the marriage re-dedication ceremony, and we joined the church. While this didn't solve our problems, it did lead me to a men's group called Bold. Due to Bold, I became friends with other men from all walks of life. The difference between me and some of those men was that they had *Hope*. They were okay with being broken and many of them had dealt with their crap. As for me, I was still pretending I didn't have any crap to deal with.

The leader of Bold was a man named Scott. While I don't know if this is true, I suspect he took one look at me and saw right through the facade I had plastered all around me. In hindsight, he gave me some of the best advice anyone has ever given me.

Scott: "You need to sign up for Encounter Weekend."

Me: "I sure do, yeah… What is that exactly?"

Scott never told me what it was, just that I needed to go. I can tell you now that he was right!

I cannot give away the secrets to this ministry event, so I am going to have to gloss over a lot of details and focus on the point of how I learned my true identity.

I arrived at the host-house and, when I entered, was greeted by several men I knew from Bold. I felt way more at ease about this mysterious event given the familiar faces. Guys were gathered around talking to one another while they prepared food. It seemed like this was going to be a fun weekend after all. In addition to those I already knew, I also got to meet several new men, some that I still keep in touch with today.

One of the leaders told me to take my stuff upstairs and find a bed that was empty. Encouraged, I ran up the stairs to find my place so I could come back down and hang out with the guys. As I entered the last room on my quest for a bed, every bed had been taken except one.

Are you ready for this?

The last place available was a twin mattress on the floor in a closet full of Christmas decorations. I always wanted to love Christmas, but due to my childhood and adulthood experiences, I resented Christmas.

I said within myself, "Sleeping alone, with a Christmas tree! Seriously God? If this is a joke, I don't find it funny."

I sat my stuff down in the closet and tried to make sure the plaster of falseness hadn't fallen off my face as I raced back downstairs to socialize. After we all ate and visited with one another, we moved into the living room to truly kick off the 'Encounter' process. Because I don't want to say too much and give away the effectiveness of this ministry, I will cap this part off by saying that for the first time in my life, I confessed all my sins before God and man. Each of the men who went after me later shared that they appreciated my bravery in saying the things I said because it gave them the courage to share their sins, too.

Once we finished up as a group, we were dismissed to do as we pleased. I visited with some of the men and eventually made my way up to the closet where I would sleep. I went in, closed the door, and shook my head in disbelief. In addition to the Christmas tree, there were a ton of cheerful Christmas decorations that filled the rest of the room.

I knelt in a small crevice of unused space, placed my Bible on my knee, and began to speak to the Lord. I was inviting Him to speak to me; asking Him to share a verse of scripture with me. Out of nowhere, verses began to fill my mind one at a time. I thumbed through my Bible and read the verses. Each one of them was from a part of the Old Testament where God was raining down hell fire and brimstone on people that, truthfully, probably deserved it. But I gotta tell you, friend. It didn't inspire confidence in me.

In fact, it validated what I had always believed about God. "*He must really be pissed at me!*" Verse by verse, this trend continued. The more verses I read, the more discouraged I got. The more discouraged I got, the angrier at God I became. Finally, like a powder keg finding a flame, I lashed out at Him and let Him know exactly what I thought about His angry verses. In the middle of my diatribe against the Almighty, I said something profound.

"Look, I don't even care that I don't know who I am any more. The question I want answered is, who do *you* say I am?"

As the words fell off my lips, my Bible flew off my knee. With it, all my papers that were neatly placed in their *appropriate places* scattered all over that tiny closet. I immediately became so pissed off that I was ready to throw that Christmas Tree out of a window. Alas, I was in a closet... there were no windows for me to break!

Mumbling expletives, I crawled around on my hands and knees, collecting my folded papers. The last one to be retrieved was a postcard that was valuable to me. I had placed it in a particular place in my Bible, and I couldn't remember where I had it. Having reached my tipping point, I did something I shouldn't have done. I picked up my Bible, shoved that postcard between some random pages, and slammed my Bible on the floor.

Out of frustration and anger I said to God, "F**k you... I am going to bed!"

The next morning when I awoke, I apologized to God for speaking to Him that way and asked Him if we could start over. I told Him I just needed answers because I had been through so much. I couldn't remember ever being in a place where I didn't feel like I had an identity. I felt so pointless and lost, like I was falling apart and just needed Him to show up and tell me who I was to Him. And, because He didn't talk to me in that second voice in my head, I assumed He didn't answer me.

Has anything like this ever happened to you?

Do you have a second voice that shares insights with you?

It's okay if you do and it's okay if you don't. We all have different spiritual gifts and not everyone experiences the voice of God the same way.

Some people say, I hear Him.

Some people say, I feel Him.

Some people say, I just know I should do X or Y.

So, my real question is – How do you think God speaks to you?

If your immediate response is, "He doesn't speak to me, weirdo!", well, I get it. I used to say the same thing to *weirdos* like me. Truth is though, God does speak to us all in a variety of ways. We just have to be willing to be still and listen.

On with my story...

Several months went by and I experienced God in ways that if I shared the experiences in detail with you, you would likely discount me as insane. At the same time, while my relationship with God was beginning to blossom, my marriage and home life were crumbling down around me.

In September of 2015, my marriage came to a screeching halt. I am not going to go into any details as I don't believe it is relevant to what I am trying to share with you here in this chapter. While my personal life looked like Normandy in 1942, my relationship with God had never been in a better place. I began waking up each morning at 5 AM so I could create a quiet time with God. I set up my *War Room* in my closet with various verses of scripture and encouraging letters from friends on the wall. Over time, my place on the floor in the closet shifted to sitting at the bar in my kitchen and writing in a journal.

One day, I sat back in my chair, and instead of writing I spoke out loud.

Me: "You never answered my question!"

God: "Yes, I did!"

Me: "I haven't even told you which question I am referring to, so how do you know you answered it?"

God: "I answered you."

Me: "I asked you who I am to you, and you left me hanging. I just realized you never answered me."

God: "You know what your problem is?"

Me: "There are many, I am afraid. Which one are we speaking of?"

God: "You always begin at the end of things, and you never begin at the beginning of things."

Me: "You know what your problem is? You talk to me in riddles, and I don't understand what you are trying to tell me."

God: "Go open your Bible and you will figure it out."

I sat there for a moment and attempted to engage with Him, but He went silent. I finally got up and stormed into my office, got my Bible, and returned to my place at the bar.

When I opened my Bible, it opened directly to where I randomly placed that postcard several months earlier in that Christmas closet. I stared at the pages, trying to solve the riddle.

"You always begin at the end of things, and you never begin at the beginning of things."

I thought back to Encounter and remembered opening my Bible that next morning after my argument with God and seeing Psalm 5 and 6 on the right side of the book binding. I recalled thinking God must have been talking to me in those verses. As I stared at the pages, it was as if I was back in that closet. My eyes only went to the right side of the book, so I tracked backwards in an effort to explore His riddle. It was then that I landed on the top of the left side of the page and found my life verse.

Psalm 2:7 New King James Version

I will declare the decree:
The Lord has said to Me,
Today you are My Son.
Today I have begotten You.

As the words settled into my mind and my heart, I began to cry.

You see, friend, never in my life had I felt like I had belonged to anyone. I had always felt like I was an orphan. I had always felt like God was angry with me and that He was just waiting for the right time to throw me in the abyss.

But I was wrong!

God wasn't angry at me, and He didn't want me to be apart from Him. He had been so patient with me, and He had allowed me to talk so terribly to, and about, Him. He had taken all my punishment for things He was not guilty of. Figuratively and literally, on the cross of Calvary, He had paid *that* price for me.

It was in that moment I finally realized the answer to the question I have been asking you.

Who are you?

My answer:

I am a son of the living God. And according to Genesis 1:26 (you should go read it), I came to this conclusion:

I have never not been a son!

So, friend, I am going to leave you the same way I found you in this section of the book.

John 1:12
But some people did accept him. They believed in him, and he gave them the right to become children of God.

This will be the last time I am going to ask you this question.

Who are you?

Accepting Truth, Finding Hope!

Part 3: Security

Why Are You So Insecure?

A Dash Between Two Dates

I give them eternal life, and they will never perish, and no one will snatch them out of my hand.

John 10:28 English Standard Version

Where do you find refuge?

In the previous section of this book, I told you that I graduated from Texas State University with a degree in Criminal Justice. What I didn't tell you was that I minored in Sociology. I am fascinated with people's stories, and I had to take several courses in Sociology as part of my Criminal Justice major, so a minor just seemed to make sense. One of my upper-level courses in Sociology focused on how certain cultures deal with their dead. In the US we tend to bury our loved ones when they pass away. Then we leave a marker at the place of burial called a headstone that usually has the person's name, date of birth, a dash, and the date of death carved into the stone. In my Sociology course I was mentioning, we spent a few weeks focused on the epitaphs that are commonly added to headstones. We even had a class project where we had to go to different cemeteries and read the epitaphs. Let me tell you, there were some truly clever ones, some sad ones, and some that just didn't make any sense to me. I am guessing that's because it was an inside joke between the headstone scribe and the person who had passed on. I enjoyed reading the epitaphs because it opened a small window into the life of the person buried there. As I studied many headstones, for what most would call an odd university project, one small detail stood out time and time again. It appeared on nearly 100% of the headstones I studied. The only exception to this small detail was when the headstone was blank.

Do you know what that small detail was?

A dash between two dates.

It's sad to me to think that the vast majority of lives ever lived will be summed up on a headstone in a dash between two dates. We live a lot of life this side of eternity. But our triumphs and failures will likely end up buried alongside our bodies. Whether you intend to or not, you are creating a legacy that will either be remembered for good, for bad, or merely forgotten once you step into eternity.

While observing this small detail, I also picked up on the pun that is so apropos to each of our lives. A *dash*, or a mad rush, between the day we are born and the day we die. It seems we are all in a great big hurry to grow up, graduate from high school, go to college, get a job, meet our spouse, have children, become successful, retire, and grow old. At some point along this timeline, I believe each of us will look back and realize we rushed through too much of this life. I believe most of us will end up wishing we hadn't *dashed* between those two dates.

In this chapter of the book, I will open the dash and reveal the stories of a man who is very famous in most cultures of the world. Whether you are a Christian or not, you are likely familiar with various portions of the legacy he created. For those of you who grew up in church, or those of you who study the Bible, you likely have a decent portrait painted in your mind's eye of the life and times of this same man. My hope is that I will be able to share at least one story from his dash that you have never heard before. The stories I plan to share will reveal his struggles, failures, and triumphs with Acceptance, Identity, Security, and Purpose.

Friend, please allow me to introduce you to King David.

Are you familiar with King David? If you don't know who I am talking about, maybe the *king* part is throwing you off. Let me rephrase the question. Are you familiar with the story of David and Goliath? In case you are still stumped, it's the story about a shepherd boy who walks out onto the field of battle, pulls a smooth stone from his bag, loads his slingshot, and kills a giant named Goliath for bad-mouthing the God of Israel.

I wasn't brought up in the church, but I bet I heard that story a hundred times when I was a kid. And you know something else, the way that story was always told it made it sound like David was about ten years old when he killed Goliath. Well, if you don't know how the story ends, that shepherd boy grew up to be the King of Israel. That's the King David I am talking about. He is one of my all-time favorite characters from the Bible and I believe he has one of the most interesting dashes that needs exploring.

"Why is David one of your favorite characters from the Bible?", you might be wondering.

Well, I identify with David's triumphs and failures as a man, a father, and a husband. I also identify with his love for God. Up until recent, I thought that his epic highs and dramatic lows told in the biblical accounts were all that could be known about the man. But then the Lord led me to a portion of David's story that I believe is likely unknown to most Christians. It was completely unknown to me until I began studying to *re-write* this chapter.

Before we jump into the unknown portions of David's dash together, I am going to create a historical framework in the order in which the events happened in the Old Testament. You might not realize it, but the Bible is not always in chronological order. As you read below, you will likely notice that I switched the order of two of the stories. I did this, and added story headers, so this chapter flows and makes sense to you. To truly understand the message, I am to convey to you, the context about what is happening in Israel around the time David was born will be of the utmost importance. This context will help you see why David's life was not only important for Israel in 1000 BC, but for all of us even today. I believe once you grasp that notion, it will help you see that God was absolutely in control of all things then, just as He is now.

Every life is precious to God. Every life has a distinct purpose for being created at that exact moment in history. He wants each of us to find our security in Him. He wants to be our rock and our refuge. Friend you and I are far more than a dash between two dates!

Israel Demands a King
In the book of 1 Samuel, Chapter 8, the nation of Israel demanded that the Prophet Samuel appoint them a king. At that time, every nation had a king. So, what was the problem with Israel having a king, too?

Well, in Deuteronomy 17:14-20, long before the time we are speaking about, God addressed this very issue to the nation of Israel. God said, "Be sure to appoint over you the king the Lord your God chooses." God's choice for king, not man's choice. Unfortunately, Israel did not seek the Lord in this decision, nor did they remember the counsel God gave them on the subject. So, when the nation of Israel wanted to be just like all the other nations and be ruled by a worldly king, God felt rejected by His people, and rightfully so!

Just like you and me, Israel had a short memory when it came to God's provision and security. In response to His children's demands, God told Samuel to warn Israel that the king they would receive wouldn't be the king they truly wanted in the end. Samuel delivered the prophetic message of warning and Israel refused to listen. Just like Adam and Eve before them, Israel wanted to rule and reign without God getting in the way.

Saul Chosen as King of Israel
In 1 Samuel 10, God, working through the prophet Samuel, appointed Saul as Israel's king. From here, I will let you read the rest of that story in the biblical account, and I will deliver the message I am sent to deliver to you.

Israel had no king because God wanted to be their King. However, just like in the Garden of Eden, man chose to rule with Satan instead of ruling with God. When given the choice between the Tree of Life and the Tree of the Knowledge of Good and Evil, Israel, like Adam and Eve, did not choose God to be their King.

This story in 1 Samuel is a parallel to Genesis 3. Satan's jealousy and pride were the motivating factors that caused him to rebel against God and form a coup in an effort to prevent God from ruling with man. Satan wanted to be God, not serve God and man ruling together. So, it was Saul. He wanted to be God, not listen to the voice of God. Saul rejected God because he was more interested in self-worship. He even built a monument in his own honor (1 Samuel 15).

The Lord Rejects Saul
1 Samuel 15 English Standard Version

²² And Samuel said,
"Has the Lord as great delight in burnt offerings and sacrifices,
as in obeying the voice of the Lord?
Behold, to obey is better than sacrifice,
and to listen than the fat of rams.
²³ For rebellion is as the sin of divination,
and presumption is as iniquity and idolatry.
Because you have rejected the word of the Lord,
he has also rejected you from being king."

Before we move on, I want to explain some word meanings to you, as they have appeared in several verses from the Bible used in this book for reference. Above, the heading says *The Lord Rejects Saul*. So, doesn't that seem to imply that God walked out on Saul because Saul made some bad choices? No. If you drew that conclusion, you would be incorrect. Let me explain why through the word meanings that stand out in scripture.

When you read the Bible, you will encounter terms like:
Angel of the Lord
Word of the Lord
Voice of the Lord
The Word became flesh
Son of Man
Son of God

These terms, often used in the Old Testament, but also in the New Testament, mean Jesus Christ. These terms refer to God himself, usually in His physical form as Jesus, appearing to, but also speaking with various people at various times. In the case of Jacob, Jesus wrestled him to the ground. In the case of King Saul above, it says *"Because you have rejected the word of the Lord, he has also rejected you from being king."* Saul rejected a relationship with God, and God refused to allow Saul to remain His appointed leader over His children.

Imagine if you placed someone in a position of authority over someone you loved. Now imagine you discovered that this person had betrayed your wishes with respect to how she cared for your loved one. Would you allow this person to remain in this position of authority? Or would you find someone else who truly reflected your heart for your loved one?

Saul did not share God's heart for God's people. God knew it, and God loved His people too much to allow Saul to represent Him in a position of authority over His children. Therefore, God told Samuel that He had found a king for Himself in verse 16 below.

David, the Anointed King in Waiting
1 Samuel 16 English Standard Version

16 The Lord said to Samuel, "How long will you grieve over Saul, since I have rejected him from being king over Israel? Fill your horn with oil, and go. I will send you to Jesse the Bethlehemite, for I have provided for myself a king among his sons."

David was born into a very prominent family. His father Jesse was the Head of the Sanhedrin. The Sanhedrin was the Supreme Court of the Torah. So, in today's terms, Jesse was the equivalent of a Supreme Court Justice. Not only did his father have a prominent professional role, but he was also considered one of the most distinguished men of his day. David was the eighth son and a late-stage child born to his mother Nitzevet, who had also bore Jesse seven older sons. At the end of the chapter, we will cover more intimate details of David's early childhood.

When David was around 12 years of age, Samuel went to the town of Bethlehem to meet with Jesse, per the Lord's instruction. Upon arrival, Samuel invited the elders, Jesse, and his sons to join him in a sacrificial feast. He consecrated them but did not tell them he was there under God's instruction to anoint the future King of Israel. For God told Samuel, "I will show you what to do. You are to anoint for me the one I indicate."

The first moment that Samuel laid eyes on Jesse's eldest son, he thought to himself, "Surely the Lord's anointed stands here before the Lord." But God said to Samuel, "Do not consider his appearance or his height, for I have rejected him. The Lord does not look at the things people look at. People look at the outward appearance, but the Lord looks at the heart." Samuel then asked Jesse to have each son pass in front of him, and with each one Samuel said, "The Lord has not chosen this one." Confused, Samuel asked Jesse an interesting question. In most of the biblical translations of today, the text does not capture what Samuel *actually* said to Jesse, nor does the text do justice to Jesse's response. In <u>Nitzevet, Mother of David: The Bold Voice of Silence</u>[2], author Chana Weisberg provides us with this telling of the account:

At last Samuel said to Yishai (Jesse), "Are there no lads remaining?"
He answered, "A small one is left; he is taking care of the sheep."

1 Samuel 16 English Standard Version

[12] And he sent and brought him in. Now he was ruddy and had beautiful eyes and was handsome. And the Lord said, "Arise, anoint him, for this is he." [13] Then Samuel took the horn of oil and anointed him in the midst of his brothers. And the Spirit of the Lord rushed upon David from that day forward. And Samuel rose up and went to Ramah.

While scripture is clear that Samuel anointed David's head with oil, the most interesting part is what isn't said. Samuel made no mention to any of the guests in attendance about the significance of the anointing, nor its meaning. Not even to David. It is believed by most biblical scholars that only God and Samuel were aware that David had been anointed **nagid**, the *king in waiting*. And waiting he would do, as it would take roughly 18 years before David would assume the throne as Israel's King.

Did you notice that David was not originally invited to the sacrificial feast? He had to be sent for after Samuel asked, "*are there no lads remaining?*". And what about his father's response, "*a small one is left…*"? We will cover more on this topic in **A Mother's Secret** below.

David and Goliath

The people of Philistia, called the Philistines, were coastal neighbors to Judah. Today, Philistia is known as Palestine. Judah was one of the 12 tribes of Israel, located in the southern region of the Levant. The Levant is a historical geographic term that describes the area where the kingdoms of Israel, Ammon, Moab, Judah, Edom, and Aram; and the Phoenician and Philistine states were located in the Old Testament of the Bible. The Philistines came to the Levant from the Aegean and brought with them a religion, and a desire for expansion, that was very different from their Israeli neighbors. This clash of cultures was what ultimately led to them being enemies. Not much has changed in this regard in our modern day. They are still waring against one another. You've likely heard of the area where the Philistines settled, today that area is referred to as the Gaza strip.

In 1 Samuel 17, you will read that the Philistines had gathered their armies for battle and had established an encampment on a mountain within the borders of Judah. In response, Saul gathered his armies, and they established an encampment on an opposite mountain and drew up in line of battle against the Philistines. Below them both, was the Valley of Elah.

1 Samuel 17:4-11 English Standard Version

[4] And there came out from the camp of the Philistines a champion named Goliath of Gath, whose height was six[a] cubits[b] and a span.[5] He had a helmet of bronze on his head, and he was armed with a coat of mail, and the weight of the coat was five thousand shekels[c] of bronze. [6] And he had bronze armor on his legs, and a javelin of bronze slung between his shoulders.[7] The shaft of his spear was like a weaver's beam, and his spear's head weighed six hundred shekels of iron. And his shield-bearer went before him. [8] He stood and shouted to the ranks of Israel, "Why have you come out to draw up for battle? Am I not a Philistine, and are you not servants of Saul? Choose a man for yourselves, and let him come down to me.[9] If he is able to fight with me and kill me, then we will be your servants. But if I prevail against him and kill him, then you shall be our servants and serve us." [10] And the Philistine said, "I defy the ranks of Israel this day. Give me a man, that we may fight together." [11] When Saul and all Israel heard these words of the Philistine, they were dismayed and greatly afraid.

For 40 days Goliath repeated this same pattern, taunting any Israeli soldier who dare meet him on the battlefield. But none were brave enough to step forward. Instead, they all shrunk back and shivered in their armor.

David's three eldest brothers, Eliab, Abinadab, and Shammah had followed Saul to the battlefield. Each day, David would travel back and forth between Bethlehem and the Valley of Elah, as he had to feed his father's sheep and then return to the field of battle.

One fateful day, David overheard Goliath mouthing off across the valley floor. He also overheard the soldiers discussing something King Saul had shared with the men of his armies.

1 Samuel 17:25-28, 32-37, 43-58 English Standard Version

²⁵ And the men of Israel said, "Have you seen this man who has come up? Surely he has come up to defy Israel. And the king will enrich the man who kills him with great riches and will give him his daughter and make his father's house free in Israel."

David, not catching the whole story, asked them to tell him again what King Saul had promised. When Eliab, David's eldest brother, heard David inquiring of the men, he became angry with David.

²⁸ ... "Why have you come down? And with whom have you left those few sheep in the wilderness? I know your presumption and the evil of your heart, for you have come down to see the battle." ²⁹ And David said, "What have I done now? Was it not but a word?"

Saul happened to overhear David's inquiry, and his brother's rebuke, and Saul called David over to him.

³² And David said to Saul, "Let no man's heart fail because of him. Your servant will go and fight with this Philistine." ³³ And Saul said to David, "You are not able to go against this Philistine to fight with him, for you are but a youth, and he has been a man of war from his youth." ³⁴ But David said to Saul, "Your servant used to keep sheep for his father. And when there came a lion, or a bear, and took a lamb from the flock, ³⁵ I went after him

and struck him and delivered it out of his mouth. And if he arose against me, I caught him by his beard and struck him and killed him. ³⁶ Your servant has struck down both lions and bears, and this uncircumcised Philistine shall be like one of them, for he has defied the armies of the living God." ³⁷ And David said, "The Lord who delivered me from the paw of the lion and from the paw of the bear will deliver me from the hand of this Philistine." And Saul said to David, "Go, and the Lord be with you!"

Saul placed his armor onto David and sent him out to face down Goliath. Goliath was insulted that a ruddy and handsome youth, of about 20 years of age, had stepped onto the field of battle to face him.

⁴³ And the Philistine said to David, "Am I a dog, that you come to me with sticks?" And the Philistine cursed David by his gods.⁴⁴ The Philistine said to David, "Come to me, and I will give your flesh to the birds of the air and to the beasts of the field." ⁴⁵ Then David said to the Philistine, "You come to me with a sword and with a spear and with a javelin, but I come to you in the name of the Lord of hosts, the God of the armies of Israel, whom you have defied. ⁴⁶ This day the Lord will deliver you into my hand, and I will strike you down and cut off your head. And I will give the dead bodies of the host of the Philistines this day to the birds of the air and to the wild beasts of the earth, that all the earth may know that there is a God in Israel, ⁴⁷ and that all this assembly may know that the Lord saves not with sword and spear. For the battle is the Lord's, and he will give you into our hand."

⁴⁸ When the Philistine arose and came and drew near to meet David, David ran quickly toward the battle line to meet the Philistine. ⁴⁹ And David put his hand in his bag and took out a stone and slung it and struck the Philistine on his forehead. The stone sank into his forehead, and he fell on his face to the ground.

⁵⁰ So David prevailed over the Philistine with a sling and with a stone, and struck the Philistine and killed him. There was no sword in the hand of David. ⁵¹ Then David ran and stood over the Philistine and took his sword and drew it out of its sheath and killed him and cut off his head with it. When the Philistines saw that their champion was dead, they fled.⁵² And the men of Israel and Judah rose with a shout and pursued the Philistines as far as Gath[f] and the gates of Ekron, so that the wounded Philistines fell on

the way from Shaaraim as far as Gath and Ekron. [53] And the people of Israel came back from chasing the Philistines, and they plundered their camp. [54] And David took the head of the Philistine and brought it to Jerusalem, but he put his armor in his tent.

[55] As soon as Saul saw David go out against the Philistine, he said to Abner, the commander of the army, "Abner, whose son is this youth?" And Abner said, "As your soul lives, O king, I do not know." [56] And the king said, "Inquire whose son the boy is." [57] And as soon as David returned from the striking down of the Philistine, Abner took him, and brought him before Saul with the head of the Philistine in his hand. [58] And Saul said to him, "Whose son are you, young man?" And David answered, "I am the son of your servant Jesse the Bethlehemite."

David in Saul's Service

The Bible tells us in 1 Samuel 16:14 that, as David was anointed by Samuel, the Spirit of the Lord departed from Saul and rushed upon David from that day forward. Like the terms I mentioned to you earlier, this means that God, through the Holy Spirit, was with David, guiding David, encouraging David, just like He does for us upon our offer of acceptance to Him.

Saul, on the other hand, had rejected the voice of the Lord. He refused to answer the knock and allow God into his heart. Saul refused to offer his acceptance to God. As such, the dwelling place within Saul, that void we spoke about in the previous section of this book that is meant for God alone, ended up being filled with an evil spirit that tormented him. Saul's palace servants recommended that they find someone who could play soothing music, so Saul could find some peace during his times of spiritual torment. As only God could arrange, David was recommended to Saul.

1 Samuel 16:18-19, 21-23 English Standard Version

[18] One of the young men answered, "Behold, I have seen a son of Jesse the Bethlehemite, who is skillful in playing, a man of valor, a man of war, prudent in speech, and a man of good presence, and the Lord is with him." [19] Therefore Saul sent messengers to Jesse and said, "Send me David your son, who is with the sheep."

²¹ And David came to Saul and entered his service. And Saul loved him greatly, and he became his armor-bearer. ²² And Saul sent to Jesse, saying, "Let David remain in my service, for he has found favor in my sight." ²³ And whenever the harmful spirit from God was upon Saul, David took the lyre and played it with his hand. So Saul was refreshed and was well, and the harmful spirit departed from him.

Not only did David assist Saul in his time of need with soothing and encouraging music, but David became very close to Saul. The Bible tells us that Saul loved David greatly. Saul chose David to be his armor-bearer. In our present world, this doesn't mean very much. We envision a man who carries another man's weapons for him, like a personal valet. But this position was far greater and significant than it appears in our modern context. In the day of Saul and David, an armor-bearer was someone extremely close to a general or a king. The armor-bearer would be a tremendous fighter, a personal bodyguard, who would fight to the death and gladly give up his life for the person he served. This position of honor in Saul's military provided David a two-fold opportunity to grow as a man after God's own heart. First, David reflected the heart of God in his loyalty and service to Saul, especially when Saul was hurting and tormented by the evil spirit. Second, David gained favorable exposure to the people of Israel as he served in the military and that experience would turn him into a leader of men on and off the field of battle.

While we will not cover all of this story, Saul did keep his promise to his armies and offered David his daughter's hand in marriage for killing Goliath. So, you can add son-in-law to David's list of title's where Saul was concerned.

Saul's Jealousy of David

In 1 Samuel 18, we see Saul's insecurity become a larger part of his identity as he sinks deeper into a chasm of self-worship. After David killed Goliath and the armies of Saul were coming back home victorious over the Philistines, the Bible tells us that all the women came out from all the cities of Israel to meet King Saul singing and dancing.

1 Samuel 18:7, 9-16 English Standard Version

⁷ And the women sang to one another as they celebrated,
"Saul has struck down his thousands,
and David his ten thousands."

Saul could not stand it that David was receiving more praise than he. The servant that he once loved, the man he chose to be his armor-bearer, his son-in-law, had now become his enemy.

⁹ And Saul eyed David from that day on.
¹⁰ The next day a harmful spirit from God rushed upon Saul, and he raved within his house while David was playing the lyre, as he did day by day. Saul had his spear in his hand.¹¹ And Saul hurled the spear, for he thought, "I will pin David to the wall." But David evaded him twice.

¹² Saul was afraid of David because the Lord was with him but had departed from Saul. ¹³ So Saul removed him from his presence and made him a commander of a thousand. And he went out and came in before the people. ¹⁴ And David had success in all his undertakings, for the Lord was with him.¹⁵ And when Saul saw that he had great success, he stood in fearful awe of him. ¹⁶ But all Israel and Judah loved David, for he went out and came in before them.

Like Satan in his rebellion against God, Saul let his jealousy for David's favor from God, his success on the battlefield, and his popularity with the people of Israel rage out of control. As a result of his insecurity, Saul began plotting to kill David.

For the next decade, Saul would relentlessly pursue David in hopes he could kill him. David fled to several cities, feigned insanity in Philistine to avoid capture, lived in caves in the hills, and became a mercenary of sorts offering protection to shepherds and their flock from bandits and wild animals.

Commander of the Discontented and Distressed
In 1 Samuel 22, we find David hiding in the cave of Adullam. But if we leave 1 Samuel for a minute and turn to Psalms 142, we will find something interesting.

Psalm 142 English Standard Version

You Are My Refuge
A Maskil[a] of David, when he was in the cave. A Prayer.

142 With my voice I cry out to the Lord;
with my voice I plead for mercy to the Lord.
[2] I pour out my complaint before him;
I tell my trouble before him.
[3] When my spirit faints within me,
you know my way!
In the path where I walk
they have hidden a trap for me.
[4] Look to the right and see:
there is none who takes notice of me;
no refuge remains to me;
no one cares for my soul.
[5] I cry to you, O Lord;
I say, "You are my refuge,
my portion in the land of the living."
[6] Attend to my cry,
for I am brought very low!
Deliver me from my persecutors,
for they are too strong for me!
[7] Bring me out of prison,
that I may give thanks to your name!
The righteous will surround me,
for you will deal bountifully with me.

How do you think God answered David's pleas for help while he was in the cave of Adullam?

God sent him 400 men who were in equal, to worse, shape than David. He sent him the discontented, the distressed, and the indebted. He sent him men who thought they were too far gone to be loved by anyone, let alone God. David was an *Outlaw Disciple* given a band of men to lead who were in search of *Hope!*

David understood how these men felt, for he had been rejected by those who were supposed to love him. He had been falsely accused of crimes he did not commit. He had been forced to run, hide, and fight for his very life, at no fault of his own. The subtle difference between David and the majority of these men God gave him to lead, was that David had offered his acceptance to God long ago. God was his refuge and his rock! God was David's *Security*, even when he felt insecure.

Just as described in the Garden of Eden account, God designed a plan through His chosen vessel to defeat Satan and create a path of redemption for His children. In 1 Samuel, David eventually becomes the King of Israel, and the blood line through which Jesus Christ would come to save us all.

But, just as David was chosen by God to rule as King of Israel, he had to wait to live out his anointing after a long, difficult life of being pursued by Saul. The same goes for us. We live in difficulty being pursued by Satan trying to steal, kill, and destroy us. But one day, like David, we will get to live out our anointing as the chosen children of God and we will rule with God forever.

So, how does all of this apply to you and me on the topic of *Security*?

Saul is a picture of self-pursuit, self-reliance, and self-worship. He didn't deal with his dark side, nor did he reflect on his flaws or disobedience in a way that was genuine. Instead, he blamed David for all his troubles; much the same as Adam blamed God for creating Eve.

In contrast, David is a picture of God-pursuit, God-reliance, and God-worship. He admitted his sins and he reflected on his flaws and disobedience in a genuine way. He took responsibility for his actions, and he blamed only himself. David cried out to God for mercy and grace!

However, David was far from perfect. Let me prove to you that far-from-perfect does not mean unlovable-by-God. While David's loyal friend Uriah was out fighting a war for David, David was spying on his wife from his roof top while she was bathing. He liked what he saw, and he sent for her. They had sex and she got pregnant. So, when Uriah returned home briefly from battle David tried to cover up the pregnancy by attempting to get Uriah drunk and have him have sex with his wife so Uriah would think he was the child's father. When that plan failed, David sent Uriah to the front lines of the war so he would be killed in battle. On the heels of this adulterous and murderous event, David's son Amnon raped his half-sister, Tamar. In 2 Samuel you will read that David was furious with Amnon, but he took no real action. As a result, David's other son Absalom took matters into his own hands and killed Amnon. Absalom would later seek to usurp David's throne, resulting in his own demise.

Friend, God is not interested in your perfection. He knows full well you are going to blow it more often than you will ever get it right. He is interested in your heart. The heart of the man is what separates the Saul's from the David's of this world. Despite all his faults and failures, David was a man after God's own heart!

A Mother's Secret
At the beginning of this chapter, I said that *I identify with David's triumphs and failures as a man, a father, and a husband. I also identify with his love for God.* I waited to expound on this until now, because I believe that much of David's struggles were a direct result of wounds that occurred before he was born. These wounds continued through conception, his birth, his childhood, and into adulthood.

"How is that possible?", you may be wondering.

Throughout the many chapters of this book, we have talked about how we are wounded by the lies we are told. These lies, once received, and believed, lead us to form improper belief systems. Usually, these lies are a frontal attack on our identity, which leads us to actions, like the soothing salves of addiction we have also spoken about. Once we are on the rat wheel of insanity, consumed with ourselves, whatever security we had erodes completely. Then it's just a matter of time before we begin to question why God would ever love us, or worse yet, we begin to question if there is a God, at all.

While David loved God very much, evidenced in the 73 psalms he wrote, he had been greatly wounded by several important people in his life over many decades. When you really examine his psalms, his woundedness will begin to jump off the page. Just like you and me, at times David responded to life from his *woundedness* instead of living from his place of *Truth*.

Several years before David was born, his father Jesse had begun to question the legitimacy of his ancestry. Jesse's grandfather was a man named Boaz. Boaz had married a Moabite woman named Ruth, who had converted to Judaism. On their wedding night, they conceived a son, Jesse's father Oved, and Boaz died the next night. Although Jesse was wise in the ways of the Torah, he got in his own head and began to wonder if his grandfather's decision to marry Ruth was lawful. So, Jesse separated from Nitzevet. He rationalized that if Boaz's marriage to Ruth was unlawful, then he could not stay lawfully married to Nitzevet, a veritable Israelite woman. Although they already had seven sons together, Jesse didn't want to cause her any disgrace. By discontinuing all marital relations with his wife, he somehow was sparing her from his, *possibly*, tainted ancestry.

As you might imagine, this broke Nitzevet's heart. For context, it is important to note that each of their seven sons was aware of their marital separation. After some years went by, Jesse began to long to have a child whose ancestry would not be questionable. So, he formed a plan to marry his Canaanite maidservant. The maidservant was very aware of Nitzevet's anguish, and out of loyalty to her, she told her of Jesse's plan to take her as his wife. Nitzevet dressed in the maidservant's place for the wedding, and she conceived David that very night. Jesse never found out that the two ladies had switched places.

Approximately three months later, Nitzevet began to show. Her seven sons were enraged and wished to kill their *perceived adulteress* mother and the *perceived bastard* child she carried. Nitzevet, not wanting to embarrass Jesse with the truth of what occurred, kept her secret to herself. In <u>Nitzevet, Mother of David: The Bold Voice of Silence</u>, author Chana Weisberg provides us with this telling of the account:

Yishai (Jesse) ordered his sons not to touch her. "Do not kill her! Instead, let the child that will be born be treated as a lowly and despised servant. In this way everyone will realize that his status is questionable and, as an illegitimate child, he will not marry an Israelite."

David was treated horribly by his father and seven brothers. His mother was his only true source of companionship and encouragement. At a young age, Jesse sent David to the fields to shepherd the sheep. Jesse's hope was that this *illegitimate child* would be killed by a wild animal or by the elements.

Instead, what Jesse meant for evil, God intended for good. David formed a relationship with God while he faced unimaginable circumstances protecting his father's sheep. God became the father that Jesse never was to David. While David's wounds show up from time to time in the stories of his failures, those failures are not the legacy of his dash between two dates. Rather, the Bible tells us that David's legacy was as a man after God's own heart. An imperfect man who chose God as his refuge!

The Conclusion

Regardless of the poor choices you have made or will make in the future, and regardless of how terrible your life circumstances have been, God's promises to be faithful to you will always be kept. All you need to do is call out to Him as the Lord of your life.

Tell me friend, where do you find refuge?

Hidden in the Valley of Hopelessness

I give them eternal life, and they will never perish, and
no one will snatch them out of my hand.

John 10:28 English Standard Version

Why are you so insecure?

When I began this chapter in 2020, Coronavirus (COVID-19) had
swept the globe. Nations literally shut down, creating shelter-in-
place orders for their entire population. Grocery stores were overrun with
anxious people trying to stockpile supplies. Companies were shuttering
and millions of people lost their jobs due to their status as 'non-essential'.
In the United States, before the virus 'struck', our economy was booming,
and unemployment was at an all-time low. By the summer of 2020, unemployment surged higher than that of the Great Depression. People were
struggling to find hope in the midst of persistent isolation and the daily
uncertainty of when life would return to 'normal'. As a result, the suicide
rate soared higher than it had in 30 years.

With viral pandemics, unstable markets, civil unrest, political corruption,
and the mere difficulties that each new day brings, it is truly a sad and scary
time to be alive!

Do you believe that is true?

One might suggest this sentiment is merely a matter of perspective. When
circumstances are working out in our favor, like when the economy was

booming, we all felt secure and prosperous. But when the pandemic hit and our economy came to a screeching halt, that feeling of security began to feel like quicksand beneath our feet. Regardless of the source of circumstances that surround us, there are many *reasons* and *seasons* in life when we feel 'non-essential'. And when we adopt this label of 'non-essential' into our identity, we exit off our *Path of Purpose* and travel into the *Valley of Hopelessness*.

So, why is it that we adopt this label into our identity?

We place our trust in, and pin our hopes on, all the wrong people, places, and things. When these nouns let us down, we buy the lies that are sold to us and form inaccurate belief systems that lead us down a dead-end road in the *Valley of Hopelessness* – the *Road of Insecurity*.

Do you remember those WWJD wrist bands people wore back in the 1990s? For those of you scratching your head at the acronym, it means '*What Would Jesus Do?*'.

> *We place our trust in, and pin our hopes on, all the wrong people, places, and things. When these nouns let us down, we buy the lies that are sold to us and form inaccurate belief systems that lead us down a dead-end road in the Valley of Hopelessness – the Road of Insecurity.*

During your travels on the *Road of Insecurity*, what do you think Jesus would do if He were you in response to the circumstances that led you there?

What do you think He wants you to do in response to your circumstances?

Are you of the opinion that Jesus *is* the reason you have been stuck on the *Road of Insecurity* in the *Valley of Hopelessness*?

He is God, right?

He is in control of all things, right?

He is the almighty, omnipresent, and omniscient King of kings, right?

So, doesn't that mean He is the *reason* for your *season* of pain and discomfort?

Do you think He allowed this pandemic to sweep the globe and destroy lives as a form of punishment?

What about other natural disasters that destroy entire populations – is God using them to punish the wicked?

What about your circumstances, do you think God used them to punish you?

How can any of us truly know the answer to this question, and better yet, why will so many Christians disagree on the answer?

Don't we all serve the same God? Don't we all read from the same Bible?

So, why do we disagree so often on the character and nature of God?

The better question to ask, what *is* the character and nature of God?

To answer this one, I have to take you all the way back to the beginning.

Welcome to the Book of Genesis!

While the story about the Garden of Eden in Genesis isn't the easiest to follow, I want to submit for your consideration that it has little to do with a snake, trees, and pieces of fruit. Rather, it has everything to do with Acceptance, Identity, Security and Purpose. The wonderful metaphors used in the Garden of Eden account need to be unpacked to truly understand what happened way back then. It is the only way for you to truly understand the rest of the Bible. More important than understanding the Bible, when you get your heart, soul, and mind wrapped around what really happened in the Garden of Eden, you'll see the true character and nature of God!

Are you ready to have your mind blown?

Grab a drink, get comfortable, and turn off any distractions around you, because friend you don't want to miss anything in this chapter.

I want to take you back to something I shared with you in Judge, Jury and Executioner to help create a primer for the observations and questions that will guide you on your deep dive. Here is what I previously wrote for your consideration:

Let's examine the next thing Satan did when he couldn't get Jesus to strive for his acceptance. (Continuing in Luke 4:5-8)

⁵ And the devil took him up and showed him all the kingdoms of the world in a moment of time, ⁶ and said to him, "To you I will give all this authority and their glory, for it has been delivered to me, and I give it to whom I will. ⁷ If you, then, will worship me, it will all be yours."

Oh, this is so good Your Honor. Did you see what he did?

Satan said, "offer me your acceptance as the god of this world, and I will make sure you get all the glory."

Once again, Satan wanted Jesus to seek acceptance from him, and if Jesus would just bow down and worship him, He could receive all manner of authority and glory.

Why do you think Satan does this?

What does it mean when Satan says "…for it has been delivered to me…"?

Here is what I have learned about Satan in the biblical accounts I have read. Satan is a counterfeiter. He lacks originality and copies what the Father has put into order, but with his own twisted version. He knows that acceptance is for us to give to God, not receive from others; even he was responsible for offering God acceptance. But his pride got in the way, and it is my opinion and understanding that he thought he would be ruling with God, not Adam and Eve. When Satan realized that Adam and Eve, lower life forms than he as a Cherubim, were chosen to rule with God, he rebelled against this plan and refused to serve God and man as they ruled together. As such, in the Garden of Eden, Satan convinced Adam and Eve to choose to rule this present world with him, instead of with God. I believe that the fruit they ate was the lie he told them that they could be like God, and they could rule this present world without a need for God to be in it. It's my belief that in Satan's mind, if he couldn't rule with God, then God would't get to rule with man as intended. Therefore, I believe, he tells Jesus that all the kingdoms of this world were delivered to him. Adam and Eve delivered this authority to him when they chose the fruit of the Tree of the Knowledge of Good and Evil (Satan) over the fruit from the Tree of Life (Jesus). So, Satan tried to get Jesus to accept him as God, the same way he convinced Adam and Eve – through deceitful promises of power and glory.

With the stage set for how I believe the story should be told for the reason for the fall, apply this notion as you read through the scriptures below.

Genesis 2:1-25 English Standard Version

The Seventh Day, God Rests
2 Thus the heavens and the earth were finished, and all the host of them. [2] And on the seventh day God finished his work that he had done, and he rested on the seventh day from all his work that he had done. [3] So God blessed the seventh day and made it holy, because on it God rested from all his work that he had done in creation.

The Creation of Man and Woman
[4] These are the generations of the heavens and the earth when they were created,
in the day that the Lord God made the earth and the heavens.
[5] When no bush of the field[a] was yet in the land[b] and no small plant of the field had yet sprung up—for the Lord God had not caused it to rain on the land, and there was no man to work the ground, [6] and a mist[c] was going up from the land and was watering the whole face of the ground— [7] then the Lord God formed the man of dust from the ground and breathed into his nostrils the breath of life, and the man became a living creature. [8] And the Lord God planted a garden in Eden, in the east, and there he put the man whom he had formed. [9] And out of the ground the Lord God made to spring up every tree that is pleasant to the sight and good for food. The tree of life was in the midst of the garden, and the tree of the knowledge of good and evil.
[10] A river flowed out of Eden to water the garden, and there it divided and became four rivers. [11] The name of the first is the Pishon. It is the one that flowed around the whole land of Havilah, where there is gold. [12] And the

gold of that land is good; bdellium and onyx stone are there. ¹³ The name of the second river is the Gihon. It is the one that flowed around the whole land of Cush. ¹⁴ And the name of the third river is the Tigris, which flows east of Assyria. And the fourth river is the Euphrates.

¹⁵ The Lord God took the man and put him in the garden of Eden to work it and keep it. ¹⁶ And the Lord God commanded the man, saying, "You may surely eat of every tree of the garden, ¹⁷ but of the tree of the knowledge of good and evil you shall not eat, for in the day that you eat[d] of it you shall surely die."

¹⁸ Then the Lord God said, "It is not good that the man should be alone; I will make him a helper fit for[e] him." ¹⁹ Now out of the ground the Lord God had formed[f] every beast of the field and every bird of the heavens and brought them to the man to see what he would call them. And whatever the man called every living creature, that was its name. ²⁰ The man gave names to all livestock and to the birds of the heavens and to every beast of the field. But for Adam[g] there was not found a helper fit for him. ²¹ So the Lord God caused a deep sleep to fall upon the man, and while he slept took one of his ribs and closed up its place with flesh. ²² And the rib that the Lord God had taken from the man he made[h] into a woman and brought her to the man. ²³ Then the man said,

"This at last is bone of my bones
 and flesh of my flesh;
she shall be called Woman,
 because she was taken out of Man."[i]

²⁴ Therefore a man shall leave his father and his mother and hold fast to his wife, and they shall become one flesh. ²⁵ And the man and his wife were both naked and were not ashamed.

Genesis 3:1-24 English Standard Version (ESV)
The Fall
3 Now the serpent was more crafty than any other beast of the field that the Lord God had made.
He said to the woman, "Did God actually say, 'You[a] shall not eat of any tree in the garden'?" ² And the woman said to the serpent, "We may eat of the fruit of the trees in the garden, ³ but God said, 'You shall not eat of the fruit of the tree that is in the midst of the garden, neither shall you touch it, lest you die.'" ⁴ But the serpent said to the woman, "You will not surely die. ⁵ For God knows that when you eat of it your eyes will be opened, and

you will be like God, knowing good and evil." ⁶ So when the woman saw that the tree was good for food, and that it was a delight to the eyes, and that the tree was to be desired to make one wise,[b] she took of its fruit and ate, and she also gave some to her husband who was with her, and he ate. ⁷ Then the eyes of both were opened, and they knew that they were naked. And they sewed fig leaves together and made themselves loincloths.

⁸ And they heard the sound of the Lord God walking in the garden in the cool[c] of the day, and the man and his wife hid themselves from the presence of the Lord God among the trees of the garden. ⁹ But the Lord God called to the man and said to him, "Where are you?"[d] ¹⁰ And he said, "I heard the sound of you in the garden, and I was afraid, because I was naked, and I hid myself." ¹¹ He said, "Who told you that you were naked? Have you eaten of the tree of which I commanded you not to eat?" ¹² The man said, "The woman whom you gave to be with me, she gave me fruit of the tree, and I ate." ¹³ Then the Lord God said to the woman, "What is this that you have done?" The woman said, "The serpent deceived me, and I ate."

¹⁴ The Lord God said to the serpent,

"Because you have done this,
cursed are you above all livestock
and above all beasts of the field;
on your belly you shall go,
and dust you shall eat
all the days of your life.
¹⁵ I will put enmity between you and the woman,
and between your offspring[e] and her offspring;
he shall bruise your head,
and you shall bruise his heel."
¹⁶ To the woman he said,
"I will surely multiply your pain in childbearing;
in pain you shall bring forth children.
Your desire shall be contrary to[f] your husband,
but he shall rule over you."
¹⁷ And to Adam he said,
"Because you have listened to the voice of your wife
and have eaten of the tree
of which I commanded you,
'You shall not eat of it,'
cursed is the ground because of you;

in pain you shall eat of it all the days of your life;
¹⁸ thorns and thistles it shall bring forth for you;
and you shall eat the plants of the field.
¹⁹ By the sweat of your face
you shall eat bread,
till you return to the ground,
for out of it you were taken;
for you are dust,
and to dust you shall return."
²⁰ The man called his wife's name Eve, because she was the mother of all living.[g][21] And the Lord God made for Adam and for his wife garments of skins and clothed them.
²² Then the Lord God said, "Behold, the man has become like one of us in knowing good and evil. Now, lest he reach out his hand and take also of the tree of life and eat, and live forever—" ²³ therefore the Lord God sent him out from the garden of Eden to work the ground from which he was taken. ²⁴ He drove out the man, and at the east of the garden of Eden he placed the cherubim and a flaming sword that turned every way to guard the way to the tree of life.

I don't pretend to fully understand all of this at the level of detail that I want to. But, as I have spent months reading the first three chapters of Genesis repeatedly, and as I have sought the Lord on the meaning of all of this, I have received several *downloads* I hope will help you to unpack this story in a new way so you can begin to see the true character and nature of God.

My intention here is not to give you *all* the unpacked answers, because I do not know them all. I am not the source, God is! But I will pose several observations and questions that I hope will lead you on a *Security Quest* to dive deep on your own with the living God.

Before I share my observations with you, I want to ask you a couple of questions about Genesis Chapter 3.

Why do you think Adam and Eve hid from God in the middle of the Garden of Eden?

Why do you think they focused on their nakedness in this moment?

As for me, I think they felt guilty about their plan to betray God with the *deal they made with the Devil*. A deal that caused them to take off their identity in God when they offered their acceptance to Satan. Remember when Peter took off his identity in John Chapter 21? Remember when the Pharisees paraded the woman caught in the act of adultery before the living God, and how I suggested it was these men, and not this woman, who were standing naked before the Lord in John Chapter 8?

I think this is why they felt insecure. I think this is why they hid in hopelessness and began to blame everyone but themselves for the choice *they made*. The choice to be the gods of their own lives and to rule with Satan instead of with the living God.

One final question on this train of thought.

Since we are discussing the character and nature of God in this chapter, did you notice what God did *for them* after they made their choice to betray Him and rule this present world with Satan?

He prepared them for their journey!

"How?", you may ask.

God explained to them what life would be like without His security. Many see this as Him *cursing them*. I now see it as God explaining to them what they had chosen over Him. In addition, God created clothing for them out of animal skin. Prior to this, no animal had been sacrificed for the sake of man being clothed. Our selfishness is the reason paradise was lost. We chose a lie, that tasted good and looked terrific, over *Truth*!

During the betrayal, God made it clear He refused to give up on us. As such, He did something amazing. He placed enmity (hostility or animosity) between us and Satan and enacted a plan of salvation so we would always have a way to change our minds about this decision to rule with Satan.

He could have forced us to stay with Him, but He didn't. He also could have let us die in sin as a result of our rejection of Him, but He didn't.

So, why didn't He do either of these things? Why did He instead choose to offer us a way out of our sin through salvation?

Simply put because love is a choice, and He chose to love us even though we didn't choose to love Him.

Let that sink in for a moment. He loves you, even if you never choose to love Him back! The character and nature of God is to teach and to love!

> *He loves you, even if you never choose to love Him back! The character and nature of God is to teach and to love!*

Want me to prove it to you?

Let's listen as Jesus personally describes His character for us, shall we?

Matthew 11:29 New Living Translation

²⁹ Take my yoke upon you. Let me teach you, because I am humble and gentle at heart, and you will find rest for your souls.

Please think about that as I continue to share with you what happened in the Garden of Eden.

Many people, myself included for decades, missed the part about salvation in this story. Let me explain it to you in case you missed it, too.

During His conversation with Adam and Eve in Genesis 3, God made it known that He would prepare a way for us to rule with Him again one day if we would humble ourselves and offer acceptance to Him. He would pay the price for us. God would sacrifice it all just to be in relationship with us. Just like in the Prodigal Son story, the father willingly gave his son the inheritance he demanded from him and then refused to give up on the idea that his son would one day come back home!

> *God would sacrifice it all just to be in relationship with us.*

"Where do you see that in the Garden of Eden story?", you might be asking me.

Genesis 3:15 English Standard Version (ESV)

¹⁵ I will put enmity between you and the woman, and between your off-spring[ε] and her offspring; he shall bruise your head, and you shall bruise his heel."

Jesus' *head* was *bruised* for you when He died for your sins. And one day His *heel* will be *bruised* when He defeats Satan and takes His rightful place as King. Then those of us who accepted Christ, we will rule with Him for eternity.

While you consider all of this, I want to share some additional observations I have made in my study on this subject.

Observations:

Acceptance

Adam and Eve chose not to seek out and offer their acceptance to Jesus and eat from His fruit of *Truth*. Jesus was available to them in the Garden of Eden, and He is referred to as the *Tree of Life*. Instead, they chose to seek acceptance for themselves and chose to rule with Satan and eat from his fruit of *Lies*. Satan was available to them in the Garden of Eden, and he is referred to as the *Tree of the Knowledge of Good and Evil*.

They wanted to receive acceptance (glory) for themselves. Adam and Eve bought the lie of all lies and wanted to be gods instead of ruling with God.

Friend, from which of these trees are you seeking fruit to eat?

Identity

Adam and Eve were names that came after the fall. So, does that mean that they, like Peter, surrendered their true identities when they bought the lie from Satan?

I wonder if it is possible that Satan called man Adam and man accepted that identity as his own. I also wonder if that is why God referred to man as Adam *after* the choice to betray God was made.

Isn't that exactly what God did when Peter took off his identity and Jesus referred to him as Simon, son of John?

Or is it possible that God called His creation Adam because He formed him from the Adamah – the dust of the earth?

Scripture doesn't tell us exactly how Adam received his name, but it is clear that Adam named Eve after the fall. God never gave her that name.

Despite the name you have been given from birth, who are you?

In what, or in whom, is your identity defined?

Security
Adam and Eve were given a life of perfection in paradise with God as their *Security*. But they wanted to be the gods of this world instead of being in relationship and ruling with the living God.

They wanted to be their own security instead of living in the security of the Father.

Are you hidden in the *Valley of Hopelessness* as a result of trying to be your own security?

Tell me friend, why are you so insecure?

Purpose
Adam and Eve were created to rule and reign with God, but they chose to rule and reign with Satan instead.

I believe this is why God placed enmity between them (us) and Satan – He wanted His children back, and He made a way for us to come back home to Him.

While we haven't yet arrived at this part of the book, I want to ask you this question now.

What is your purpose for being alive?

Why did God create you when He did?

I hope you will give real consideration to these observations and questions I have presented to you. If you need to take a moment and reflect on each of them, do so now. When you are done reflecting, we will continue to discuss the concept of security together from Genesis 3. I will wait here with you until you are ready.

I am not saying I have read all the Bible or even understand all that I have read. But here is what stands out to me from my study. The beginning (Genesis) mirrors the end (Revelation); the choices Adam and Eve made are the same choices we all make. But *Truth* (Jesus) gives us a way of escape from our bad choices. When Jesus left His throne and came to this world for the sole purpose of dying so that we wouldn't have to, grace covered us. There is no sin debt left to pay. Yours has been paid by Jesus. All you have to do is respond to the knock on your heart's door by accepting Him. You don't have to clean up your life or stop sinning before you accept Him. All you have to do is eat of the fruit from the Tree of Life, which simply stated means to accept *Truth* and you will find *Hope*!

Let's quickly examine Genesis 3:22 in light of what I have just shared with you about the character and nature of God.

²² Then the Lord God said, "Behold, the man has become like one of us in knowing good and evil. Now, lest he reach out his hand and take also of the tree of life and eat, and live forever—"

I submit for your consideration that if Adam and Eve had been allowed to stay in the Garden of Eden, they could have *saved themselves* by then choosing (secondarily and through the sin of self-preservation) to eat the fruit of *Truth* through a relationship with Jesus after having first chosen a relationship with Satan.

Is it possible that God would not allow Adam and Eve to save themselves and that is why God prevented re-entry to the Garden of Eden after they chose to leave and rule earth with Satan?

The Bible says that God drove them out of the Garden of Eden. When you read the text without understanding the character and nature of God, it sounds like He angrily forced them out of the Garden of Eden and slammed the gate closed so they could never come back. But that doesn't align with God's character and nature, now does it?

Is it possible that God would not allow Adam and Eve to save themselves and that is why God prevented re-entry to the Garden of Eden after they chose to leave and rule earth with Satan?

So, here is a new word picture I want you to consider. While cars were not yet created, I see our loving Father offering to *drive them out* of the Garden of Eden because He loves them, and He wants to see them off on their journey that they chose to take without Him.

I believe if Adam and Eve had changed their minds in that moment, it would have been to save themselves out of desperation and the sin of self-preservation, not out of genuine love for God.

Imagine if someone ended a relationship with you, and as you drove them to where they wanted to go, you explained to them what they had just given up. Then, they tried to *have their cake and eat it, too,* by manipulating their way back in so they didn't lose something they only sought out of selfish ambition instead of genuine love.

Question for you, my friend:

Would you protect your heart in that moment, like God did the Garden of Eden, or would you just let this person manipulate you?

I believe this is what God meant when He said, "…lest he reach out his hand and take also of the tree of life and eat, and live forever—"

Earlier in this chapter, and in Part 1: Acceptance, I explained what I think happened when Satan rebelled against God. But what were the motivating factors that would lead him to want to spite God so badly?

I think Satan was jealous of Adam because he was made in the image of God, meaning Adam looked the way God looks. The same is true for all of us, and we were all made to rule with God over the heavens and the earth, the spiritual beings, and the living creatures. However, we were made *lower* than the spiritual beings, which means we don't have the same abilities they possess. But it also means we have a path for redemption with God, while spiritual beings do not. That is right, we can be saved by God from our poor choices, and they cannot!

Friend, read that paragraph again. Really allow that to soak into your heart and mind before we continue.

Contrary to man, Satan is a Cherubim, also known as a Cherub. In paintings, these *angelic beings* are pudgy, childlike creatures with wings and harps. But this is not how the Bible describes them at all. Believe it or not, a Cherubim is more akin to a beast, than a chubby baby!

That is right. Lucifer, whom we call Satan, is not an angel. He is a Cherubim.

Ezekiel 28:13-14 English Standard Version (ESV)

Here is some context for this chapter which is often misunderstood: Ezekiel 28:1-12 addresses the Prince of Tyre (the earthly king), while verses 13-19 address the King of Tyre – Lucifer, or Satan. Satan is the king of this world, the authority of which he received from Adam in Eve during the fall of man. Ezekiel tells us the backstory of Satan through God's message of lament for the King of Tyre.

[13] You were in Eden, the garden of God;
every precious stone was your covering,
sardius, topaz, and diamond,
beryl, onyx, and jasper,
sapphire,[b] emerald, and carbuncle;
and crafted in gold were your settings

and your engravings.[c]
On the day that you were created
they were prepared.
[14] You were an anointed guardian cherub.
I placed you;[d] you were on the holy mountain of God;
in the midst of the stones of fire you walked.

Okay, so what is the distinction between an angel and a Cherubim?

Let me show you what the Bible says about the Cherubim.

Ezekiel 10 New Living Translation (NLT)

The Lord's Glory Leaves the Temple
10 In my vision I saw what appeared to be a throne of blue lapis lazuli above the crystal surface over the heads of the cherubim. [2] Then the Lord spoke to the man in linen clothing and said, "Go between the whirling wheels beneath the cherubim, and take a handful of burning coals and scatter them over the city." He did this as I watched.
[3] The cherubim were standing at the south end of the Temple when the man went in, and the cloud of glory filled the inner courtyard. [4] Then the glory of the Lord rose up from above the cherubim and went over to the entrance of the Temple. The Temple was filled with this cloud of glory, and the courtyard glowed brightly with the glory of the Lord. [5] The moving wings of the cherubim sounded like the voice of God Almighty[a] and could be heard even in the outer courtyard.
[6] The Lord said to the man in linen clothing, "Go between the cherubim and take some burning coals from between the wheels." So the man went in and stood beside one of the wheels. [7] Then one of the cherubim reached out his hand and took some live coals from the fire burning among them. He put the coals into the hands of the man in linen clothing, and the man took them and went out. [8] (All the cherubim had what looked like human hands under their wings.)
[9] I looked, and each of the four cherubim had a wheel beside him, and the wheels sparkled like beryl. [10] All four wheels looked alike and were made the same; each wheel had a second wheel turning crosswise within it. [11] The cherubim could move in any of the four directions they faced, without turning as they moved. They went straight in the direction they

faced, never turning aside. [12] Both the cherubim and the wheels were covered with eyes. The cherubim had eyes all over their bodies, including their hands, their backs, and their wings. [13] I heard someone refer to the wheels as "the whirling wheels." [14] Each of the four cherubim had four faces: the first was the face of an ox,[b] the second was a human face, the third was the face of a lion, and the fourth was the face of an eagle.

[15] Then the cherubim rose upward. These were the same living beings I had seen beside the Kebar River. [16] When the cherubim moved, the wheels moved with them. When they lifted their wings to fly, the wheels stayed beside them. [17] When the cherubim stopped, the wheels stopped. When they flew upward, the wheels rose up, for the spirit of the living beings was in the wheels.

[18] Then the glory of the Lord moved out from the entrance of the Temple and hovered above the cherubim. [19] And as I watched, the cherubim flew with their wheels to the east gate of the Lord's Temple. And the glory of the God of Israel hovered above them.

[20] These were the same living beings I had seen beneath the God of Israel when I was by the Kebar River. I knew they were cherubim, [21] for each had four faces and four wings and what looked like human hands under their wings. [22] And their faces were just like the faces of the beings I had seen at the Kebar, and they traveled straight ahead, just as the others had.

So, since Satan is a Cherubim, he looks nothing like God. I believe when Adam was created in the image of God with the intention of ruling with God, but created lower than all the spiritual creatures, it pissed Satan off to no end!

It is my contention that Satan thought *he* was supposed to rule with God, and when he learned that he would, instead, be forced to serve Adam and God ruling together, he rebelled, taking 1/3 of the angels with him.

"Why would 1/3 of the angles follow Satan?", you may ask.

I can only believe it was because *they* didn't want to serve Adam ruling with God, either. They wanted the place of Adam. They desired to be equal to God.

While this is my belief based on my study, I cannot say my interpretation is 100% accurate. You're welcome to disagree with me, and we can still be friends.

But here is what I do know with absolute certainty.

God is consistent. He does what He says He will do. He is who He says He will be. Adam and Eve, on the other hand, (like all of us) are inconsistent (at best). We allow the wind and waves of life to toss us about. In the Garden of Eden, Adam and Eve had all the security they would ever need. They had God. They walked with God. They talked with God. They had access to *Hope* because they had direct access to *Truth*. So, what made them decide to choose to live in the *Valley of Hopelessness* over the Garden of Eden? The easy answer that I surmise from scripture is that they bought the lie from the enemy – they bought the lie of all lies!

I believe New Testament scripture validates this notion.

Romans 5:12-21 English Standard Version (ESV)

Death in Adam, Life in Christ

[12] Therefore, just as sin came into the world through one man, and death through sin, and so death spread to all men[a] because all sinned— [13] for sin indeed was in the world before the law was given, but sin is not counted where there is no law.[14] Yet death reigned from Adam to Moses, even over those whose sinning was not like the transgression of Adam, who was a type of the one who was to come.
[15] But the free gift is not like the trespass. For if many died through one man's trespass, much more have the grace of God and the free gift by the grace of that one man Jesus Christ abounded for many. [16] And the free gift is not like the result of that one man's sin. For the judgment following one trespass brought condemnation, but the free gift following many trespasses brought justification.[17] For if, because of one man's trespass, death reigned through that one man, much more will those who receive the abundance of grace and the free gift of righteousness reign in life through the one man Jesus Christ.

[18] Therefore, as one trespass[b] led to condemnation for all men, so one act of righteousness[c] leads to justification and life for all men. [19] For as by the one man's disobedience the many were made sinners, so by the one man's obedience the many will be made righteous. [20] Now the law came in to increase the trespass, but where sin increased, grace abounded all the more, [21] so that, as sin reigned in death, grace also might reign through righteousness leading to eternal life through Jesus Christ our Lord.

Romans 15:13 English Standard Version (ESV)

[13] May the God of hope fill you with all joy and peace in believing, so that by the power of the Holy Spirit you may abound in hope.

Based on what I have presented, what would you say is the true character and nature of God?

Is He a mean and cruel creator who kicked Adam and Eve out of the Garden of Eden because they simply made one mistake due to the lies of a talking snake?

Or is God a loving Daddy who allows His children to betray Him, yet offering them a way to come back home when they are ready?

Here is what I believe, my friend.

When you place your *Security* in Jesus Christ by accepting Him as the *Truth*, then, and only then, will you find *Hope*!

Are you tired of being on the dead-end *Road of Insecurity*?

> **When you place your Security in Jesus Christ by accepting Him as the Truth, then, and only then, will you find Hope!**

Do you realize you don't have to stay hidden in the *Valley of Hopelessness*?

If God is freely offering you, His security; tell me friend, why are you so insecure?

Finding Hope in Hopeless Conditions

> I give them eternal life, and they will never perish, and
> no one will snatch them out of my hand.
>
> John 10:28 English Standard Version

What are you so afraid of?

During my Quest in February of 2015, God took me to a hilltop and called me Philemon. Prior to calling me Philemon, He also called me Barnabas, but I misunderstood Him and thought He called me Barabbas. Barabbas was a notorious murderer and insurrectionist from Matthew 27:16. Barnabas, on the other hand, is known as the son of encouragement. In Acts Chapter 9, Barnabas took up for Saul of Tarsus, later named Paul, when the disciples weren't sure if they should trust him. This offer of encouragement from Barnabas came soon after Paul's road to Damascus experience, where God knocked him off his *ass* onto his *ass*. Scripture doesn't actually say Paul was riding on a donkey the way it is depicted in "Jesus movies", and many paintings suggest he was on horseback. But that is neither here nor there. The point is, God got his attention, and we all need that experience with God. You can read this story in its entirety in Acts Chapter 9, and we will cover parts of it together in Part 4: Purpose.

Are you familiar with the small book in the New Testament called Philemon?

Consisting of one chapter and 25 verses, it is a small but powerful book. Ironically, it is similar to our main character in this chapter of the book you are reading, Gideon. We will explore a portion of Gideon's story together as we address how we are to find hope in the midst of a hopeless condition.

"So, why did God call you Philemon?", you may be asking me.

Well, I think He did because I have had a lot of people intentionally hurt me and leave me, *and* it's up to me to let them go, forgive them, and move on!

How about you? Have you had this experience, too?

I bet you can recall many incidents in your life where this has been true. I know I can.

So, who is Philemon and why would God choose this name for me?

Well, Philemon was a wealthy man from Colossae, and he owned a slave named Onesimus. Onesimus ran away from Philemon, and while it is not explicitly stated, it is presumed that Onesimus stole from Philemon, too.

While on the run, Onesimus met Paul in Rome. Paul taught the gospel message to Onesimus, who accepted Jesus Christ as his Lord and Savior. While the text doesn't give us full details of the account, I imagine somewhere in this timeline Paul asked Onesimus to tell him his story. Probably with his head hung low, Onesimus told Paul how he betrayed his master by running away to Rome in search of a new life.

To Paul's amazement, and only as God can do, he knew Onesimus' master. In fact, Paul had led Philemon to salvation in Jesus Christ. So, Paul penned the letter that we call Philemon in the Bible, explaining to Philemon that Onesimus had been with him, that he accepted Jesus Christ as his Lord and Savior, and that he was now much more than a runaway slave. Paul called Onesimus a son of the living God, and to Philemon, a brother in Jesus Christ.

Paul explained in the letter that while Onesimus had not been much use to Philemon, he had been of great use to Paul. But Paul didn't want to keep Onesimus in service to him without Philemon's consent. So, he sent Onesimus back to Philemon, in hopes that he would forgive him, consider him a brother instead of a runaway slave, and let him return to service with Paul preaching the good news about Jesus Christ.

Take a minute and really ponder this story for yourself.

Who is your Onesimus?

If this person willingly came back to you and genuinely sought your forgiveness, would you offer this person freedom from your scorn, or would you bind this person in your resentment causing you both to be slaves?

If this person willingly came back to you and genuinely sought your forgiveness, would you offer this person freedom from your scorn, or would you bind this person in your resentment causing you both to be slaves?

Remember, I didn't say you would have to be 'buddies' with this person ever again, nor did Paul ask this of Philemon. In fact, God doesn't require that of you, either.

The request is to forgive.

So, friend, if you were Philemon, would you forgive Onesimus and let him go?

Wait. Before you answer I want you to hear something else, and I hope you really listen to me!

I think the parallel here is this:

If Philemon acted like King Saul, blaming Onesimus for his troubles the way King Saul blamed David, he wouldn't be able to reflect on his own flaws or find *Hope* for himself in Jesus Christ. But, if he let Onesimus go, he would be able to find freedom from those wounds of betrayal. By offering forgiveness to Onesimus, he would be able to unlock the slavery-chains of betrayal and find freedom in the *Hope* and *Security* he had in the very forgiveness offered to him by Jesus Christ.

Now, with that as the context for the question, what will you do with your Onesimus?

I pray you take time to really consider this question before you read on. It might just mean the difference between being a slave in the *Valley of Hopelessness* or finding freedom to pursue your *Path of Purpose.*

Speaking of finding hope in a hopeless condition, let's talk about the main character of this chapter - Gideon. In Judges 6, the angel of the Lord appeared to a man named Gideon while he was hiding from the Midianites at the bottom of a winepress.

Do you remember who *the angel of the Lord* refers to in scripture?

Jesus Christ!

Beyond the fact that God, Himself, appeared to Gideon at the bottom of a winepress, a truly amazing part of this story is what God said when He appeared.

"Mighty hero, the Lord is with you!" (Judges 6:12)

So, why do you think God would leave His throne to come to earth to hang out with Gideon? And why would He choose to immediately refer to Gideon as a mighty hero when he was hiding at the bottom of a winepress in cowardice?

God gets a bad rap for how He treats His creation. But God is not the bully we sometimes claim Him to be. Because Gideon was terrified of the Midianites killing him, he hid in his hopelessness at the bottom of a winepress so he could thresh his wheat in peace. God, in His amazing grace and mercy, chose to join Gideon in his hardest time and, instead of telling him how much of a coward he was or how he could not possibly be the right man for the job, God offered him a word of encouragement. That is how He works. He loves us unconditionally and completely, enough to leave His throne and come sit with us at the bottom of a winepress. He loves you enough to meet you right where you are!

Let me ask you a serious question. What are you so afraid of that has you hiding at the bottom of your winepress?

As you consider this question in light of *Security*, I want to segue into the lesson God wants you to hear about how He handled our friend Gideon. He wants you to hear this message so you know that this is what you should expect from Him, too.

Lesson #1: God Will Show Up!

When you call out to God for help, like Israel did when they wanted a Judge, God will show up. When you feel overrun by the Midianites of your life and you feel like you have to hide away at the bottom of a winepress, God will show up. When you need a word of encouragement to help you see you can make it through this day, God will show up.

Lesson #2: God is Patient and Kind!

When you doubt that God has spoken to you or called you to do something and you ask Him for a sign, He is willing to be patient with you and provide you a sign to help your faith. When you feel afraid that God won't show up or be there like He has already proven to you He will, hear Him say, "I will stay here until you return." When you become overwhelmed by fear and feel like you are doomed, hear Him say, "It is alright… Do not be afraid."

Lesson #3: God is a Way Maker!

Friend, when God gives you a task, He will provide you a way to make it happen. Even when you think you need 30,000 troops to accomplish the task and God makes you reduce the numbers to 300, like He did with Gideon, it is because He wants you to rely on Him and nothing else to accomplish that task. He wants you to seek Him, and Him alone, for your *Security*. You can count on Him to provide the way, and you don't have to strive to make it happen!

Here is the point of this chapter.

You can trust God!

He is a faithful source of security that will never leave you nor forsake you. And even when you doubt Him, curse Him, or abandon Him, He will deal with you patiently and lovingly, offering you grace and mercy as you walk out your relationship with Him.

I know how hard it is to overcome doubt when you are sitting on the floor of your winepress starving and hopeless. I have been there. And guess what? God showed up for me just like He did for Gideon.

Look here at Gideon's doubt.

Judges 6:13-14 NLT

[13] "Sir," Gideon replied, "if the LORD is with us, why has all this happened to us? And where are all the miracles our ancestors told us about? Didn't they say, 'The LORD brought us up out of Egypt'? But now the LORD has abandoned us and handed us over to the Midianites." [14] Then the LORD turned to him and said, "Go with the strength you have, and rescue Israel from the Midianites. I am sending you!"

When Gideon expresses fear about the mission he's been given, the Lord says, "Go with the strength you have, and rescue Israel… I am sending you!" Similarly, in the New Testament, when Jesus prepares His own disciples for their fearsome mission, He addresses their fears by promising that He is the one sending them (John 20:21-23).

Do you know what that means for you?

You can find *Hope* in your hopeless condition. Gideon had little strength, but God called him mighty, and He prepared the way for Gideon to overcome his fear and his enemy.

When we give into fear, we lose hope! When we can't see a way out of our circumstances, and doubt about God's willingness to help us creeps in, we become filled with distrust. When we lose hope and begin to distrust, we blame God instead of worshiping Him.

If you are going to give in to something, give in to God's amazing grace and mercy.

Give in and allow God to be your security!

Tell me friend, what are you so afraid of?

Learning to Sleep
Through the Storm

**I give them eternal life, and they will never perish, and
no one will snatch them out of my hand.**

John 10:28

Have you ever prayed for weakness instead of strength?

It has been one year and three months since I began writing "Falling
Apart or Falling Into Place?". Let me tell you friend, what a difference
a year makes!

In case you don't recall the details of that chapter, let me remind you. I had
just finished writing Part 1: Acceptance, and I was about to begin writing
Part 2: Identity. I had planned to begin the first chapter of that section by
re-asking that oh-so poignant question of you, my reader, "*Who are you?*".
When out of the clear blue sky I had a dramatic, life-changing *situation*, and
I had to answer this question for myself in your presence.

I was in a relationship with a woman who agreed to marry me, but she
wasn't the chosen woman that God had promised me. I had an executive
role for a company I never felt connected to but stayed at because they paid
me well. Last, but certainly not least, I had just purchased my dream car,
a 2019 Corvette Z06, and I loved going to car shows and car meets. This
became my one and only hobby and social outlet.

You know what, friend? At this time of my life, I truly thought things were good. The strange part is, I thought it was good even though I wasn't fulfilled in the relationship or the job. I was settling for far less than I was worth in both areas of my life because I was striving to be my own *Security*; I thought *good* was *good enough*.

I mean, why should I expect anything better than what I had in the present?

Do you ever feel that way about your relationships, career, or circumstances?

Once again, I was striving. Once again, I was trying to be the god of my own life. I was my *Security*, but I couldn't see it for myself at the time. The forest of my pretended contentment was too dense to notice the trees of idolatry standing tall all around me. Today, I thank God almighty He sent that hurricane of a storm that swept it all away in May of 2019.

As you read, in the midst of that storm, I truly thought my life was falling apart. But it wasn't. In fact, God was doing me one of the greatest favors of my life. In a minute, I will

> *The forest of my pretended contentment was too dense to notice the trees of idolatry standing tall all around me.*

share the struggles of that time with you and reveal how God brought restoration when I least expected Him to show up.

For the moment, I want to transition the conversation to a Bible story I woke up thinking about. I feel like it needs to be added to this chapter and we both need to truly soak in its meaning.

Matthew 8:23-27 English Standard Version (ESV)

Jesus Calms a Storm

[23] And when he got into the boat, his disciples followed him. [24] And behold, there arose a great storm on the sea, so that the boat was being swamped by the waves; but he was asleep. [25] And they went and woke him, saying, "Save us, Lord; we are perishing." [26] And he said to them, "Why are you afraid, O you of little faith?" Then he rose and rebuked the winds and the sea, and

there was a great calm. [27] And the men marveled, saying, "What sort of man is this, that even winds and sea obey him?"

So, why do you think God placed this verse in my heart for us both?

Take a minute and share with me (out loud or in a private thought if you are in public or mixed company) what you are facing right now.

What storm are you in?

Do you think God has abandoned you and left you to perish the way the disciples thought in the story above?

Are you calling out to God to save you?

Or are you digging your heels in, trying everything within your power to control the wind and waves of your storm?

What if you learned in the deepest, darkest hour of your storm that God was sleeping while you were begging Him for help?

What would that knowledge do to your faith?

Would you feel like God was for you, or would you assume He really doesn't care about what you are facing?

Take a minute and process this with me.

In the midst of the storm, is God going to let you sink and drown?

Will He just watch you perish without a care in the world?

Let me ask this another way.

Is this your first storm of life, or have you been in something similar before?

What was the outcome previously?

Did God show up and bring you safely through the calamity?

When I ask this question, I don't mean *did God give you your wish for an outcome*. I mean did God show up and carry you through the storm and provide for you, even if it wasn't the outcome you wanted?

Do you think the disciples always got the outcomes they wanted?

Can you name one person in the Bible, or this life, that did?

So, with all of that in mind, what does this verse mean in light of the storms we all face?

It means God is in full control of every aspect of your life. He knows your heart's desire before you tell Him, and He knows how your story will ultimately end. Every day you live He has a plan and purpose for your life, and He is actively carrying out that plan and purpose on your behalf, for His glory. He wants you to be so secure in Him that when the strongest storms of adversity come your way and you get rained on so hard your lifeboat is beginning to swamp, instead of focusing on the storm, you find a place next to your Daddy and draw so close to Him that you fall asleep in His *Security*.

So, I ask you again. Do you think God has abandoned you and left you to perish the way the disciples thought in the story above? Or has He, instead, prepared a place next to Him for you to sleep until He tells the wind and waves of your storm to be still?

While you give this serious thought, I will take you back to the summer, fall, and winter of 2019 to share how I handled it when my lifeboat was taking on serious amounts of water.

So, I ask you again. Do you think God has abandoned you and left you to perish the way the disciples thought in the story above? Or has He, instead, prepared a place next to Him for you to sleep until He tells the wind and waves of your storm to be still?

I wish I could tell you I was a picture of perfect faith, but I would be lying to you if I did. I freaked out worse than the disciples did. I was on a rollercoaster of emotions and had very high points of anger followed by super depressing lows. I was terrified that I was about to lose everything I had worked so hard to earn, and for what? You see, I helped some people by giving them money when they needed it and was told to go fly a kite when they were supposed to pay me back. I got caught in the trap of, "If you had only been smart, then you wouldn't be in this boat you are in." But I chose to do what I chose to do. My decisions to be good to others backfired on me financially and I no longer had my job, my relationship, or my Corvette, and my 401k had been drained to zero in the process. I felt really stupid for trusting that people would do right by me, only to have them screw me over. I began to beat myself up emotionally, allowing thoughts of suicide to creep in from time to time as I sat alone playing with my "sack of regrets".

If I correctly budgeted each month, I would have just enough money to carry me from June of 2019 to June of 2020. My checking account would run dry at the end of March 2020. Then, I would have to pull what remained from my savings account to make it until June when I would be completely broke.

I was terrified I was going to be homeless!

In an effort to make money, I started a business with my friend Michael, who was also laid off at the same time. Reluctantly, I used some of the money I had to live on to build a website and pay for business email addresses for us. We hustled and did our best to build a $6 million pipeline for our start-up, but it seemed that with every opportunity we found, there was always a reason the money couldn't flow to us. It was as if it was being blocked.

I knew God was there and I knew He had a plan, but I was at a loss for what was happening. You see, He had promised me for several years that my time of good fortune and love would be coming, and that I needed only to trust Him. Friend, I tell you, I tried to trust Him, but I discovered along the way that I didn't trust Him at all. I began to lash out at Him and falsely accuse Him of being a bully and a mean-spirited God that cared nothing for His creation. The deeper I sank into depression, the madder I got and the more I reminded myself of all the hell He had put me through over the course of my life. Then, in an act of what I felt was righteous indignation, I began comparing how I loved my daughter to what I believed was His lack of love for His son. I told Him He was a horrible Daddy; that He could learn a thing or two from me because I would never, never, treat my daughter the way He was treating me. I even went so far as to tell Him to shove this book up His a** and find someone else to be His preacher because I was quitting. I wanted nothing more to do with Him and His abuse. I was so tired of feeling beaten up and left for dead that I couldn't take it anymore.

Every day when I woke up, I would try to avoid Him, being intentional not to pray or spend any quiet time alone with Him. Instead, I would watch pornography or get on dating apps and try to soothe my aching soul with salves of addiction.

Then, I would get a belly full of myself and I would feel the tug of the Holy Spirit to come back to Him. And, every time, I would come crawling back on my hands and knees begging Him to love me. This was my pattern for several months. I felt like I had no *Hope* at all, and I questioned what *Truth* looked like. If it hadn't been for the downloads, He gave me to write on *Identity*, I probably would have lost my mind. It was His never-ending-faithfulness that brought me back to a place of *Hope* every time. Like Gideon before me, He ministered to me at the bottom of my winepress and never gave me up on me, no matter how much I yelled obscenities at Him.

Have you ever felt like I did?

Have you ever felt like your life was pointless and that God didn't care for you at all?

Have you ever wished He would just smite you and get it over with, so you don't have to deal with the hell you find yourself in anymore?

That is exactly how I felt.

As I grappled with how I was going to bail all that water out of my boat and deal with my fears of being homeless and alone with no ability to take care of my daughter, I came to an important realization. I did not trust God and I did not believe He would show up for me. After all He had done for me, I still saw Him the way I saw my parents, and I don't trust them any further than I can throw them. When push came to shove, I had always been the source of my pretended security. The hardest part of this realization is that I had to admit He wasn't the one at fault. It was me!

You see, friend, I wanted strength to make it through these storms of life and I had prided myself on being able to take all the proverbial beatings and still get back up. I refused to surrender, and I thought that was a good thing. But I was seeing it all wrong, again! It wasn't strength I needed. It was weakness.

Have you ever prayed for weakness instead of strength?

If you're anything like me, that probably sounds like a terrible idea.

Why the hell would anyone want to be weak?

The strong survive this life, right?

No. They die, too. No one escapes with their life.

So, then what are we supposed to do?

Easy answer - you are supposed to surrender to God.

What does that even mean?

Jesus said, "we must deny ourselves, take up our cross, and give our lives for Him (Matthew 16:24-25; Mark 8:34-35; Luke 9:23-24).

When faced with a similar set of circumstances, Paul (2 Corinthians 12:8-10) called out to the Lord and asked Him to remove a "thorn" from him three times. God simply told him, "My grace is sufficient for you, for my power is made perfect in weakness."

Look, I get it. When you are in the midst of the crucible, Bible verses don't always do much for you. Unless of course they remind you to take your eyes off your storm and place them upon *Truth*. The key to surrender is to live each day from your place of *Truth* instead of responding to life from your woundedness. While I had taught this concept to Kylie, I hadn't fully accepted it for myself.

To trust God meant I had to surrender all my hopes and dreams as well as my fears. And if homelessness was what He wanted for me, then how could it be a bad thing?

Extreme, I know, but I had to fully surrender it all to Him and trust that He would show up and take care of me.

I'll fast-forward this story to January of 2020. I had one client who was barely paying me, much less providing enough for me to make ends meet. My bank account was slowly reaching its end and I was finding it hard to live from a place of *Truth* each day unless I made it my priority to do so. As I finished the last chapter in Part 2: Identity, I began my studies on the subject of *Security*, as it relates to God. Then, something incredible happened. He introduced me to a wonderful woman named Amy who is now my wife. He opened a door for me professionally that allowed me to keep my home and support my family. And, just like only God can do, He fulfilled a prophetic promise to me and has given us a son, Bennett Asher.

My life is still far from perfect, and my faith still wains from time to time, but I know who I am, and I know to whom I belong. I can look back and review the record and see how He allowed that storm to teach me to rely on Him. My hope is that I can eventually come to a place in my life that, when the storms roll in, I learn to fall asleep next to my Daddy instead of throwing a holy fit.

How about you, friend? Do you think you will surrender it all to God and learn to sleep through your storm?

I hope you will choose to pray for weakness over strength and allow Him to be the only source of *Security* you will ever truly need!

A Pause Before Your Purpose

I give them eternal life, and they will never perish, and
no one will snatch them out of my hand.

John 10:28

Do you take time to enjoy the blessings and security that God offers you?

Welcome to the last chapter in Part 3: Security. I hope you have found
the lessons we have covered insightful, and I hope they have given
you pause. If you haven't done so already, I pray you will do a *Security Deep
Dive* on your own with the Lord. It is important to do so, lest the circumstances of this present age steal your joy!

With that in mind, I want to set the stage for our final *Security* conversation.
If you're anything like me, you have taken these lessons to heart in one hand,
but you haven't really paused to reflect on all it means to you in the other
hand. Chances are, you have cried, made some promises to change things
you now realize about yourself, or maybe you have made the decision to
trust the Lord with your eternal salvation. All good things. But do you find
yourself hurrying about to conquer the next chapter of this book, and your
life, only to realize you haven't stopped to enjoy the blessings and security
God offers you each and every day?

If this describes you, well friend, you're in fantastic company because I do
the same dang thing!

Before we jump into this final lesson, I have some questions for you.

Do you ever get so busy that you just cannot see past the tip of your own nose?

Does the stress of preparing for a big event steal your joy?

How about the holidays? Do you truly enjoy the moments you should, or does the stress of the season bring out the worst in you?

Ever pray for a miracle of sorts, receive it, and then hurry on to the next thing you need solved?

I don't *think* we all do this; I *know* we do!

It is part of our striving mentality that is difficult to break. No matter how spiritually mature, or immature, you may be, you will find yourself on this hamster wheel of insanity more times than you wish.

So, how does that play into this conversation?

Isn't that all the stuff we covered in Part 1: Acceptance of this book?

We are at the end of Part 3: Security, so why is this coming back up?

Well, because it is all connected, that's why.

Do you try to please people?

I certainly do!

Do you know why you do it?

As for me, and for the lady in the story below, it is less about being caught up in oneself and more about wanting to win the favor of those we love. When it comes to God, though, all we need to do is relax. But that is counter to how we live and likely to how we have been taught all our lives.

Luke 10:38-42 from The Message (MSG) version

Mary and Martha

[38-40] As they continued their travel, Jesus entered a village. A woman by the name of Martha welcomed him and made him feel quite at home. She had a sister, Mary, who sat before the Master, hanging on every word he said. But Martha was pulled away by all she had to do in the kitchen. Later, she stepped in, interrupting them. "Master, don't you care that my sister has abandoned the kitchen to me? Tell her to lend me a hand."

[41-42] The Master said, "Martha, dear Martha, you're fussing far too much and getting yourself worked up over nothing. One thing only is essential, and Mary has chosen it—it's the main course, and won't be taken from her."

As I contemplated this chapter, God (Daddy) gave me the title and the subject matter to present to you. In addition, here is what I heard is meant for your consideration.

Martha wanted so badly to please Jesus. She was hoping to make everything just right. She wasn't caught up in herself as much as people think. Rather, she was caught up in striving to please Jesus. All she had to do was relax. But the insecurity of that moment caught her attention.

I do it, too. We all do it. None are exempt!

So, instead of striving, stop, relax, and come sit at the feet of Jesus, or as I would say, 'in Daddy's lap', and just love on Him and let Him love on you. That is all you need to do in that moment.
God is not looking for you to please Him with your meager attempts at perfection or performance. He is seeking your devotion and your love. He simply wants you to choose Him, for He has already chosen you.

Make that moment about God.

So, when you find yourself hurrying about to conquer the next chapter of your day or your life, stop and take the time to enjoy the blessings and *Security* God offers you each and every day.

Do it now, before you hurry on to your *Purpose*.

I Am the Way, and the Truth, and the Life

14 "Let not your hearts be troubled. Believe in God;[a] believe also in me. 2 In my Father's house are many rooms. If it were not so, would I have told you that I go to prepare a place for you?[b] 3 And if I go and prepare a place for you, I will come again and will take you to myself, that where I am you may be also. 4 And you know the way to where I am going."[c] 5 Thomas said to him, "Lord, we do not know where you are going. How can we know the way?" 6 Jesus said to him, "I am the way, and the truth, and the life. No one comes to the Father except through me. 7 If you had known me, you would have known my Father also.[d] From now on you do know him and have seen him."

8 Philip said to him, "Lord, show us the Father, and it is enough for us." 9 Jesus said to him, "Have I been with you so long, and you still do not know me, Philip? Whoever has seen me has seen the Father. How can you say, 'Show us the Father'? 10 Do you not believe that I am in the Father and the Father is in me? The words that I say to you I do not speak on my own authority, but the Father who dwells in me does his works. 11 Believe me that I am in the Father and the Father is in me, or else believe on account of the works themselves.

12 "Truly, truly, I say to you, whoever believes in me will also do the works that I do; and greater works than these will he do, because I am going to the Father. 13 Whatever you ask in my name, this I will do, that the Father may be glorified in the Son. 14 If you ask me[e] anything in my name, I will do it.

John 14:1-31

Accepting Truth, Finding Hope!

Part 4: Purpose

What is Your Purpose for Living?

Heathen Sailor, or Hateful Prophet?

I cry out to God Most High, to God who will fulfill his purpose for me.

Psalm 57:2

What is your purpose for living?

A rguably, this is going to be the toughest part of this entire book. I mean, seriously, how can I possibly know the purpose of your life if you don't have a clue what it is?

Or maybe I am wrong, and you have it all figured out.

Tell me, friend. What is the purpose of your life?

I mean, why were you even born?

What is the point of all the pain and turmoil that has led you to this very day in your life?

On a positive note, why do you have the talents and abilities you possess?

Were you a planned pregnancy by your parents or did they wrongly refer to you as an *accident*? Because you're not an accident, if they did call you that. They may not have planned you, but I promise you God did!

Are you extremely social or do you prefer to be alone?

Are you single, married, or divorced?

Do you have any children?

Were you born with any so-called *disabilities?*

What about secret sins? How many of those do you have?

Are you building sandcastles on the secret beaches of your life like I did?

What about your identity? Have you come to the place where you truly know who you are?

Or are you still striving on that hamster wheel of acceptance trying to figure it all out?

Do you believe God is for you and that He loves you?

Or are you buying lies and stealing thrones?

Last question, at least for the moment.

Are you living on purpose each day, or are you just existing?

I don't know about you, but I wonder all the time what this God-sized social experiment called life is *really* all about.

Here is a question I want you to ask God.

What future do You have for me?

We all hear or perceive God differently, so pay attention for His answer. It might not come right away, and it might not come in the way you expect. I am certain though that He will answer you if you ask Him.

"Ricky, how can you be so sure God really does have a specific destiny for each of us?", you might be asking me.

Good question, friend. Let me pile on and add a few thoughts here before I answer.

Is it possible that when you took that left turn in life when you were supposed to go right, that you somehow missed out on the *"one opportunity"* God had in store for you because of the decision(s) you made?

What about that secret sin you were (or maybe still are) holding onto that no one knows about? Did you somehow miss out on the *"one opportunity"* God had in store for you because of your secret sin?

Do you seriously think that you are so *special* and *powerful* you can screw up God's plan?

If I had to guess, you are holding onto something you said, did, or didn't do right now that makes you think God is keeping score. And because of this *thing*, you cannot possibly ever reach your full potential or be included in the fulfillment of *"what used to be"* your destiny.

Do you remember me telling you the story of when God told me to "shut up"? Do you want to know why I believe He said that? If you recall, my immediate response in the moment was to be offended and say, "I really thought you would be more polite!".

I need to put something in the light for both of our benefit, so I am going to confess something I just realized while writing this chapter. I held a grudge against God over this exchange for roughly six years. I was angry with Him for what I perceived was Him being ugly and treating me harshly. I was offended by what He said to me because that is the same way my parents would have spoken to me, and neither of them would have done it from a place of love. So, I projected my insecurity and the residual hurt from old wounds onto God. Once I realized it, I went to Him and confessed it.

As a result of dealing with this wound, here is what I *now* believe He meant.

"Ricky, you never spend quiet time alone with *just* me. You are too busy being busy, and too busy talking to listen for my voice of *Truth!*"

You see, friend, when He told me to shut up, I had already bought the lie of all lies. And in my striving behavior, I was frantically responding to life instead of living from any place of real *Truth*.

God, because He loves me so much, did what He needed to do to get my attention. He made it clear He didn't want to compete for my time any longer. He also made it clear that He had made a way for me to let go of my secret sins which were holding me hostage. He told me He had already freed me from the bondage, but I had to decide to walk away from it.

My question for you, friend, is if God has opened the jail cell door and freed you from yourself, then why haven't you chosen to leave and live from that place of freedom He offers you today?

The only thing standing between you and your *destiny* is your decision to forgive yourself and your willingness to trust God. While you ponder this reality, I am going to share a Bible story with you about men, like you and me, who found themselves in a place where God showed up and fulfilled His purpose in their lives.

Hang on to your hat, this chapter is about to get interesting.

Jonah:

I am not sure how much you know about the prophet Jonah, but I can guarantee that you will not find my version of this story in your local Sunday school curriculum. Jonah was not the typical prophet who was excited to do the Lord's work. In fact, one could argue that Jonah was angry with God for being too compassionate toward his enemies; he wanted to see his enemies burn instead of being saved!

Doesn't that sound just like the *typical, churchy*, churchgoer? Always smiling to your face in that holy and sanctimonious way, but secretly hoping you won't show up to their church on Sunday because they truly believe you deserve Hell for the way you live your life. Well, that's Jonah! That's exactly how he felt about the people of Nineveh.

Jonah was an arrogant, pompous, jerk. He rejected what God told Him to do and he placed others in harm's way because of his disobedience. He even went as far as asking some sailors to kill him so he wouldn't have to obey God. When that didn't work, he resorted to asking God to kill him.

Let's look at this story together.

Jonah 1:1-16 English Standard Version

Jonah Flees the Presence of the Lord

1 Now the word of the Lord came to Jonah the son of Amittai, saying, ² "Arise, go to Nineveh, that great city, and call out against it, for their evil[a] has come up before me." ³ But Jonah rose to flee to Tarshish from the presence of the Lord. He went down to Joppa and found a ship going to Tarshish. So he paid the fare and went down into it, to go with them to Tarshish, away from the presence of the Lord.
⁴ But the Lord hurled a great wind upon the sea, and there was a mighty tempest on the sea, so that the ship threatened to break up. ⁵ Then the mariners were afraid, and each cried out to his god. And they hurled the cargo that was in the ship into the sea to lighten it for them. But Jonah had gone down into the inner part of the ship and had lain down and was fast asleep. ⁶ So the captain came and said to him, "What do you mean, you sleeper? Arise, call out to your god! Perhaps the god will give a thought to us, that we may not perish."

Jonah Is Thrown into the Sea

⁷ And they said to one another, "Come, let us cast lots, that we may know on whose account this evil has come upon us." So they cast lots, and the lot fell on Jonah. ⁸ Then they said to him, "Tell us on whose account this evil has come upon us. What is your occupation? And where do you come from? What is your country? And of what people are you?" ⁹ And he said to them, "I am a Hebrew, and I fear the Lord, the God of heaven, who made the sea and the dry land."¹⁰ Then the men were exceedingly afraid and said to him, "What is this that you have done!" For the men knew that he was fleeing from the presence of the Lord, because he had told them.
¹¹ Then they said to him, "What shall we do to you, that the sea may quiet down for us?" For the sea grew more and more tempestuous. ¹² He said to them, "Pick me up and hurl me into the sea; then the sea will quiet down for you, for I know it is because of me that this great tempest has come upon you." ¹³ Nevertheless, the men rowed hard[b] to get back to dry land, but

they could not, for the sea grew more and more tempestuous against them. ¹⁴ Therefore they called out to the Lord, "O Lord, let us not perish for this man's life, and lay not on us innocent blood, for you, O Lord, have done as it pleased you." ¹⁵ So they picked up Jonah and hurled him into the sea, and the sea ceased from its raging. ¹⁶ Then the men feared the Lord exceedingly, and they offered a sacrifice to the Lord and made vows.

How far have you gone to avoid the calling upon your life that you don't want to answer?

What about that continuous knock on your heart's door? Are you running from it?

Are you disobedient for the sake of rebellion, or are you simply oblivious to what God wants you to do?

In our reading above, I am certain you saw what Jonah did and how his disobedience impacted the lives of the sailors on the boat. But did you see what God did in His mercy?

Do you remember me asking you in Part 3: Security about the true character and nature of God? Do you remember me walking you through classic stories in an unconventional way to explain how things unfolded, and weaved into the fabric of that story was God loving His creation in an unconditional way? The same is true of this story. I will unpack it for you, so you don't miss the point I am trying to make.

Jonah knew God on a first name basis, but he hated the people of Nineveh more than he loved God. His disobedience is obvious and needs no explanation. However, even in Jonah's disobedience God was able to reach lost people for His glory. You see, God loved those sailors and He wanted to capture their hearts as much as He wanted to capture the hearts of the people of Nineveh. So, what Jonah intended for evil, God used for good!

Do you see it now?

In only the way God can, He showed up in the lives of men who worshiped many gods, and through a storm, He captured their attention. While they didn't know Jehovah God the way Jonah did, He gave them discernment to see His hands at work in their lives through Jonah's disobedience. While the storm they were caught up in wasn't their storm, God allowed them to get rained on in hopes they would surrender their hearts to Him.

Did you notice what it said the heathen sailors did next?

They offered their acceptance to the living God, and they worshipped Him!

I don't know where you find yourself right now, but maybe you are far from God like these sailors were. If so, are you prepared to surrender to Him in the midst of the storm you find yourself in?

Or maybe you are running away from God because you don't want to minister to the least of these, not believing they truly deserve His grace and mercy.

"Okay, Ricky. What if I am just like the hateful prophet? What will God do in response to my disdain for those He wants me to love whom I find unbearable to love?", you might be contemplating.

Great question. Let's see what God did in response to Jonah's repeated angst towards God for showing his enemies compassion.

Jonah 4:1-11 English Standard Version

Jonah's Anger and the Lord's Compassion
4 But it displeased Jonah exceedingly,[a] and he was angry. ² And he prayed to the Lord and said, "O Lord, is not this what I said when I was yet in my country? That is why I made haste to flee to Tarshish; for I knew that you are a gracious God and merciful, slow to anger and abounding in steadfast love, and relenting from disaster. ³ Therefore now, O Lord, please take my life from me, for it is better for me to die than to live." ⁴ And the Lord said, "Do you do well to be angry?"
⁵ Jonah went out of the city and sat to the east of the city and made a booth for himself there. He sat under it in the shade, till he should see what would become of the city. ⁶ Now the Lord God appointed a plant[b] and made it come up over Jonah, that it might be a shade over his head, to save

him from his discomfort.[c] So Jonah was exceedingly glad because of the plant. [7] But when dawn came up the next day, God appointed a worm that attacked the plant, so that it withered.[8] When the sun rose, God appointed a scorching east wind, and the sun beat down on the head of Jonah so that he was faint. And he asked that he might die and said, "It is better for me to die than to live." [9] But God said to Jonah, "Do you do well to be angry for the plant?" And he said, "Yes, I do well to be angry, angry enough to die." [10] And the Lord said, "You pity the plant, for which you did not labor, nor did you make it grow, which came into being in a night and perished in a night. [11] And should not I pity Nineveh, that great city, in which there are more than 120,000 persons who do not know their right hand from their left, and also much cattle?"

Do you see how angry Jonah was and the contrast of how compassionate God was to him and the people of Nineveh?

I think the question God is asking the *hateful prophet* reading this message today is, will you offer that same compassion, mercy, and grace that you continually receive from God, without merit, to those whom you privately admit you wouldn't piss on if they were on fire?

Oh wait, you're not that hateful. You just don't think a gay couple should be sitting next to you and your children in church, right?

Or what about that young woman who uses abortion as birth control? She has no business coming into your Sunday school class, right?

Not to mention the drug addicts, alcoholics, adulterers, or whores, right?

Tell me, *hateful prophet*. Do you do well to be angry?

I think the question God is asking the *heathen sailor* reading this message today is, will you finally accept the compassion, mercy, and grace He continually bestows on you, without merit, even when it's delivered by someone you are *certain* is judging you for how you live your life?

Will you choose to call out to God when you do notice Him at work in the storm of your life, even if He is working through the unintended ministry of a *hateful prophet?*

Or will you continue to say you won't ever show up at that church because of all the *hypocrites* that worship there?

Tell me, *heathen sailor,* do you do well to be angry?

If you truly want to know your purpose in this life, you are going to have to deal with whichever version of *you* is described above.

Why, you may ask?

Jesus was asked once what the greatest commandment was by a Pharisee. His answer was simple, yet profound. Listen close!

Matthew 22:36-40 English Standard Version

[36] "Teacher, which is the great commandment in the Law?" [37] And he said to him, "You shall love the Lord your God with all your heart and with all your soul and with all your mind. [38] This is the great and first commandment. [39] And a second is like it: You shall love your neighbor as yourself. [40] On these two commandments depend all the Law and the Prophets."

God made you to be in relationship with Him. One of His purposes for you is to love Him with all your heart, soul, and mind. Another purpose of His for you is to love others as much as you love yourself.

Until you relinquish your selfishness, you cannot possibly love God with all your heart, soul, and mind.

Until you can love God with all your heart, soul, and mind, you cannot possibly love yourself.

Until you can truly love yourself, you cannot possibly love anyone else the same way you love yourself.

Before you can live from your place of *Truth*, you must resolve within you to stop being a hateful prophet and/or a heathen sailor.

To stop being a hateful prophet and/or a heathen sailor, you must know your true identity.

To know your true identity, you must have opened the door and accepted Jesus Christ as your Lord and Savior.

You see, it is all connected!

God created you to rule and reign with Him. You are His Bridegroom. This is your truest purpose for living.

Within this macro purpose, you have several micro purposes, as well. But if you ever hope to understand what your micro purposes are for living, you must be able to choose your love for God over everything, and everyone, else. Including that all important love for self!

The next question is, will you choose God even if it doesn't benefit you the way you hope it will?

Tell me, friend, are you content with being a hateful prophet and/or a heathen sailor?

Or do you want to be all God has created you to be?

If the latter is true for you, then ask God this question.

What future do you have for me?

Too Far Gone for God to Save?

I cry out to God Most High, to God who will fulfill his purpose for me.

Psalm 57:2

Who's will, shall be done?

All of us, at one point in our lives, suffer from being a hateful prophet and/or a heathen sailor. I would argue that we all begin as a heathen sailor. We buy the lie of all lies and refuse to believe there is any *Hope* for people like us. Then, at some point or another, some of us take a shot of religion and begin to hate the very people we used to be, in the name of God of course. And just like that, we transform from a heathen sailor into a hateful prophet with murderous ambition for those we deem unworthy of grace, just like the prophet Jonah.

Some people actually murder others with implements of death. You may be one of them reading this book from behind bars, possibly on Death Row. The rest of us simply murder others with our vicious words and wishes for them to die a slow, horrible death.

But why aren't *we* placed on Death Row?

Aren't we just as guilty as the man or woman who pulled the trigger, thrusted the blade of a knife, or savagely beat someone until they took their last breath?

Why do we think we get to be God and decide who lives or dies?

Are we willing to serve the same sentence we pronounce upon others when our hearts are in a murderous state due to jealousy, envy, or wrath?

What about righteous indignation?

Don't some people just deserve the fiery flames of Hell because they are too far gone for God to save?

Imagine with me for a moment that you bought a ticket to a movie and are sitting all alone in the theatre. As the lights dim and the curtain slowly opens, the flicker of the projector's light places the first image on the screen. It's a question for you from the screen writer.

Is there Hope for someone who murders another in cold blood?

The question disappears and the screen is black as coal. Then, another question appears on the screen.

Is there Hope for someone who murders the unborn in the name of birth control?

The question disappears and the screen is black as coal. Then another question appears on the screen.

Is there Hope for someone who murders another with their words or thoughts because of something this person might have said, or done, or for how this person lives in this life?

The question disappears and the screen is black as coal. Then another question appears on the screen.

How can there possibly be any shred of Hope for a murderer like YOU?

Then, the narrator addresses you directly in a loud and convicting tone.

"That's right, YOU are a murderer!"

The screen goes black again and you are left in the deafness of the darkness that surrounds you.

Hey, friend, do I have your attention yet?

You see, I am no different than you are. I might not have plunged my blade into the heart of another, but I have wished for death, and I have damned others to Hell as if I have the authority only God can possess to take life from another.

I am an idolatrous murderer!

Are you willing to admit this with me?

Or are you still too prideful, like Jonah, to ever admit your desire to destroy another is anything but righteous?

Maybe you are willing to admit this but unwilling to forgive yourself because you are convinced that you are too far gone for God to save.

Either way, you are an idolatrous murderer!

While you give this thought, I want to introduce you to another idolatrous murderer from scripture named Saul of Tarsus.

Saul of Tarsus (AKA: Paul the Apostle):

Acts 7:54-60, 8:1-3, and 9:1-22 English Standard Version

The Stoning of Stephen
[54] Now when they heard these things they were enraged, and they ground their teeth at him. [55] But he, full of the Holy Spirit, gazed into heaven and saw the glory of God, and Jesus standing at the right hand of God. [56] And he said, "Behold, I see the heavens opened, and the Son of Man standing at the right hand of God." [57] But they cried out with a loud voice and stopped their ears and rushed together[b] at him. [58] Then they cast him out of the city and stoned him. And the witnesses laid down their garments at the feet of a young man named Saul. [59] And as they were stoning Stephen, he called out, "Lord Jesus, receive my spirit." [60] And falling to his knees he cried out with a loud voice, "Lord, do not hold this sin against them." And when he had said this, he fell asleep.

Saul Ravages the Church

8 And Saul approved of his execution.

And there arose on that day a great persecution against the church in Jerusalem, and they were all scattered throughout the regions of Judea and Samaria, except the apostles. ² Devout men buried Stephen and made great lamentation over him. ³ But Saul was ravaging the church, and entering house after house, he dragged off men and women and committed them to prison.

The Conversion of Saul

9 But Saul, still breathing threats and murder against the disciples of the Lord, went to the high priest ² and asked him for letters to the synagogues at Damascus, so that if he found any belonging to the Way, men or women, he might bring them bound to Jerusalem. ³ Now as he went on his way, he approached Damascus, and suddenly a light from heaven shone around him. ⁴ And falling to the ground, he heard a voice saying to him, "Saul, Saul, why are you persecuting me?" ⁵ And he said, "Who are you, Lord?" And he said, "I am Jesus, whom you are persecuting. ⁶ But rise and enter the city, and you will be told what you are to do." ⁷ The men who were traveling with him stood speechless, hearing the voice but seeing no one. ⁸ Saul rose from the ground, and although his eyes were opened, he saw nothing. So they led him by the hand and brought him into Damascus. ⁹ And for three days he was without sight, and neither ate nor drank.

¹⁰ Now there was a disciple at Damascus named Ananias. The Lord said to him in a vision, "Ananias." And he said, "Here I am, Lord." ¹¹ And the Lord said to him, "Rise and go to the street called Straight, and at the house of Judas look for a man of Tarsus named Saul, for behold, he is praying, ¹² and he has seen in a vision a man named Ananias come in and lay his hands on him so that he might regain his sight." ¹³ But Ananias answered, "Lord, I have heard from many about this man, how much evil he has done to your saints at Jerusalem. ¹⁴ And here he has authority from the chief priests to bind all who call on your name." ¹⁵ But the Lord said to him, "Go, for he is a chosen instrument of mine to carry my name before the Gentiles and kings and the children of Israel. ¹⁶ For I will show him how much he must suffer for the sake of my name." ¹⁷ So Ananias departed and entered the house. And laying his hands on him he said, "Brother Saul, the Lord Jesus who appeared to you on the road by which you came has sent me so that you may regain your sight and be filled with the Holy Spirit." ¹⁸ And immediately

something like scales fell from his eyes, and he regained his sight. Then he rose and was baptized; [19] and taking food, he was strengthened.

Saul Proclaims Jesus in Synagogues

For some days he was with the disciples at Damascus. [20] And immediately he proclaimed Jesus in the synagogues, saying, "He is the Son of God." [21] And all who heard him were amazed and said, "Is not this the man who made havoc in Jerusalem of those who called upon this name? And has he not come here for this purpose, to bring them bound before the chief priests?" [22] But Saul increased all the more in strength, and confounded the Jews who lived in Damascus by proving that Jesus was the Christ.

Why do you think God would have mercy on a man like Saul?

Saul took great pleasure in persecuting Christ's followers, and he took great pleasure in watching Stephen be stoned to death. I mean, the people who threw the rocks at Stephen paid Saul some sort of sick homage by placing their garments at his feet (seeking his acceptance of them for their works), as if he were God! Then, they murdered Stephen because they didn't like what he said and wanted Saul's acceptance.

Like you and me, friend, they too, were idolatrous murderers!

So, tell me something. Why would God offer a man like this His amazing grace?

More important than that, why would God offer a person like you His amazing grace?

Aren't you simply too far gone for God to save?

Can you answer these questions?

Let me answer them for you. God loves you!

That is why He offers you His amazing grace. That is also why He never gives up on you and He will fulfill His purpose in your life regardless of your willingness to participate.

The evidence for this is clear in the life of Jonah and the life of Saul of Tarsus. While we don't have the rest of the story on Jonah, it sure appears that he died a hateful prophet. Saul, on the other hand, made a different choice than Jonah. As a result, God gave him a new name, and Paul went on to be the most influential follower and teacher of Jesus Christ.

So, tell me, friend. If there is *Hope* for Saul, a murderer of Christians, then is it possible that there is also *Hope* for you?

If God can fulfill His purpose through a man like Paul and use all his evil deeds for good, then is it possible that God can do the same through your life?

I guess the real question is, who's will, shall be done in your life?

Your will or God's will?

Which character in your story do you want to be? Jonah or Paul?

Either way, my friend, God will fulfill His purpose in your life.

If you still have breath in your lungs, you still have time to make the choice.

You are NEVER too far gone for God to save!

Check out this note Paul left you under the inspiration of our Lord Jesus Christ:

> *Be careful how you live. Don't live like fools, but like those who are wise. Make the most of every opportunity in these evil days. Don't act thoughtlessly, but understand what the Lord wants you to do.*
>
> *EPHESIANS 5:15–17*

Undeniable Proof of His Presence

I cry out to God Most High, to God who will fulfill his
purpose for me.

Psalm 57:2

What chapter of your purpose are you in?

Welcome to another chapter in this book and, subsequently, in my purpose for living. In this chapter, I am going to share *undeniable proof of His presence in my life*. If you choose to see it the same way, you can. If you choose to see if a different way, that is okay, too. My job isn't to convince you. It is to share *Truth* with you, that you may find *Hope*!

What would you say if I told you I encountered an angel in a bar when I was twenty-two years old?

For the smart alecks among you, I am certain I don't have enough pages left to document all the crazy questions or comments you want to insert here. So, I will address the most lingering question and move along.

No, I don't mean the winged variety wearing a white robe and shining of the glory of God.

I had just graduated from college and was back in my small hometown of Red Oak, TX. A few of my buddies invited me to go bar hopping with them and one of them picked a place we all knew well. The official name of this club was *Borrowed Money's Crystal Chandelier*.

On this particular night, it seemed like a high school reunion because I remember recognizing every person that was drinking in this place as someone with whom I went to high school. My buddies and I kept to our small circle. We walked around a bit together, but eventually found our standing place where we huddled up to talk and throw back longneck beers.

I cannot remember how long we were there, but I remember the encounter like it happened to me yesterday. For an unknown reason, I turned out of the huddle and faced directly toward one of the bars. It was then that I saw this waitress making a beeline right for me. When she approached, her tray was empty and there wasn't one water ring on it from where a drink had been. Perfectly arranged napkins and a black ink pen were all that was on her tray. She started a conversation with me but didn't ask me what I wanted to drink. Rather, she began talking to me about God. In response, I grabbed a napkin and the pen, and wrote down this poem, and slid it to her to read.

Oh, What A Day That Will Be

Oh, what a day that will be,
When all God's children are free.

Free from the temptation,
That drives us to sin.
Free from the condemnation,
Of devoting our lives to Him.

Free from hate,
That burns within.
Differences we create,
Over the color of skin.

Free from lust and greed,
Consumed in the pride of life.
Satan's flourishing seed,
In a desolate field of strife.

An invitation to eat,

At the Lord's table above.
Reserved is our seat,
Through His covenant of love.

A life in Heaven for all eternity,
Oh what a day that will be!

Ricky D. Sluder
Copyright ©2003 **Ricky Dale Sluder**

She never even looked at it and said, "I know. You will be a minister one day, but not until you are in your forties." Astounded by the words just spoken to the broken mess that was me, I turned away from her and got the attention of one of my friends.

Me: "Dude, you gotta hear what she just said to me!"
Scott: "What do you mean, you weren't talking to anyone. You're drunk!"

As I turned back toward her, she was gone! My friend and I had a legit argument in that moment. I know what I saw and heard, but he was convinced I was standing there alone talking to no one. So, I searched the bar high and low. I even went into the women's restroom in an attempt to find her, but to no avail.

For weeks afterward I thought I was crazy. How could I have a full-blown conversation with someone, write a poem on a napkin, and have my friends tell me they didn't see her? That all they saw was me standing there alone.

Again, my job in telling you this story is not to convince you I met an angel. Rather, I am sharing my experience with you about a loving God who wanted my attention. I didn't know it yet, but I had a whole lot of *stuff* to go through, and this encounter was the one thing I could point back to without any other explanation than, *but God!*

You see, friend, I would spend the next 17 years pursuing the dreams I wanted to accomplish. I spoke to God on occasion, but I wasn't truly interested in walking with Him the way I do today.

I wasn't interested in Him having His way. Not really. I just wanted to live the dream and find the *happiness* I always hoped was waiting for me in this life. I wrapped my purpose up in my career, which, ironically, was also my identity and my security.

If you are a guy, you have likely done the exact same thing. Chances are, as you are reading this book, this is where you might find yourself.

If you are a lady, you aren't exempt! I am going to guess your identity, security, and purpose have been hijacked by your role as a mom, sister, friend, significant other, or provider. Chances are, you too are on the hamster wheel of insanity striving for acceptance right now.

Am I right?

The answer to this question is rhetorical, but, depending on where you are in this growth paradigm, it will determine your ability to see it for what it really is or is not.

After the angel incident, I left for Texas DPS. I have already told you my story of struggle and striving to belong and prove em' all wrong. But if you go back and re-read that chapter it will become clear that God was with me every step of the way. From telling me to resign, to challenging me to trust Him with my money, to showing me grace and mercy during the height of my striving, to getting my full attention with the gift of my daughter, and all the other storms of life that came and went that led me to surrender.

All of it served as undeniable proof of His presence in my life.

Let me tell you, friend. I am not special or unique. If you will spend time interrogating the scriptures of the Bible, you will see this same pattern in every story. God desires our attention and affection. He simply wants us to be in relationship with Him. Along the way, He allows hardship and adversity to come so we will stop striving for acceptance for ourselves and seek Him instead.

I don't know your story, but if we ever meet, I do want to hear it. In the interim, I promise you that the only reason you relate to my story is because

God has been right there with you, too. His purpose for me is the same purpose He has for you.

"Wait, you mean God has a singular purpose or all of us?", you might be thinking.

I would argue that God has many purposes for our lives, but until you grasp the main purpose, He has for all of us, it will be next to impossible for you to discover each of the micro purposes that are just for you.

As you reflect on the past and present, can you see the undeniable proof of God's presence in your life? If this is a struggle for you, let's make it easy. Start by looking in the mirror. If you see a reflection, then the evidence is right in front of you.

Tell me, friend. What chapter of your purpose are you in?

CREATED ON PURPOSE, FOR A PURPOSE!

I cry out to God Most High, to God who will fulfill his purpose for me.

Psalm 57:2

WHAT DOES THE BIBLE SAY IS GOD'S MAIN PURPOSE FOR YOU?

As I ended the last chapter, I gave you two thought-provoking questions to ponder. Whether you caught it or not, I also gave you a third item to ponder in the form of an imperative. As we walk the halls of your purpose together in this chapter, we are going to focus on the imperative.

Do you remember that *one thing* I said was of vital importance in the last chapter?

Hang on to your hat. It is time for one of those dream sequence moments you see in the movies when everything gets wavey on the screen.

Here it is…

*"I would argue that God has many purposes for our lives, **but until you grasp the main purpose, He has for all of us**, it will be next to impossible for you to discover each of the micro purposes that are just for you."*

Now you remember, right?

So, just as the title states, my friend, God created you on purpose, for a purpose!

Do you know what the Bible says is God's main purpose for you?

If you paid close attention, you would remember that I answered this question for you in an earlier chapter. Do you remember what I said?

You know, it's a really good thing that there isn't a pop quiz at the end of this book. Just kidding, let me remind you. And no, we don't have to do the dream sequence thing again, unless of course you are a nerd like me and think it's fun.

Here it is...

"If you truly want to know your purpose in this life, you are going to have to deal with whichever version of you is described above (heathen sailor and/or hateful prophet).

Why, you may ask?

Jesus was asked once what the greatest commandment was by a Pharisee. His answer was simple, yet profound. Listen close!

Matthew 22:36-40 English Standard Version

[36] "Teacher, which is the great commandment in the Law?" [37] And he said to him, "You shall love the Lord your God with all your heart and with all your soul and with all your mind. [38] This is the great and first commandment. [39] And a second is like it: You shall love your neighbor as yourself. [40] On these two commandments depend all the Law and the Prophets."

God made you to be in relationship with Him. One of His purposes for you is to love Him with all your heart, soul, and mind. Another purpose of His for you is to love others as much as you love yourself.

Until you relinquish your selfishness, you cannot possibly love God with all your heart, soul, and mind.

Until you can love God with all your heart, soul, and mind, you cannot possibly love yourself.

Until you can truly love yourself, you cannot possibly love anyone else the same way you love yourself.

Before you can live from your place of truth, you must resolve within you to stop being a hateful prophet and/or a heathen sailor.

To stop being a hateful prophet and/or a heathen sailor, you must know your true identity.

To know your true identity, you must have opened the door and accepted Jesus Christ as your Lord and Savior.

You see, it is all connected!

God created you to rule and reign with Him. You are His Bridegroom. This is your truest purpose for living.

I didn't always understand this truth, though. Here is what a younger version of me would have said in response to what I have presented to you.

"I get that God created me to worship Him and all that jazz, and that's great, really. But, if I am being honest, I want to know if there is something in it for me, too. I didn't ask to be born, but I have done the best I can to manage this life. I didn't ask for the hardships I have literally had no control over, but I have figured out a way to, for the most part, make it through them. I didn't ask for any of this to happen to me. What I have done is work hard to be a good person despite circumstances I didn't choose for myself. Some of which, left me with no way out! So, if the whole point of this life is for me to suffer and be miserable so God can have a friend when I die, then that is a bunch of crap! What kind of loving God would create us, leave us alone to hopefully figure out that He does actually exist, punish those who don't figure it out with an everlasting Hell that will probably resemble this life, and reward those who do figure it out with a daily walk around the universe forever holding His hand? So, what the heck is that about? What I am trying to say is this life is really hard. If God is as amazing as He is made out to be, then it would be nice to really know Him.

But it is really hard to know someone you never see or hear from in a tangible way. So, how can I be sure there is a point to all of this that actually requires me to be involved in the process? Not just as a member of God's worship team, but something that required Him to create me on purpose. Did God really create me on purpose, for a purpose?"

Friend, this is exactly how I used to feel. Maybe you feel this way, too. If so, feeling this way is normal. I have battled my way through every one of those thoughts and questions. Many of them during my deepest and most profound times of being in relationship with God. Don't think there is a one-and-done methodology that turns you into a super-Christian so you can just grin your way through the difficulties of this life singing Amazing Grace at the top of your lungs. That isn't reality. That isn't what God wants from you, either!

Whether you feel this way or not, how about we start with why God created you. Then we can discuss why life sucks sometimes and I will do my best to help you find the *Hope* you may be struggling to find.

As tempting as it is for me to quote a bunch of scripture or tell you a profound Bible story, I am not going to do that. Instead, I am going to share some things that I think will help you see it more clearly. Then, in the next chapter, I will share some scriptures with you as proof that what I am telling you is backed up by the Bible.

Deal?

First of all, thank you for listening to me as I have put my failures, and triumphs into the *Light*. My hope is that you will do the same with someone you trust. I believe that is the best first step you can take. My prayer for you is that you will take your version of those statements and questions to God. Be as real with Him as you can be. Don't worry, He can take it, and He won't smite you for being real with Him. I am living proof that a genuine and authentic heart is honored by God, not despised.

Friend, nowhere does it state that this life will be easy or fair. I am not sure why we buy the lie that because life is difficult, it somehow means God doesn't love us. With that in mind, let me ask you a quick question about your life and the circumstances you have gone through.

Which has taught you more, the times of triumph or the times of failure?

As for me, the times I won a trophy only emboldened me to think I had it all figured out. However, the difficult times that challenged me are the times that made me grow. Now, whether I grew bitter or better was the choice I made in response to the challenging times.

Do you believe this is true for you, too?

The reason we often choose the path of bitterness over the path of betterment is because we tend to respond to life from a place of woundedness instead of living from a place of *Truth*.

To respond to life is to jump on that hamster wheel of insanity and attempt to control the outcome of the very *thing* you and I both said we didn't ask for. So, if we didn't ask for it, why on earth do you think we can control it or its outcome?

> *The reason we often choose the path of bitterness over the path of betterment is because we tend to respond to life from a place of woundedness instead of living from a place of Truth.*

I lived on this hamster wheel of insanity for the majority of my life. But when I found *Truth*, I realized I didn't have to strive to control things I was not meant to control. That, my friend, is what the cross was for!

I also understand if you find it hard to trust in that which you cannot see, touch, or interact with in a tangible way. But let me ask this of you. Are you going to float off this planet because you choose not to believe in gravity simply because you cannot see, touch, or interact with it?

The same is true of God. His tug on your life is stronger than gravity. And, regardless of whether or not you can explain all the details that make up God, or gravity, it doesn't lessen either one's impact on your life.

So, at some point we all have to suspend our disbelief long enough to have faith in something instead of making excuses for why we cannot believe in it.

What about air? Do you believe it is real? I mean, you can't touch it, but sometimes you can feel it. You can't see it, but sometimes it shows itself as evident through other substances like smoke, sand, or the clouds in the sky. You can't interact with it, but you know when it is there and when it isn't. You don't see air, yet it has a major impact on your life. Regardless of whether the wind is being pushed or pulled by an unseen force, it is there whether you want it to be or not. There is nothing you can do to control it.

And the earth. The earth is set on a very specific axial tilt spinning at a very specific speed and occupying a very specific place in relation to the sun. If any of these details were just a hair off kilter, none of us would be able to exist on this planet.

Tell me, then, how it's possible that you can believe in air, gravity, the earth's axial tilt, or any of the other millions of mysteries of this universe that you take for granted, when you cannot see them, touch them, or interact with them?

So, why is it strange to believe that the God, who created all of these things, would also work through us in a similar manner as the air we breathe?

In an unseen, untouchable, and uncontrollable way.

I used to think that God didn't speak to me, but now I see His hand and hear His voice in so many different elements of the wonderful world around me every single day. I don't have a special ability like a Marvel character, I am just paying attention and looking for Him, instead of making all of this about me in every moment. In addition, I am taking Him up on His promise that if I seek Him, I will find Him.

I think the real problem for all of us can be summed up in one question.

Do you want to rule and reign with God, or do you want to *be* God?

If you want to be in control of all things, you want to be God. Welcome again to idolatry!

As you think through that one, let me share with you what God told me when He gave me the four words that make up the foundation of this book and the ministry that will come from it.

I was a member of a church in north Fort Worth called Northwood Church. Do you remember me telling you how I discovered it in my second marriage? Well, after joining the church I discovered they had a men's group called Bold. I started attending Bold, which is what eventually led me to Encounter and Quest. I had a good thing going there, but after my second divorce I heard God tell me to change churches.

God: "Go to Gateway Church in Southlake."

Me: "No. I have my men's group at Northwood. And besides, Southlake people aren't my people."

God: "I am not asking you, son, I am telling you. Go to Gateway!"

Me: "Fine, I just won't go to church at all."

Can you say stubborn? It is really hard to look back at that version of me and be proud. After about six weeks or so, I finally gave in and attended Gateway Church in Southlake, TX. I surrendered my will and joined the church. My daughter, Kylie, immediately fell in love with the children's ministry, and I truly enjoyed the worship experience and the teaching of Pastor Robert Morris. I especially appreciated his willingness to share how he was a drug user when God found him in a hotel room and called him to ministry. As I soaked up the lessons taught, and gave in to hand-raising worship, I began to feel at home in this church. It turns out, Southlake people are my people.

Then, on February 12, 2017, Pastor Jimmy Evans walked out on the stage and said that Robert was sick, and he was filling in on short notice. Jimmy then said something that would change my life forever. He said, "There are four needs that only God can meet in each of us. They are Acceptance,

Identity, Security, and Purpose." My ears perked up like a dog hearing a whistle and I placed those words into my notes on my iPhone. Then, Jimmy started teaching his lesson on the seven benefits of the Holy Spirit, which had nothing to do with his introductory statement.

As I left church, I couldn't get those four little words out of my head. I thought about them continuously night and day. In my quiet time with God, I asked Him why those four words were resonating in my head and heart. He said He had given these four words to me as my ministry. Because I tend to think a little too well of myself, I got offended.

Me: "You don't trust me with more than four words as a ministry?"

God: "Get in my Word, son, and you will see the meaning."

Me: "I don't ever remember seeing this in your Word, so where should I start looking for them?"

God: "Begin in Mark."

Me: "Mark? Who wants to read Mark?"

And so, this nearly five-year journey began. The more I dug into God's Word, the more evident it became that these four words were bigger than me!

Me: "Daddy, I am sorry I thought I was bigger than these four words. I now realize that they are so much bigger than me and I don't know why you would ever choose a man like me to teach them. Help me understand why these four words were given to me."

God: "Do you know what your problem is Ricky?"

Me: "That is a loaded question, can you be more specific?"

God: "You have spent your life seeking the acceptance of others. You go around knocking on heart's doors, seeking anyone who will let you in. But the moment they let you in, they let you down. Then, you leave and go knock on another heart's door, seeking acceptance from them. This behavior is what led you to create the false identity that has always defined you. This false identity is what led you to the false sense of security you have clung to. This false sense of security shaped your false sense of purpose. What I am trying to get you to see is that acceptance is not for you to receive. Do you know what Revelation 3:20 says?"

Me: "No."

I looked up the verse in the Bible and it reads:

Revelation 3:20 English Standard Version
[20] Behold, I stand at the door and knock. If anyone hears my voice and opens the door, I will come in to him and eat with him, and he with me. God: "Ricky, I have already accepted you. I did so at the cross of Calvary. What I am seeking is your acceptance of me. You were never intended to go around knocking on heart's doors. Instead, you are to offer me your acceptance. When you do, I will inform your identity. When you finally learn who you are in me, then, and only then, will you begin to find your security in me. When you learn to trust in me and the security of my promises, then I will lead you to your purpose. You see son, you, and everyone else around you, have been living this backwards. It is the enemy's counterfeit to my truth."

Do you see it friend?

It took me a while to wrap my head around it, but it finally sank in. I still have my days of striving and I still struggle with trust. I still have moments of depression and still struggle with wanting to be God and be in control. But I have finally found the secret to cracking the code for *Hope*!

Accept Jesus as the God of your life. Learn who you are in Him. You are a child of God! Practice trusting Him by relying on Him to be the source of your security in this insecure world. And when you do, He will lead you to your purpose.

When I dissect my statements and questions above from the earlier version of me, I hear the hurt of a hopeless person desperately trying to understand the scars that have been left behind from a difficult life.

So, why do you think God allowed all of that to happen?

In a word, relatability.

Why should you trust me to speak into your life through this book? Are my stories and confessions relatable? Does it help to know that a man like me can be loved by God? Does it give you *Hope* that God not only can, but does love you, too?

Accept Jesus as the God of your life. Learn who you are in Him. You are a child of God! Practice trusting Him by relying on Him to be the source of your security in this insecure world. And when you do, He will lead you to your purpose.

You see friend, we have all gotten it backwards. It began in the Garden of Eden when Adam and Eve bought the lie of all lies. Since then, we have all been running on the hamster wheel of insanity trying to be the gods of our own existence. Seeking acceptance in others. Creating identities that aren't actually true. Becoming the security for ourselves and missing out on understanding our truest purpose.

If you still find yourself in that place, when you get tired of this hamster wheel God will be waiting there to show you a better way to live. Chances are, He has already tried to show you a few hundred times over the course of your life. So, if you want to know why you were born and what the pain is all for, take it up with the God of Creation. He has an answer for you.

And when you do, He will show you the purposes you seek.

If you never do, He will still fulfill His purposes in you.

So, what is the point of giving you a choice?

Easy. He wants to know if you will choose Him over yourself to spend eternity with.

Think about it for a minute. Why does life suck sometimes?

Why will Hell suck all the time?

Because a life centered around selfishness, and selfishness alone, can't do anything but suck. A life without love, which is a life without the presence of God, has no lasting purpose. Thus, Jesus's answer about the greatest commandment. I invite you to go back up and read it.

Friend, He created you on purpose, for a purpose! It is up to you to find out why. If you truly want to know *what is in it for you*, seek the answer for yourself from the *One* who created you.

I did, and I finally understand my *Purpose*. I finally understand the point of all the pain. I finally understand that by accepting *Truth*, I have found the greatest *Hope* of all.

So, tell me friend, will you accept *Truth* in order to find the *Hope* you truly seek?

ACCEPTING TRUTH, FINDING HOPE!

Time to Make a Decision!

The End, Let There Be Light!

Insanity

"Insanity is doing the same thing, over and over again, but expecting different results."

— Narcotics Anonymous

C ongratulations, you made it to the end of this book. If you truly plan to apply the principles, I have shared with you, then your work has just begun.

Do you know why I chose this title to close out our time together?

At the beginning of the Bible in Genesis 1:3, God said "Let there be light…". It is my contention that God wrote the *Book of Life*, and when He penned *The End*, it was then that He said, "let there be light"!

That is another tough concept to digest, so take a minute and read these scriptures I promised to share with you in the previous chapter on *Purpose*. As usual, it all ties together.

Genesis 1:26 English Standard Version

26 Then God said, "Let us make man[a] in our image, after our likeness. And let them have dominion over the fish of the sea and over the birds of the heavens and over the livestock and over all the earth and over every creeping thing that creeps on the earth."

Jeremiah 1:5 English Standard Version

⁵ "Before I formed you in the womb I knew you,
and before you were born I consecrated you;
I appointed you a prophet to the nations."

Ephesians 1:4 English Standard Version

⁴ even as he chose us in him before the foundation of the world, that we should be holy and blameless before him. In love

Matthew 25:34 English Standard Version

³⁴ Then the King will say to those on his right, 'Come, you who are blessed by my Father, inherit the kingdom prepared for you from the foundation of the world.

While you ponder these truths, let me ask you an important question.

Did you answer the four questions I presented to you in *It's Time to Get Real with Yourself*?

I hope you did. As I pointed out in that chapter, here is the second opportunity for you to ask yourself these four questions again. Chances are, you will have a different perspective on each of them, even if your answers haven't changed... yet.

Take a minute and answer them for yourself once again.

1. Why are you striving for acceptance?

_____

_____

_____

_____

_____

2.   Who are you?

_____

_____

_____

_____

_____

3.   Why are you so insecure?

_____

_____

_____

_____

4.   What is your purpose for living?

_____

_____

_____

_____

_____

By chance, did you notice the definition I placed at the beginning of this chapter?

Or did you skip over it in haste?

Tell me, friend. Are you tired of doing the same thing and expecting a different result?

Are you tired of responding to life on the hamster wheel of insanity?

Are you ready to live from a place of *Truth* and allow God to fulfill these four needs in your life?

My prayer is that God has used this book to remove the veil, or scales, from your eyes. I hope that if you were blind at the beginning of this book, now you see. I hope that by placing all my junk into the light, it has motivated you to live in the light, too. By sharing my struggles with trusting God, I hope you will choose to admit your struggles with trusting Him, too.

Revelation 3:20 English Standard Version

[20] Behold, I stand at the door and knock. If anyone hears my voice and opens the door, I will come in to him and eat with him, and he with me.

Tell me, friend. Are you ready to accept *Truth?*

I know with all my heart, soul, and mind that *Hope* awaits you if you will simply answer that knock on your heart's door.

ACCEPTING TRUTH, FINDING HOPE!

An Invitation Specifically Addressed to You!

THE REMNANT MOVEMENT

So too at the present time there is a remnant,
chosen by grace.

Romans 11:5

WILL YOU JOIN THE REMNANT MOVEMENT AS AN OUTLAW DISCIPLE FOR JESUS CHRIST?

D o you remember what it means to be an Outlaw Disciple for Jesus Christ?

Here is the definition I wrote of an Outlaw Disciple:

"An unlikely sheepdog of the Shepherd, Jesus Christ, born into darkness and raised with wolves, but drawn to the Light with a heart to leave the 99 in search for the one who is lost. A broken vessel with rough edges that lives in the refining fires of adversity; fed up with legalism and masks of religiosity, walking boldly through the valley of the shadow of death proclaiming hope through a message of grace to the walking wounded among us."

Are you tired of the religiosity and legalism that is handicapping the body of Christ from fulfilling the Great Commission?

Are you ready to step out on faith and become a part of something that is bigger than you?

Are you ready to be *in* the world but not be *of* the world?

Are you ready to be the remnant chosen by grace?

271

Before you commit to your "yes" or your "no", I want to show you that your answer has been spoken about in scripture.

Take a look for yourself!

Romans 11:1-10 English Standard Version

The Remnant of Israel

11 I ask, then, has God rejected his people? By no means! For I myself am an Israelite, a descendant of Abraham,[a] a member of the tribe of Benjamin. ² God has not rejected his people whom he foreknew. Do you not know what the Scripture says of Elijah, how he appeals to God against Israel? ³ "Lord, they have killed your prophets, they have demolished your altars, and I alone am left, and they seek my life." ⁴ But what is God's reply to him? "I have kept for myself seven thousand men who have not bowed the knee to Baal." ⁵ So too at the present time there is a remnant, chosen by grace. ⁶ But if it is by grace, it is no longer on the basis of works; otherwise grace would no longer be grace. ⁷ What then? Israel failed to obtain what it was seeking. The elect obtained it, but the rest were hardened, ⁸ as it is written,

"God gave them a spirit of stupor,
 eyes that would not see
 and ears that would not hear,
 down to this very day."

⁹ And David says,
"Let their table become a snare and a trap,
 a stumbling block and a retribution for them;
¹⁰ let their eyes be darkened so that they cannot see,
 and bend their backs forever."

Dear friend, if it is by grace, it is no longer on the basis of works. That means you don't have to strive any further. Your hope rests in the grace and mercy of our Lord Jesus Christ. So, let your "yes" be yes; accept *Truth* and claim the *Hope* you seek.

But, if your "no" is no, then know that your heart will be hardened just as the scripture says above.

The question I have for you now is, what decision will you make?

Will you choose to be a member of the remnant chosen by grace?

If you have accepted *Truth* and found the *Hope* you have sought, what will you do with that hope now that you have it?

Will you keep it for yourself?

Or will you share it freely with as many people as you possibly can?

Matthew 28:16-20 English Standard Version

The Great Commission

[16] Now the eleven disciples went to Galilee, to the mountain to which Jesus had directed them. [17] And when they saw him they worshiped him, but some doubted. [18] And Jesus came and said to them, "All authority in heaven and on earth has been given to me. [19] Go therefore and make disciples of all nations, baptizing them in[a] the name of the Father and of the Son and of the Holy Spirit, [20] teaching them to observe all that I have commanded you. And behold, I am with you always, to the end of the age."

Each of us is equipped with spiritual gifts and each of us has a mission to fulfill as part of our purpose for being alive. The body of Christ is referred to as a body because each of us has a different part to play. Arms and legs function differently than kidneys and lungs, and so it is with each of us relative to the Great Commission.

Whether you are a Christian of thirty years or have accepted Jesus Christ as your Lord and Savior just this minute, the invitation I hold in my hand is specifically addressed to you. You are cordially invited by God to be a part of *The Remnant Movement*. Please join us so we can continue to reach the heathen sailors and hateful prophets that desperately need to find rest in the grace and mercy of our risen King!

At TRM, we seek to be more than a ministry. We seek to be a movement! We want to walk in the light with you; to shepherd you as you grow in your faith and disciple you so you can disciple others. This is what is meant when Jesus asked Peter to feed His lambs, tend His sheep, and feed His sheep.

This book is the first of many exciting things to come. If you want to know more about The Remnant Movement and if you want to answer God's call to action to be His remnant chosen by grace, please join us at www. WeAreTRM.com.

I do hope you will accept the invitation to join us as we journey together through the darkest valleys in search of those lost sheep that desperately need to come home.

Matthew 16:24 English Standard Version

Take Up Your Cross and Follow Jesus

[24] Then Jesus told his disciples, "If anyone would come after me, let him deny himself and take up his cross and follow me."

I look forward to meeting you and hearing your story!

Your brother-in-Christ,

Ricky D. Sluder

ENDNOTES

1   http://www.bibleinfo.com/en/questions/who-wrote-the-bible

2   Nitzevet, Mother of David: The Bold Voice of Silence, author Chana Weisberg

All scripture is for reference purposes and all scripture references were from BibleGateway.com

CPSIA information can be obtained
at www.ICGtesting.com
Printed in the USA
BVHW081305210222
629664BV00008B/226